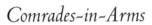

Comrades-in-Arms

Comrades-in-Arms

*The World War I Memoir
of Captain Henri de Lécluse,
Comte de Trévoëdal*

EDITED BY

Roy E. Sandstrom

TRANSLATED BY

Jacques F. Dubois

The Kent State University Press

KENT, OHIO, AND LONDON, ENGLAND

© 1998 by The Kent State University Press, Kent, Ohio 44242
All rights reserved
Library of Congress Catalog Card Number 98-12951
ISBN 0-87338-608-6
Manufactured in the United States of America

04 03 02 01 00 99 98   5 4 3 2 1

Library of Congress Cataloging-in-Publication Data

Lécluse, Henri de, 1867-1945.
    Comrades-in-arms : the World War I memoir of Captain Henri de
    Lécluse, comte de Trévoëdal / edited by Roy E. Sandstrom :
    translated by Jacques F. Dubois.
        p.   cm.
    Includes bibliographical references and index.
    ISBN 0-87338-608-6 (cloth : alk. paper) ⊖
    1. Lécluse, Henri de, 1867-1945.   2. World War, 1914-1918 —
    Campaigns — Western Front.   3. World War, 1914-1918 — Personal
    narratives, French.   4. France. Armée — Biography.   5. Soldiers —
    France — Biography.   I. Sandstrom, Roy E.   II. Title.
    D530.L39   1998
    940.4'144 — dc21   98-12951

British Library Cataloging-in-Publication data are available.

To my parents, Kaarlo and Eva Sandstrom

CONTENTS

PREFACE

Many historians hope to discover an original manuscript that might shed new light on a major historical event. *Comrades-in-Arms* is such a find. The original, handwritten manuscript of a French cavalry officer, Captain Henri de Lécluse, was found at an estate auction in Grinnell, Iowa. The auction of the property of Odette de Lécluse, the author's daughter and only survivor, was conducted by the Powesheik Bank in Grinnell. Professor Emeritus of French John Kleinschmidt of Grinnell College, a friend of both the author's wife and daughter, assisted the bank officers. Two substantial handwritten manuscripts were found in a trunk of personal effects sold to Harley McIlrath of Cedar Falls, Iowa. The first was a hastily scribbled combat diary of 573 pages, written on both sides of onion-skin paper. The second was a carefully written memoir of 313 pages, bound in a lined notebook. There were also some collections of published military poems and an original sketch. In the unbound pages of the combat diary were a series of handwritten "working maps," some of which were the author's own work, as well as a few newspaper clippings. There was also one printed copy of a play and two copies of a song published by the author.

It was obvious from the beginning that Lécluse was an accomplished writer who had literary ambitions. But he was not famous, nor was he describing one of the great battles of World War I. Instead, he seemed to be relating a series of very personal anecdotes that often had little to do with combat. Moreover, his fierce patriotism, religiosity, and hatred of the enemy seemed at odds with the great majority of the diaries and memoirs published by ordinary soldiers. On the other hand, there are relatively few undiscovered memoirs from World War I, and Lécluse had the ability to create interesting and even eloquent images of daily life at the front.

Fortunately, one of my good friends, Professor Jacques Dubois of the University of Northern Iowa, is an accomplished translator and offered to translate the text. As I began background reading, I discovered that many of the opinions expressed by Lécluse that seemed jarring on

first reading were actually quite characteristic of the way other French
line officers of his age and rank tended to describe their own experiences
in World War I. Additionally, Lécluse's descriptions of life at the front
seemed quite consistent with those found in a number of other untrans-
lated French war diaries and memoirs available in print.

Most readers will not be familiar with the small villages and ham-
lets described by Lécluse in his text. Yet, many of these communes were
located in regions where much of the fighting took place in 1914–16,
including Artois, Champagne, and Lorraine. To assist the reader, we
have created a series of maps showing specific locations mentioned by
the author as well as nearby cities, towns, rivers, and modern highways.

ACKNOWLEDGMENTS

As is often the case, the list of those who deserve special thanks for their contribution to this book is quite long. In a rough chronological order corresponding to the sequence of their contributions, I want to begin by thanking Professor John Kleinschmidt, Professor Emeritus of French at Grinnell College, for his kindness and generosity. Dr. Kleinschmidt proved enormously helpful in gaining information about the family's experiences in the United States. He also introduced me to the author's next of kin, his nephew, the vicomte Adéhmar de Lestrade de Conty, who resides in Paris.

Permission to publish the memoir was obtained from M de Lestrade.[1] M and Mme de Lestrade were extremely helpful and generous in sharing family documents and artifacts. Their son, Stéphane, the grand-nephew of Captain de Lécluse, is the family genealogist. He transcribed both the personal letters written during WWI by the author to his wife as well as the combat diary, which provided useful information regarding Captain de Lécluse's daily activities.

Mr. Fouad Miahi-Nesi, a former graduate student in French language and literature at the University of Northern Iowa, transcribed the memoir into word-processing files and did a commendable job of deciphering the author's handwriting. The book was translated from the French version by my friend and colleague Jacques F. Dubois, Assistant Professor of French Language, Literature and Culture at the University of Northern Iowa. Mr. Andrew Hupp and Ms. Lisa Garlisch prepared the maps used in this book under the direction of Professor Fred Fryman of the Department of Geography of the University of Northern Iowa.

The author's official military record was obtained from the Archives Militaires at the Château de Vincennes in Paris (*Dossier d'un officier,* N° 150,378) along with the *Historique anonyme* of the Third Regiment of

---

1. The family tree indicating the evolution of the name of the Lécluse family and its relationship to the Lestrades is contained in Appendix I.

Dragoons and the *Journal des Marches et des Opérations (JMO)* of the regiment. The *Historique* is a printed summary of some of the major events in the history of the regiment and was especially useful for tracing its movements in the early days of the war. The *JMO* is the regimental daily log and was the basis for the *Historique*.

I want to extend special thanks to M le colonel Paul Gaujac, Chef du Service Historique de l'Armée de Terre, and Mme Marie-Annick Hepp, Conservateur en Chef et Chef de la Division des Archives, for their assistance in obtaining this dossier. I would also like to express my gratitude to the staff of the Archives Militaire for their kindness and assistance. Photographs of the author and his wife were obtained from the Lestrade family archives from their château at Badefols d'Ans[2] in the Dordogne. Other photographs were obtained from the photographic archives of the Service Historique de l'Armée de la Terre (SHAT) at Fort d'Ivry.

I also want to thank the University of Northern Iowa, which was most generous in granting a professional development leave, and Dr. David Walker, Associate Dean of the Graduate College, for providing a travel grant to visit the military archives in Paris. I owe a particular debt of gratitude to Mrs. Judith Dohlman and Mrs. Vickie Hanson, secretaries in the Department of History, for assistance in preparing the text and in resolving various and persistent problems with word-processors, printers, and computer hardware. My graduate assistant, Mr. John Wolfe, deserves thanks for his careful proofreading of the manuscript. I want to thank several colleagues who were extremely supportive and who offered invaluable advice on a variety of technical matters, especially John Baskerville, Andrew Burstein, Fred Fryman, John Johnson, Charlotte Kelsey, Jay Lees, Ken Lyftogt, Robert Neymeyer, Timothy O'Connor, Donald Shepardson, and Charlotte Wells.

---

2. Badefols d'Ans (24021) is located in the Dordogne in the arrondissement of Périgaux in the canton of Hautefort. Numbers following commune names are unique for all communes in France. They begin with a two-digit code indicating the department number, arranged alphabetically. Communes are then numbered alphabetically within each department. These numbers have been obtained from the *Dictionnaire national des communes de France: donnant la nomenclature complète des communes et des principaux villages, hameaux, écarts, et lieux dits habités avec le canton, et les renseignements sur la population, les perceptions, la poste, les chemins de fer voyageux, les télécommunications, les messageries, les zones industrielles, la distance à la bretelle d'autoroute la plus proche et le code postal* (Paris: A. Michel, Berger-Levrault, 1992).

Finally, I want to thank three military historians who went far beyond the call of duty in helping to clarify complicated points of military organization in the 1914-16 period: Bullitt Lowry of the University of North Texas, Mark Conrad from Monmouth, New Jersey, and Mark Hayes of the Naval Historical Center.

TRANSLATOR'S NOTE

The author, Henri de Lécluse, was an entertaining and gifted writer. My primary goal in this translation has been to preserve as much as possible the linguistic artistry of the original manuscript. One of the reasons I chose to translate this journal, aside from my friendship with the editor, was the impact that the text had on me. I found Lécluse's entries extremely moving and enjoyable reading. The Lécluse text, however, presented a series of challenges for translation.

As an unedited manuscript, the author displayed remarkable command of the French language. What appear to be rare mistakes of punctuation, spelling, or grammar may, in fact, be attributable to the difficulty in deciphering his handwriting. If there were occasional passages that seemed less polished in comparison to the rest of the manuscript, I am sure that Lécluse would have made the necessary changes to get the manuscript ready for publication. Occasional, first-person intrusions by the author were translated directly since they seemed likely to survive an author's editing of his own manuscript.

As an accomplished author, prone to use colloquialisms, metaphors and similes, Lécluse used expressions that might seem stilted and artificial today. A choice had to be made to use a translation that would recapture the elegance (or awkwardness) of the original or a modern translation that might be more pleasing to the reader. I chose to try to preserve the style of the original manuscript as much as possible and to avoid anachronisms. There were times, however, when the use of such terms as "potholes," "bulkhead doors" and "trying for a bull's eye" seemed to communicate better than the direct English equivalent. Similarly, I left the term "Indian file" unchanged instead of substituting a less pejorative phrase, such as "single file," since this is what the author actually used and indicates for the reader a term in common use at that time.

At times, Lécluse wrote using sustained images such as in chapter 9, "Forgetting About Time," when he referred to magic, magicians, and fairies, among other things. Another example is his use of the image of a wheat field and a "harvest of martyrs" in chapter 12, "Brothers-in-Arms." Again, in chapter 27, "Brambles," he compares barbed wire to brambles, each snaring its own victims in full flight. (That chapter has been reprinted in appendix 2 in French for the sake of those who might like to read the author's original prose style.)

As is often the case with French writers, Lécluse often composed long sentences, separated by commas, which needed to be broken down into a more acceptable form of English usage. A particularly clear example can be found in chapter 5, "The Good Thieves," where the author's first sentence runs some sixty-five words. Another example would be the fifty-eight word sentence that concludes chapter 8, "Moment of Anguish." A third example is found in chapter 12, "Brothers-in-Arms," where the author has a single sentence consisting of seventy-eight words.

The author's excessive use of ellipsis points presented little difficulty. Except where the text required them, unnecessary ellipsis points were eliminated. His use of exclamation points, however, was more problematic. For a matter of emphasis or surprise, the exclamation points were retained. When exclamation points seemed unnecessary, they were replaced by periods.

In chapter 17, "The Mad Escapade," the author accented the speech of Lung, Blanchard's Alsatian friend. He also accented the speech of a Senegalese soldier in chapter 26, "Mama Pleya, Rifleman." It would have been easy to remove all accents and to allow Lung and Mama Pleya to speak proper English. But that would have created a very different impression of how Alsatians and Senegalese might have sounded to Lécluse. Since foreign accents were not encountered as frequently in France at the turn of the century as they are today, it was felt that it would be appropriate to show how the author reacted to differences in accent, race and geographic origins. In chapter 17, for example, the original text reads "Beud-edre, mais c'est bas de da vaude." The correct French text should read "Peut-être, mais ce n'est pas de ta faute." Here, the French *p* sound has been transformed into a *b*, the *t* has become a *d*, and the *f* has become a *v*. In English, the same transposition of *p* to *b*, *t* to *d* and *f* to *v* creates the same impression of accented speech.

Translation from French requires communicating to a modern English-speaking audience what the author intended to say to his French audience without radical alteration of the stylistics of the prose text. For example, in chapter 19, "The Farewell," the author is walking through the ranks, saying good-bye to each of his men. As he proceeds through, he makes mention of those soldiers who had been killed in action. During roll call, those who were dead or missing obviously could not respond. Lécluse, in a gesture of affection and sentimentality, had these names called out at the appropriate spot in the ranks which had been left empty by a recent loss. On this occasion, he made reference to that practice. Two very subtle ideas had been combined in the original French text. To be able to keep the same linguistic subtlety and complexity, the word *alluded* had to be substituted for the word *said,* which would have been more correct in a purely technical sense but which would not have conveyed the true meaning of that marvelous sentence.

The French text reads:

J'évoquais dans les rangs, à leur place accoutumée, ceux dont je faisais parfois appeler les noms, les jours d'appel general, nos chers camarades tombés à leur poste de combat. . . .

while the English text reads:

As I walked through the ranks, I alluded to the men who had stood on that very spot and whose names I still had called out during general assembly, men who had lost their lives at their combat posts. . . .

As with any translation from French to English, the difference in placement of adverbs demands care as does the placement of adverbial phrases. In several cases, however, Lécluse's word order could be misinterpreted as a matter of personal style rather than a matter of something particularly French. In such cases, I used an inverted word order in English for purposes of emphasis. On occasions, words such as *clayey* in chapter 1, "The Mud," were transformed from adjectives in a long adjectival series to nouns that communicated the same point but did so less awkwardly. On other occasions, when Lécluse ended a sentence with a preposition, it was often left unchanged since French style permits such an ending, and changing the word order would alter the tone of the original text. Toward the end of chapter 18, "A Winter in Lorraine," the author's use of alliteration created the challenge to retain the use of hard *c* and *k* sounds in English. Thus the original French text reads:

> Bientôt ton Kaiser exécré, écrasé sous le poid de ses crimes et de la
> malédiction du monde, s'écroulera à son tour, et roulera, comme
> toi, dans le fossé!

while the English translation follows:

> Soon, your execrable Kaiser, crushed under the weight of his
> crimes and the curse of the world, will crumble in turn, and will
> end up, like you, in a ditch!

On occasion, where there was no English equivalent, a word or phrase
has to be used with minimal translation. One example is the phrase
Messieurs the Boches in chapter 10, "In Chalkland." Another is the use of
the French word *adieu* in chapter 12, "Brothers-in-Arms," where the original used two words for *good-bye* that conveyed a very different meaning.

    While Lécluse would never be compared to Charles Péguy, Victor
Hugo, or Henri Bataille, his poetry is far better than average. There are
five more of Lécluse's poems contained in his personal papers: "Les
Morts vivants," "La Fée," "Le 1,000ᵉ jour de la guerre," "Plus tard," and
"Le Collier." He chose the alexandrin,[1] a twelve-meter scheme that was
extremely popular among nineteenth-century French poets. The French
classify poetry as "poor," "sufficient" or "rich" based on the number of
elements contained in rhymes. Lécluse's rhyme schemes, for example, are
at least "sufficient" and sometimes "rich." His original French text for
chapter 33, "The Living Dead," has been reprinted in appendix 3 for the
benefit of readers interested in the captain's abilities as a poet.

    Henri de Lécluse's work makes a powerful contribution to the col-
lection of memoirs from World War I. It gives insight into the thoughts
and reactions that the events of war had on a man who was not just a
military officer but also a sensitive person able to express his feelings in a
stirring and, at times, poignant fashion. I felt from the beginning that it
would be most unfortunate if this journal were not made available to
others and am pleased to have been able to offer this translation to English-
speaking readers.

Jacques F. Dubois

---

1. A favorite of a number of poets whom he had read and copied in his personal papers.

Introduction

The War

The First World War, a catastrophic event in European history, continues to fascinate both professional historians and the general public. It was the first great, modern war that mobilized millions of soldiers and consumed vast quantities of human, physical, and financial resources. A traumatic shock for combatants and civilians alike, it severely damaged the foundations of European economic, military, and colonial strength. In its wake, the confidence and optimism that had characterized the fin de siècle in Europe gave way to the deep cultural despair that was to be reflected in art, literature, and philosophy.

World War I also destroyed the aging monarchies of Germany, Austria, and Russia and created a series of new independent states in Eastern Europe. It ushered in an era of communism and fascism that dominated the history of the period between 1917 and 1945. The Treaty of Versailles, which tried to resolve disputes between the great powers and ensure a lasting peace, became instead a source of contention between the great powers that contributed substantially to the outbreak of a second world war in 1939.

The so-called Great War began amid the cheers and well-wishes of friends and family, who shared the illusion that this new war would be relatively brief and bloodless. After fifty-one months of some of the most horrendous slaughter ever known, those soldiers fortunate enough to survive returned to their homes shattered by that experience, carrying both physical and psychological scars that would last for the rest of their lives.

The story of the war itself has been told in two very different ways. One approach has been to focus on military strategy and tactics. In the standard military histories, there is usually extensive discussion of Germany's Schlieffen Plan and France's Plan XVII as well as detailed analyses of the tactics of the various field commanders responsible for

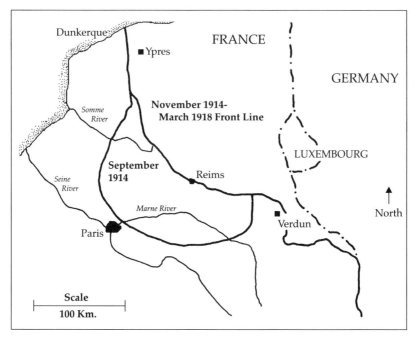

Map 1. Western Front, 1914-18

carrying out those plans. Official documents, the personal papers of leading generals and politicians, and eyewitness accounts have proven vital sources of information and have contributed greatly to our understanding of the war plans of the great powers and the importance of specific battles in the history of that conflict. But a second, very different approach to the history of World War I focuses on the experience of common soldiers in the trenches. Personal diaries, letters, memoirs, and reminiscences written by soldiers of various ranks and nationalities have been enormously helpful in describing the horrible conditions men endured at the front, their sense of hopelessness and despair, and the disillusionment that characterized many of the combatants by war's end.

The war began on 3 August 1914 as the Germans implemented the Schlieffen Plan, which called for a rapid advance through Belgium and the encirclement of Paris. The French responded with Plan XVII, which called for a quick counterattack in Alsace and the Ardennes. Losses were high on both sides in the first few months of war, commonly called the "War of Movement." Among the memorable battles of this first phase were the Battles of the Frontiers (14-25 August), the Battle of Lorraine

(14-22 August), the Battle of the Ardennes (20-25 August), the Battle of the Sambre (22-23 August), and the Battle of Mons (23 August).

The four-day Battle of the Marne (5-10 September) halted the German advance and led to what was called the "Race to the Sea" (15 September-24 November), wherein enemy forces tried to outflank each other. The Battle of Ypres (29 October-15 November) marked the end of that phase of the war, the last chance to outflank the enemy had ended, and the War of Movement gave way to the immobility of trench warfare, sometimes called the "War of Position." The heaviest rains in thirty-eight years deluged the battlefields in December 1914 and turned trenches into rivers of mud. The last major battle of that year was the First Battle of Champagne on 20 December 1914. In the last five months of 1914, the French army suffered 22 percent of its total casualties in World War I.

By the end of 1914, there were 475 miles of trenches stretching from the North Sea to the Swiss border. The Belgians held the first fifteen miles of the front while the British and Commonwealth armies held the next eighty-five miles. The French held the remaining stretch of approximately 375 miles. The tactics and strategies of trench warfare developed rapidly over the next several months and left posterity with a persistent image of failed attacks and horrendous slaughter.

By 1915, the failure of the grand strategic plans of the prewar period led to a focus on ways to gain tactical advantage. Military strategists, still wedded to old theories, spent much of 1915 in futile and costly efforts to resume the attack. While there were few memorable battles in 1915, there were many small-scale ones that were enormously wasteful in terms of human lives. The allies attempted to resume the offensive during the 1 January-30 March period in Artois and Champagne, sometimes considered part of the First Battle of Champagne. The Battle of the Woëvre (6-15 April), the Second Battle of Ypres (22 April-25 May), the Second Battle of Artois (May-June) the French assault at Vimy Ridge (16 May-June 30) and the Second Battle of Champagne and the Third Battle of Artois (25 September-26 November) are known primarily to military historians. Yet in those "campaigns of local interest," as they have been called, the French lost 1,292,000 men (some 27.7 percent of all the casualties suffered by the French army during the First World War), while the Germans lost 612,000 and the British 279,000.[1]

In 1916, the Germans launched a massive attack at Verdun (21 February-18 December) while the British and French mounted their own offensive at the Somme (24 June–13 November). The Germans theorized that the French would defend Verdun at all costs and intended to bleed French armies sent to reinforce the key point in their eastern defenses. Unfortunately for the Germans, the attack on Verdun proved almost as costly as defending it. At the Somme, the British and the French hoped to break through German lines aided by a massive assault. That effort failed miserably as well. By the end of 1916, all armies had suffered horrendous casualties and were exhausted. Strategies of attack were abandoned in favor of more cautious efforts. In a year famed for its carnage, the French army suffered 19.9 percent of its casualties.

Nineteen seventeen was infamous for the French army mutiny. The unending slaughter at the Somme and at Verdun broke the morale of the troops, who realized that to take the offensive was in essence to commit suicide. Thus, when orders were given to attack once again in April and May 1917, many units refused to advance. Although French troops had panicked and fled in total disorder as early as August 1914 (and other units had failed to carry out orders in 1915 and 1916), the mutiny of 1917 far surpassed previous numbers.

By 1918, the arrival of large numbers of American troops shifted the balance in favor of the allies. Fresh troops and weapons proved the decisive advantage. The Germans made one last attempt to attack in May 1918. After that, American troops arriving by the tens of thousands pushed the enemy back, and the stalemate on the western front was finally broken. By Armistice Day, 11 November 1918, the French controlled 59 percent of the western front, the British 19 percent, and the Americans 22 percent.[2]

The First World War had an utterly demoralizing effect on the lives of ordinary soldiers,[3] described vividly by historians such as Tony Ashworth, Denis Winter, Jean Norton Cru, Stéphane Audoin-Rouzeau, and Paul Fussell.[4] Ashworth reminds us that there were two types of battles, "intermittent large-scale battles" such as those of Verdun, the Somme, and Passchendale, and "continuous small-scale attacks." According to Ashworth, the official military histories devote at least fifteen times more space to the great battles than to trench warfare.[5] Yet the typical experience of soldiers day after day on the western front, he argues, is best described in terms of small-scale action and life in the trenches.

Each army organized its trenches differently, and trench systems varied according to the terrain. Ashworth and Winter described the British system as one with a fire trench some twenty yards ahead of the

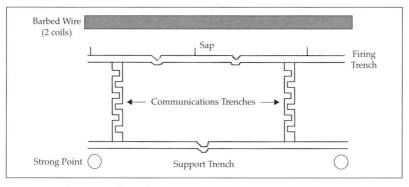

Fig. 1. French system of trenches.

command trench. The support trench lay seventy to one hundred yards behind the command trench. Some four hundred to six hundred yards to the rear lay the reserve trenches. Each line was protected by flanking strong points manned by at least one hundred men. In general, the French used two main trenches, a firing trench and a support trench[6] (see figure 1).

Although the popular impression is that life at the front was an uninterrupted hell, combat soldiers had widely varying experiences. Some were under enemy fire for extended periods of time while others were in relatively quiet sectors where little fighting took place. Moreover, specific units were rotated from one sector to another over time. Some French soldiers, for example, might spend six days in the firing trench, six days in the support trench, and six days in reserve. After a month or two of duty in the trenches, units were frequently pulled back into various encampments where they received additional training in new weaponry and tactics, usually for a week or two at a time. Rotation of units through various sectors also meant that as much as a week might be spent moving from one sector to another. Some units might be temporarily assigned to rear areas to guard prisoners or to await reorganization after suffering particularly heavy casualties. According to some estimates, only 10 percent of soldiers might be assigned to the front line trenches at any one time. The rest were in support roles or in rear areas. One diary cited by Denis Winter, for example, reveals that the diary's author saw sixty-five days of combat in front line trenches in 1916, the year of the Somme offensive and the battle of Verdun.[7]

What many readers may not fully appreciate is the degree to which soldiers were detached from their units during the war. Some soldiers were given passes to visit their families. Others were sent to aid stations and hospitals, were temporarily assigned to other units, or were permanently reassigned. Some of those serving with their units in a rear area might be temporarily reassigned to front line duty while others received additional training and instruction. Thus, diaries, memoirs, and other firsthand accounts of common soldiers are likely to record substantial periods of rest, movements from one sector to another, or noncombat experiences, in addition to horrifying moments of incredible carnage.

Not surprisingly, these diaries and memoirs are filled with evidence of the complex patterns of daily life. During periods when enemy activity was light, daily life focused around the discomforts, rather than the terrors, of the front. Coping with cold, rain, mud, rats, lice, trench foot, poor food, and boredom filled soldiers' days in quiet sectors or during periods when the enemy was unable or unwilling to mount an attack. These same diaries are also filled with descriptions of fleeting moments of pleasure, stolen from that terrible war. While these descriptions tell little about the war itself, they tell much about the heightened sense of awareness among combat troops as well as the intense emotions that could be generated by simple pleasures and moments.

Although the prevailing image of trench warfare is one of "persistent, violent and bloody conflict," Tony Ashworth claims that there were many "quiet sectors" where "life was relatively safe, tolerable, even comfortable." Informal truces between combatants were intended to preserve the peace and avoid additional casualties. He points out that the origins of informal truces on quiet sectors varied widely and might end abruptly as one unit was replaced by another. Ashworth concludes that "no single 'typical,' 'average' or 'truly common' war experience existed, but rather a number of diverse, sometimes inconsistent experiences."[8] Leonard Smith suggests that "the levels of violence in trench warfare are best thought of as a spectrum, ranging from a couple of shells or bullets lobbed each day in the general direction of the enemy trenches, to nearly constant shelling, sniping, and raids and counter-raids."[9]

As the war progressed, staff officers grew restive over inactivity in various sectors and were determined to stamp out overt fraternization with the enemy, such as in the famous "Christmas Truce" of 1914, wherein soldiers on both sides of the front lines serenaded each other with Christmas songs and even exchanged gifts in no-man's land. In time, the high command insisted that "aggression was obligatory at all times and places"[10] and attempted to spur aggression by prescribing carefully the organization of raids and bombardments. In response to these demands for greater aggressiveness, common soldiers adapted. Some ritualized combat so that they fulfilled the letter but not the spirit of their instructions. Small arms fire had little effect on an enemy protected by trenches, especially if that fire were directed toward inanimate objects. Artillery fire was far more provocative but could be directed into no-man's land or some other peripheral sector of the front. Regular bombardment at the same time in the same place each day might communicate to the enemy that no offense was intended.[11] Unfortunately, such informal truces and ritualized aggression were far too infrequent as measured by the enormous loss of life during the First World War.

Informal truces, whether motivated by self-interest or by sympathy for the enemy, serve to undermine the heroic image of the war and call into question the degree to which combatants hated each other. Jean Norton Cru studied hundreds of French diaries, letters, memoirs and reminiscences and concluded that most soldiers were thoroughly demoralized by the war. Cru was especially hostile to authors who would glorify war or tell heroic tales. He tells us that common soldiers lived in constant fear of death. They might have hated the mud, rats, lice, and cold, but they suffered imaginable torments from the carnage that surrounded them. To glorify war was an outrage; to call such men heroes was to mythologize those fighting merely to survive. To denigrate the enemy was to underestimate the dangers faced by one's own soldiers.

Under these circumstances, it was particularly galling for common soldiers to hear officers, politicians, and journalists talk of "heroes" and heroism. These soldiers were simply trying to survive, and they deeply resented propaganda intended to inspire them to throw their lives away in fruitless attacks. But the cult of heroism evidenced during and after wartime had deep roots. In France, for example, between 1870 and 1914, many patriots demanded revenge against Germany for the defeat of 1870-71. There were many who fostered the heroic myth after 1870, including teachers, writers, clerics, politicians, veterans, and journalists. Even gymnastic and shooting clubs were swept up in the "heroic contagion."[12] Thus, the cultivation of heroism was not the exclusive province of the political right wing or the military, nor was it a creation of the First World War.

The cult of heroism is closely related to nationalism. The nationalist cause was no longer the exclusive property of clerics and political conservatives. R. D. Anderson, for example, finds that nationalism "affected virtually every sector of public opinion."[13] Maurice Agulhon sees two nationalist traditions in France, one that stems from Catholicism and the other that is secular.[14] Thus, the French Revolutionary tradition of a nation in arms and the *levée en masse* combined with the late-nineteenth-century Catholic, royalist emphasis on the nation as a source of social stability, unity, and order. Raoul Girardet argues that "a large part of the young generation of intellectuals in the years immediately preceding the First World War" was influenced by this nationalism. Eugen Weber indicates that fear of war after 1911 encouraged its spread.[15]

On the other hand, there is no doubt that socialist internationalism had made deep inroads into the European working classes prior to 1914. There was, in fact, some significant resistance to the war in socialist worker enclaves.[16] Yet, a majority of socialists rallied to the defense of the national flag in each country, including France. The famous French socialist historian, Albert Mathiez, for example, abandoned his prewar pacifism and attempted to volunteer for military service but was refused because of an previous injury. Later, he wrote a series of articles in newspapers and journals defending the war effort: "German nationalism, despotism, and barbarism were responsible for the war, [Matthiez] declared, while France was fighting to preserve civilization and humanity."[17] Jean-Jacques Becker also suggests that the spirit of union, the *Union Sacrée,* which suggests a defense of country and an end, at least temporarily, to prewar animosities, found strong echoes in the common people who shared a belief that the war was caused by German aggression.[18]

The enthusiasm for the war was shared by many Catholics despite the recent and severe conflicts in France over the rights of religious congregations and the issue of separation of church and state. According to Becker, a minority of Catholics, following the lead of Pope Benedict XV, opposed the war, but most hoped that its outbreak would "provoke a considerable return to the altar." Becker also indicates that, even in dechristianized areas, there had been crowds joining in religious processions and filling the churches. The number of those taking communion had increased considerably as did the distribution of religious medals intended to protect soldiers at the front, the burning of votive candles in the sacristy, and increased throngs of pilgrims making their way to various shrines.[19]

With rare exceptions, the French Catholic Church supported the war effort as did most of the laity. Many clergy denounced the German invaders for various atrocities. In February 1915, for example, Monsignor

Turninay from Nancy denounced an enemy that "massacred the elderly, the women and the children." He then cited various "war crimes" that allegedly took place in his diocese. In April 1915, the Comité catholique de propagande française à l'étranger published a work entitled *La Guerre allemande et le catholicisme* [The German War and Catholicism.] One hundred thousand copies were distributed. The committee denounced the Germans for carrying on a "war against churches and priests." In August 1915, the *Revue du clergé français* defined the war in terms of a struggle for civilization against barbarism. The committee listed the names of sixty-nine noncombatant ecclesiastics who were victims of the enemy, and 350 chaplains, medics, and other noncombatant clergy who had been killed in the first eight months of war. It also published an album of photographs of Belgian and French churches bombarded, destroyed, or desecrated by the Germans.[20]

Despite widespread public support for the war at its outset, aided by massive propaganda efforts of the government, church, and journalists, disillusionment set in quite early in the war, and it would be reasonable to expect that those like Mathiez, who were fairly recent converts to the nationalistic cause, might be among the first to lose that new faith. However powerful these feelings of outraged patriotism may have been among common soldiers early in the war, the harsh realities of combat imposed themselves on the minds of combatants almost from the very start. Henri Desagneaux, for example, speaks of excellent morale from 3–6 August 1914 as troops headed off for the front. Crowds sang "La Marseillaise" and women handed out drinks and cigarettes to the soldiers. But by 11 August, casualties had begun to arrive, and enthusiasm for the war had begun to wane.[21]

The stark contrast between the enthusiastic response to the announcement of war in some French cities in 1914 and the mutinies of French army units in 1917 has tended to create the impression that the soldiers' morale was generally good earlier in the war but deteriorated over time, especially after the horrendous slaughter at Verdun and the Somme in 1916. Jean-Jacques Becker, looking at the postal archives, suggests that soldiers' letters home at the end of 1916 reflect a sharp loss of confidence and a steep rise in pessimism among front-line troops at that point in the war.[22] There is impressive evidence, however, that suggests massive desertions and abandonment of posts in the face of the enemy from the outset of the war. Vincent Suard, for example, cites one hundred executions in 1914 and seventy-three in 1915, many of them in the

first trimester of that year.[23] How do we reconcile two divergent inter-
pretations of troop morale in WWI? It would seem likely that the loss of
confidence in the prospects for victory (or even survival) was a direct
response to the intensity of conflict. For some soldiers, this occurred
early in the war, as early as 1914 or 1915. But for many others, the terrible
slaughter at Verdun and the Somme destroyed morale throughout the
French army.

As casualties mounted and enemy fire grew more intense, one emotion tended to overwhelm all others: fear of death. Jean Galtier-Bossière
offers powerful and disturbing testimony regarding the feelings of soldiers
awaiting the order to attack. Before an attack, men struggled to overcome
their fears.

> I cast a glance at my neighbors; breathless, shaken by nervous
> tremblings, their mouths are contracted in a hideous grin, their
> teeth are chattering; their faces convulsed with terror recall the
> grotesque gargoyles of Notre-Dame; prostrate in this bizarre posi-
> tion with arms crossed on their chests and heads down, they look
> like condemned men offering their necks to the executioner.[24]

The heightened fear of death suffered by common soldiers under fire in
front-line trenches is reflected in an infantryman's thoughts during heavy
bombardment, as described in the April 1917 edition of *La Saucisse:*

> Shells fall without interruption. He feels that his head is bursting,
> that his sanity is wavering. This is torture and he can see no real
> end to it. He is suddenly afraid of being buried alive. He sees him-
> self with his back broken, smothered, digging out the earth with
> his clenched hands. He imagines the terrible agony of death,
> wishes with all his strength that the shelling would end, that the
> attack would begin.[25]

Unending stress left its mark on all soldiers at the front. Denis Winter
suggests that "Even the best-adjusted of men might have trembling eyelids, shaking hands, nightmares or black moods to show the price they
were paying for their self-control."[26] For example, Winter describes the
Australians, who had the reputation for being tough fighters, as "shaking
like leaves and weeping . . . on their introduction to the west front
shelling." It seems incredible that anyone could survive such horror.

While fear might induce even the toughest of soldiers to break down emotionally from time to time, it could also induce other reactions, including feelings of dread, numbness, and euphoria. Winter suggests that "a state of high fear long sustained generated a sense of invulnerability or even enjoyment." Other soldiers, faced with enormous stress in a "bewildering, confusing and constantly changing environment," found that the easiest response was to "blunt the emotions and perceptions."[27] Thus, reactions to the pervasive fear, suffering, and death that permeated their daily lives might vary tremendously from one soldier to another.

Another source of information for the social historian that tends to corroborate information obtained from diaries and memoirs are the trench newspapers published at the front by common soldiers. Stéphane Audoin-Rouzeau studied 170 of these newspapers in his book *Men at War*. Some of these papers were short-lived; others were intermittent. There were some five hundred different editors who came primarily from the rank of captain or below. These papers — some handwritten, some printed — varied enormously in circulation. Many consisted of only a page or two per edition. Frequently, they were passed from hand to hand. Few of them lasted more than two years.[28] All claimed to be produced in the front lines under the harshest of conditions.

Trench newspapers reflected many of the complaints of the diaries and memoirs as they comment at length on the miseries of daily life. All indicated the problems soldiers faced, such as their homesickness, fear of death, and sense of grief when friends died. These same newspapers were often bitterly critical of the staff officers, civilian journalists, politicians and slackers. They criticized army pay, poor food, rest camps, sanitary facilities, war profiteers, inadequate leave, and pointless physical labor.

Trench newspapers bitterly denounced the civilian press, often parodying their articles and editorials. Soldiers resented civilian journalists who depicted soldiers as suffering silently from their wounds or waiting joyously for the enemy to attack. They were particularly critical of those who denigrated the enemy. As Audoin-Rouzeau explains: "To present the Germans as cowards was thus not only a travesty of the truth, it offended the French troops and denigrated their courage." In several respects, trench newspapers seem to closely parallel combat diaries and memoirs in their depiction of the common soldier's mentality.[29]

In fact, trench journals tended to paint an idealized portrait of morale at the front,[30] stressing discipline, harmony between the ranks, and camaraderie between soldiers. They extolled the "brotherhood of the trenches," such as the sharing of food, drink, and personal items among the soldiers and the mutual friendships that developed between comrades. In that sense, trench newspapers sought to make a contribution to the war effort by maintaining soldiers' morale.

Although social historians display remarkable unanimity in describing the physical conditions of life at the front, they often disagree over some very important aspects of the soldier's mentality. One school of thought can best be represented by Tony Ashworth and Jean Norton Cru, who read hundreds of French and British soldiers' diaries and memoirs. In their opinion there is strong evidence of the common soldier's fear of death, his dislike for the general staff, and his respect, even empathy, for the enemy. Ashworth and Cru found little evidence of conventional religion[31] or jingoist patriotism. They argue that those sentiments were usually expressed by journalists, politicians, and the general public. But these conclusions are hotly debated by other historians.

David Englander, Denis Winter, and Jean Norton Cru are at the center of a particularly sharp dispute regarding the degree to which common soldiers hated the enemy. Cru is quite specific on this point: Common soldiers may have feared the enemy, but they did not hate them. In many cases, they even sympathized with them. Yet Englander insists that "a fierce and undying hatred of the enemy remained a pronounced feature of correspondence from the front."[32] Winter, taking a middle course between these extremes, suggests that there were a number of exceptions where soldiers remained extremely hostile to the enemy for prolonged periods of time. He argues that some regiments tended to be more bellicose than others, especially elite army units. Soldiers often carried out vendettas motivated by earlier combat or loss of comrades. Since elite units tended to be more aggressive than regular units, the degree of danger was more likely to be heightened and to be sustained for longer periods of time. Similarly, elite units often suffered from heavy casualties, which could explain hostility based on a desire for revenge. Winter concludes that "regardless of . . . individual differences, all men behaved with bitter hatred in situations involving mortal fear and direct confrontation."[33]

A second source of lively debate between historians has taken place over atrocity legends spread during and after World War I. Some tend to regard these as fabrications by propaganda machines designed to intensify hatred of the enemy. However, according to Ruth Harris, a French commission of inquiry into war crimes was particularly care-ful in obtaining corroborating testimony and found many instances of women being raped, towns burned, civilians murdered, and churches desecrated.[34] Similarly, Joseph Bédier used German soldiers' war dia-ries to document his claims of widespread atrocities carried out against the French population by invading German armies.[35] John Horne and Alan Kramer have examined the evidence of such atrocities and con-cluded that about half the incidents involved the shooting of civilians and the burning of homes and villages, one-third involved "pillage and incendiarism," and the rest involved the killing of wounded Allied soldiers and prisoners of war. Thousands of French and Belgian citi-zens were shot as the German army was swept by a "franc-tireur para-noia." Horne and Kramer also attribute some of the atrocities to "fierce anti-Catholicism," which encouraged the belief that "convents and monasteries were . . . diabolical places where . . . mutilations were practiced on hapless wounded German soldiers."[36] As a result, churches and church towers were believed to be used by partisans to signal French and British forces or even to conceal machine guns to be used for shooting German troops.

The execution of hostages, the burning of towns, and the desecra-tion of churches in towns such as d'Allarmont, Andenne, Arlon, Badonviller, Gerbéviller, Luvigny, Namur, Nomeny, Sermaize, and Vexiancourt by German soldiers during August 1914 provoked angry reactions from French soldiers and civilians alike.[37] Many soldiers re-turning from the front told of atrocities, such as that contained in chap-ter 25, "Settling a Score." Other incidents such as the deliberate shelling and desecration of churches as described in chapter 5, "The Good Thieves," and chapter 16, "The Heartbroken Christ," are commonly found in many diaries and memoirs. Anger over such incidents seems to have persisted among the French civilian population but appears to have dissipated over time among most common soldiers. In the Lécluse mem-oir, when the author visits towns devastated by war, the result of reprisals being carried out by German soldiers against French civilians, his anger and hatred for the enemy is quite evident. Yet, he shows compassion upon encountering the bodies of individual German soldiers. Thus, be-cause attitudes toward the enemy may fluctuate due to the heightened emotion generated by events immediately surrounding a specific diary entry, they need to be treated with some caution.

A third issue hotly disputed by social historians is whether soldiers at the front tended to be patriotic. In direct contradiction to Jean Norton Cru, who regarded expressions of patriotism as a sign of an inauthentic witness, Audoin-Rouzeau writes: "Over the four years of the war, patriotism remains in general unfailingly evident." As evidence, he cites the 15 March 1916 issue of *L'Argonnaute:* "Every fragment [of this land] soaked with blood of our brothers, is a sort of sacred clay." In his opinion, that the sufferings and death of comrades-in-arms must be remembered reinforced soldiers' patriotism.

Perhaps the differences between Cru and Audoin-Ronzeau can be attributed to the fact that Cru read soldiers' diaries, letters, and memoirs, while Audoin-Rouzeau read trench newspapers. One point is clear, however: officers' diaries tended to be more overtly patriotic than those of enlisted men. Similarly, ardent nationalists before the war might be expected to exhibit those feelings more intensely and more persistently than their socialist, antimilitarist counterparts whose support for the war tended to be short-lived. Thus, rank, politics, personality, and experience may have played a powerful role in shaping the attitudes of combatants toward the enemy.

Time was another important factor affecting the soldiers' mentality. Denis Winter sees a subtle evolution of the soldier's and the civilian's mentality toward the war over time. At the outset, he argues, there was little overt hostility toward the Germans. Most people assumed the war would be brief and relatively bloodless. There were many volunteers in 1914 who joined out of a love of country or desire for adventure. Lack of employment or a sense of duty brought others to enlist. A few got drunk, joined up, and regretted their decision later.[38] By the end of 1916, after twenty-nine months of horrible losses at the front, the seemingly endless character of the war and the deprivations at home transformed the way both soldiers and civilians viewed the conflict. By war's end, disillusionment became widespread. Some soldiers may have hated the enemy; others may have sympathized with them. But all were sick of the fighting and wanted it to end.

Jean Norton Cru did a masterful job of analyzing his sources according to the type, the date of publication, the combat theater, and the rank of the author. His impulse to disaggregate the data is extremely useful to historians. It is reasonable to assume that combatants' accounts might vary by the year of the war (1914, 1915, 1916, 1917, or 1918); by the sectors where they served (Ypres, Arras, the Somme, the Marne, Verdun, the Ardennes, or Alsace); by the combat specialties of the writers (infantry, cavalry, artillery, intelligence, transportation, medical corps, etc.); by the ranks of the authors (private, corporal, sergeant, second lieutenant, lieutenant, captain, major, colonel, general); by their proximity to the front lines (firing trench, support trench, reserve trenches, rear area); by the nature of the units (active or reserve, elite or regular); by the ages of the participants (teens, twenties, thirties, forties, fifties); by the prewar politics of the soldiers (extreme left, moderate, or extreme right); by their religious preferences (or lack of same); or by the departments from which they originated. Jean Norton Cru sought to find what was commonly shared among all combatants in World War I. However, we need to consider the possibility that the experience of war and the reaction to that experience varied widely.

One issue often ignored in the secondary literature is the mentality of line officers, especially their attitudes toward their men. Line officers were responsible for transmitting instructions from the staff officers to the enlisted men. They were responsible for carrying out orders and maintaining morale. Many captains and lieutenants fought shoulder-to-shoulder with privates, corporals, and sergeants. There is little doubt that the responsibilities of command weighed heavily on these officers. They knew the men whom they sent into combat, often to their deaths. They shared many of the same hardships of life in the trenches. Officers' journals are commonly filled with expressions of affection for the men. Whether that affection was reciprocated remains open to question. Certainly, the celebrated diary of Corporal Louis Barthas suggests there may have been a deep alienation between officers and men. And Barthas was not alone in his criticism of the officer corps. While we can not resolve that issue here, the memoir of Captain Henri de Lécluse provides powerful evidence of his strong, fatherly affection for his soldiers.

The Man

The author of *Comrades in Arms*, Captain Henri-Pierre-Marie de Lécluse, was a French aristocrat who kept a combat diary during 1914-16 and later, while recovering from a gas attack, wrote an unpublished memoir. Born on 27 December 1867 in Paris, the future comte de Trévoëdal attended the French military academy of Saint-Cyr and received his cavalry training at Saumur. He married Jeanne Bertrande Labrousse de Beauregard in 1893 and gained a sudden fortune as a result of the generosity of both families.[39] In 1897, Lécluse resigned from active

Fig. 2. Captain de Lécluse, 1914–15.

duty to run the family canning business, which was the primary source of his family's wealth.[40]

It may seem surprising that the principal source of family wealth came from industry. In fact, the French aristocracy varied tremendously in rank, sources of wealth, and political affiliation. Some had modest incomes. Others were fabulously rich. Many continued to draw their incomes from landed estates while others had turned to business and finance as a source of income. While many French aristocrats were legitimists, others were Orleanists, Bonapartists, or simply conservatives. Ralph Gibson insists that "the nobility was solidly Catholic — with increasing fervor as the century progressed." Gibson tells us that French nobles often played leading roles in charitable and other church activities. However, priests and nobles came from different social classes. He explains: "Nobility and clergy regarded each other as indispensible and indeed respected each other but there was little closeness between them on a personal level."[41]

For the most part, French nobles maintained a considerable portion of their estates throughout the nineteenth century and right up to the First World War.[42] Attempting to adjust to changing conditions, they adopted a variety of strategies to preserve and enhance family property. They also remained preoccupied with lineage and family alliances. During the nineteenth century, there was a decline in the social and political influence of the nobility, but any economic decline was relative to the rapid growth of the grande bourgeoisie. Furthermore, despite the pressures to intermarry with the upper bourgeoisie, the French nobility appear to have remained relatively endogamous, marrying within their class. One study of nobles cited by Gibson, for example, concluded that, out of 146 marriages, only 11 involved a non-noble.[43] The Lécluse family was, in many respects, quite typical of the French provincial aristocracy on the eve of the Great War.

Andrew Sinclair argues that the French aristocracy tended to be even more rigid than other European aristocrats in their emphasis on manners as a distinguishing characteristic of nobility. He claims that they tended to be arrogant toward inferiors and were characterized by a "morbid wish for a final bloody solution to the class struggle" on the eve of the Great War. Sinclair concludes that the concept of *noblesse oblige* with its emphasis on dignity, taste, and restraint still prevailed.[44]

Eric Mension-Rigau described the French nobility as seeing themselves as part of a long family tradition and took great pride not only in their direct ancestors but also in their various family alliances. More inclined to refer to their line by the term *maison* (house) rather than *famille* (family), French aristocrats continued to practice the right of primogeniture, as did other European nobility; they followed a strict code regulating marriage and transmission of family property. To assure family cohesion, the head of the family regularly entertained the various cadet branches to get to know nephews, grandnephews, cousins, and so on. Family reunions were popular, especially in the summer. Burials, marriages, and baptisms provided opportunities for large family gatherings, which renewed family ties.[45]

French aristocrats tended to socialize within their own class and often belonged to exclusive clubs. Children were raised with cousins and children of family friends as companions. Associations with the children of servants and other nonelites tended to be limited to early childhood, if allowed at all. An overwhelming majority of French aristocrats were also practicing Catholics.[46] Until 1914, most aristocrats and grand bourgeois had the financial means to employ a large number of servants for highly differentiated tasks. Since French aristocrats tended to educate their children at home, great emphasis was placed on servants hired to instruct the young. Dominic Lieven tells us that most aristocrats tended to care for elderly servants in their declining years.[47]

After 1900, the great majority of aristocrats who served in the military chose careers as cavalry officers. Theodore Zeldin argues that the values of most of these aristocratic army officers included:

> physical courage, toughness and endurance; the ability to bear
> pain and extremely stressful conditions without losing one's calm
> or one's resolve. Comradeship, loyalty and a willingness to subordinate one's individuality to the demands of the group and institution were required. Leadership and example were highly valued.
> So too were certain practical skills such as horsemanship and, especially later in the century, marksmanship and an eye for ground.

For the most part, Lécluse's diary and memoir reflect those values rather well. Zeldin also sees the aristocracy as accepting a "world of hierarchy and paternalism." These same aristocrats, Zeldin insists "distrusted radical liberalism, let alone democracy or socialism." He says: "The officer believed in authority, hierarchy and discipline."[48] Unfortunately, we have no information about the politics of Captain de Lécluse, as it was uncommon for soldiers at the front to discuss partisan politics in their diaries and memoirs. His letters to his family described the war and his own activities. But, in many ways, he seems representative of his class and caste in his attitudes toward the war, the enemy, his country, and his men: He was a deeply religious man who loved his country, hated the enemy, and regarded his men as heroes.

Following his graduation from Saumur and a brief period on active duty in the area near Lunéville, Lieutenant de Lécluse continued to serve in the reserves and gained favorable performance reviews for his work in special courses designed for reserve officers. In 1910, his commandant recommended him for promotion to captain, but officers were frozen in rank before the war. Lécluse was promoted on 14 July 1914 as a captain in the territorial army. During the war, he was stationed with the reserves until 31 October 1914, when he received orders to join his regiment.

Fig. 3. Lieutenant de Lécluse, 1893.

According to his diary entry of 12 September 1914, Lécluse initially commanded a unit in the depot consisting of 543 men. On 30 October he was
informed that he would command a mixed squadron of cyclists and foot
soldiers.[49] He began organizing that new squadron on 2 November and
noted in his diary that it was equipped and ready on 5 November. His
men received their weapons on 12 November. Starting 17 November,
Lécluse drilled his men. Then, on 4 December, he received orders to head
for Dunkerque[50] with one hundred enlisted men, four noncommissioned
officers, one cook, and one medical orderly. He departed on 7 December
and arrived at Dunkerque the next day. On the eleventh, Captain Delaire
formed the Ninth Light Group[51] with four squadrons and approximately
six hundred men. Lécluse commanded the fourth squadron. The Light
Group was part of the Third Regiment (nicknamed "Bourbon"), Ninth
Cavalry Division, Thirtieth Army Corps, attached to the Ninth Infantry

Division. Lécluse commanded this unit for the next sixteen months until it was absorbed into the Second Light Group. By August 1916, the Ninth Infantry Division would be reduced to regimental status, the Second Light Group would be dissolved, and forty-nine-year-old Lécluse would be assigned as a reserve officer. For the duration of the war, he commanded a squadron assigned to the Twentieth Regiment of Dragoons.[52] His official dossier contains the following comments:

> Former officer on active duty, he commanded an infantry squadron most brilliantly at the front for more than a year-and-a-half. Sent to the depot because of his age, he commanded a reserve squadron and obtained the best results. An intelligent, serious and very zealous officer.

His colonel wrote more effusively of him:

> An excellent captain, intelligent, active, full of vigor, he organized his foot squadron which he commanded brilliantly on the front beginning 6 December 1914. Awarded the Citation of the Order of the Division for good conduct under fire in Alsace, he made proof of his courage and tenacity in Champagne at the Trou Bricot in maintaining his squadron which had lost one-third of its forces in the trenches.

The chief of squadrons for the sixth army group wrote:

> Captain de Lécluse who spent nine years in the actives is an officer of the first rank having a very good education and [is] remarkably intelligent. He has demonstrated his qualities of judgment, coolness and bravery. He formed a foot squadron which he commanded with distinction.[53]

During the war, Captain de Lécluse received a divisional citation commendation, for his courage and leadership in the battle of Ammerzviller in 1915.[54] That commendation brought with it the croix de guerre with a silver star.[55] Lécluse's service at the front was unusual only in the sense that he was already forty-seven years of age when he formed his squadron. His assignment to the front lines was typical of the experience of many other reserve officers who were forced into command positions

Fig. 4. *(from left)* Odette, Henri, and Jeanne Bertrande de Lécluse.

in late 1914 and early 1915 because of the enormous losses to line officers in the first few months of the war.

The combat diary and the memoir describe the author's experiences during sixteen months spent with the Third Regiment in three specific campaigns — in Artois, Alsace, and Champagne — from January 1915 to August 1916.[56] After August 1916, Lécluse commanded a unit at a reserve depot. Military records and family documents indicate only that he was gassed on the night of 7-8 May 1917 and spent the remainder of the war recuperating from his injury. He would receive the Legion of Honor award for this injury.

According to the family, Lécluse had hired a manager to run the family canning business during the war. Unfortunately, the business went bankrupt and, after the war, Lécluse was forced to sell his family estate, the chateau at Loquéran in Brittany, to pay the accumulated debts of the business. His son, Guy, had died in 1917 as a result of tuberculosis contracted while in the army. With his business in ruins, his family estate sold to pay creditors, and his only son dead, Lécluse, his wife Jeanne Bertrande, and their daughter Odette migrated to the United States in January 1920 and settled in St. Louis, Missouri. Eventually

Fig. 5. A familiar scene in August and September 1914. *Copyright SIRPA/ECPA France.*

naturalized as an American citizen,[57] Lécluse worked as a professor of French language and literature at Lindenwood College, then a small college for women in St. Louis, and became acquainted with the famous American newspaper publisher, Joseph Pulitzer II. In the 1920s and 1930s, Professor de Lécluse toured the United States, giving poetry readings for the Alliance Français. In 1945, he moved to Grinnell, Iowa, with his wife and daughter and died on 21 November of that year. He is buried in the Grinnell cemetery.

The Regiment

The regimental history indicates that the Third Regiment received its mobilization orders at 1600 hours on 31 July 1914.[58] It departed for the front on the night of 3 August. There were thirty-three officers, sixty-nine non-commissioned officers, 582 enlisted men, and 671 horses. The men were recruited exclusively in the western departments of France, especially in Brittany and the Vendée. The regiment was commanded by Colonel Schmidt.

During the War of Movement, the regiment was sent to the area of Bar-le-duc, south of Verdun, and arrived at Longeville-devant-Bar and

Nançois-Tronville, camping at Naives-devant-Bar. On 8 August, the regiment reached the Meuse, where it was situated between the Second and Fourth Army Corps. While reconnaissance units were dispersed ahead to locate the enemy, the bulk of the regiment was transported to Merles. On 10 August, the regiment engaged an enemy cavalry division for the first time. On the sixteenth, the Divisional Command received orders to head for Neufchâteau.[59]

On 22 August, the Eleventh Army Corps attacked at Paliseul,[60] only to be driven back. By the twenty-ninth of that month, they were retreating towards the Aisne. The official history indicates that the Third Regiment took the lead position among the Ninth and Eleventh Army Corps in the various movements associated with the early phase of the war. By 31 August, the French retreat began in earnest.

The regiment would participate in the Battle of the Marne. This was a period of almost constant action, according to the regimental history. They reached Reims on 3 September and encamped at Châlons, southeast of the aviation barracks. On 7 September, the unit engaged in heavy fighting in the area of Soudé-Sainte-Croix and Sommesous. On the eighth, the son of the commandant, a soldier named Maurice Schmidt, was mortally wounded. By the twelfth, the enemy was in retreat with the Third Regiment in pursuit. The regiment regrouped at Suippes on 13 September. The regimental history indicates that part of the village was in flames, the horses were exhausted, and the number of effective troops was substantially diminished. The advance was quickly halted north of Châlons. Some units saw the cathedral at Reims in flames. From 20 September to 8 October, the regiment encamped at Ecueil. On 8 October, the regiment moved toward Compiègne, arriving there on the 11th.[61]

Beginning on 21 October, they moved in a series of stages to the north, in what has been called the Race to the Sea. By the twenty-fifth, they were at the Belgian frontier. On 31 October, the regiment was ordered to support English troops under German attack. At Saint-Eloi, the Brigade Sailly abandoned its horses and fought on foot, led by the Third Regiment. They were positioned along the road to the Hollebeke castle[62] where they encountered strong enemy resistance. At this point, Captains Polo and Briois were killed and General de Sailly was wounded in the hand and arm. Thinking that they might be shooting at their own troops, Colonel Schmidt ordered a cease fire. Captain Leonard was killed just as he was giving the order to cease fire. Captain Ricour was also wounded. At the Heikif farm, half of the regiment occupied trenches that were raked by enfilade fire. Under heavy bombardment, the front lines were abandoned. That night, the regiment was ordered to depart for Wormezeele, where it remounted its horses and encamped to the northwest.

In that brief but bloody battle, the regiment had suffered twenty-three casualties. The brigadier general had been seriously wounded. Two staff officers (both captains) had been killed. Among the line officers, one captain and one lieutenant had been killed and a second captain and lieutenant had been wounded. Three noncommissioned officers had been killed and three others wounded, along with a second lieutenant. One enlisted man had been killed and eight others wounded.[63] These losses required reinforcements and, especially, the appointment of new officers to command existing squadrons.

The heroic image of the horse cavalry was destroyed forever by the horrible slaughter of men and horses in the first few months of 1914. As early as 14 September 1914, a combination of hot weather, continuous alerts, and enemy fire had killed 40 percent of the horses assigned to the Second Calvary Division operating in the Lunéville sector.[64] Once the War of Movement and Race to the Sea ended, cavalry units were forced to adjust to the realities of trench warfare. No longer could cavalrymen dream of heroic charges across open fields or reckless pursuit of a fleeing enemy. Reality forced most of them, little by little and against their will, to become transformed into infantry.

There were two types of cavalry units after 1914: mounted troops that were primarily used in reserve capacity, filling holes in the line left by other units rotated out of a sector, and permanently dismounted troops carrying carbines and fighting in the trenches using the same tactics as the infantry. For the mounted troops, horses were usually kept ten to twenty kilometers to the rear. When the mounted cavalry had to serve in the front lines, they typically moved their horses to within four or five kilometers of the front. These mounted units usually spent only twenty-four to forty-eight hours in the front lines before being rotated back. They then spent one or two weeks in the rear before returning to the front lines.[65] By contrast, the permanently dismounted cavalry, especially those assigned to infantry units, tended to rotate in and out of the front lines on the same basis as the infantry and to share their experiences.

On 5 November, as the War of Position began, the regiment occupied trenches along the other side of the Yser canal, across from

Bixschoote. It remained there for the next twelve days. The regiment was then transferred on 5 December to the region of Saint-Pol, where it encamped at Humières for the next six weeks. The light group of the Ninth Calvalry Division was formed during this period. The Ninth Light Group was formed out of cavalry units from different regiments within the Ninth Cavalry Division, Thirtieth Army Corps, and was attached to the Ninth Infantry Division for service in the trenches. We also find the first mention of Captain de Lécluse. The author of the anonymous historique writes: "The squadron of the Third Regiment is commanded by Captain de l'Ecluse [sic]. He will contribute substantially to the glory of the regiment."[66]

The regiment was ordered to move to Compiègne on 25 January and arrived five days later. They encamped once again at Royallieu and Jaux. From 16 February 1915 to 8 May 1915, the regiment provided a detachment of 147 men commanded by Captain de Lécluse and four of his lieutenants to occupy the trenches in the Bois des Loges.[67] Lécluse described this major assignment, his first, in his diary and memoir.

On 16 June 1915, the regiment was ordered to head for Doullens in preparation for relocation to the northeast. On 2 July, the regiment was transferred to Alsace, which it reached twenty-two days later. The troops occupied the trenches near Burnhaupt-le-Haut and Ammerzviller. It was here that Lécluse distinguished himself as the regiment repelled an enemy attack. On 28 August, the regiment was sent to Saint-Dizier[68] in preparation for the attack in Champagne in September 1915, referred to as the Second Battle of Champagne.

Following two night marches on the twenty-second and twenty-third of September, the regiment bivouacked at Saint-Julien-de-Courtisols and attacked the enemy on the twenty-fifth. By 1500 hours, they had reached the woods three kilometers north of Sommes-Suippe, where they remained for the next three days. Upon receiving orders, they returned to Saint-Julien, where they stayed until 4 October. Two days later, a single artillery shell exploded in the midst of a large group of cavalrymen huddled in the trenches, awaiting the order to attack. Twelve of Lécluse's men were killed and thirty-three others wounded, many of them severely in that incident. On 11 October 1915, the regiment was ordered to occupy the trenches on Hill 193. By 20 October, that campaign came to a halt. Describing the heavy casualties suffered between 25 September and 20 October during the Second Battle of Champagne, the regimental history indicates that "our light groups suffered a great deal."[69]

The regiment was transferred toward Lunéville on 25 October. On 26 December, they occupied a series of defensive positions near the Parroy forest.[70] On 13 and 14 February 1916, the regiment came under heavy attack. A second attack followed on the night of 23–24 February. A series of artillery bombardments and small arms fire occurred nightly until the regiment was rotated out of that sector on 27 April 1916. On 22 May, the Ninth Division received orders to dissolve. Most dismounted cavalry units were then absorbed into regular infantry units. The *Historique* indicates, however, that the Third Regiment then became a part of the Second Light Group. Lécluse indicates that this was an elite cavalry unit consisting of trained veterans and new recruits. On 18 July 1916, the Third Regiment was dissolved and was ordered to transfer the first half-regiment to the Fifty-first Infantry Division and the second half-regiment to the Seventy-second Infantry Division. Within a month, the Second Light Group was dissolved and Lécluse was reassigned to duty in a rear area. His service at the front had ended.

The *Historique* indicates that thirty-three men received the "Citation de l'ordre de l'armée," fifteen received the "Citation de l'ordre du corps d'armée,"[71] fifty-four received the "Citation de l'ordre de la division," forty-two received the "Citation de l'ordre de la brigade," and three hundred and sixty-two received the "Citation de l'ordre du regiment." Sixty-two soldiers were listed as killed during the war.

The Memoir

During the period 4 August 1914 to 24 August 1916, Captain de Lécluse kept a personal diary.[72] This material consists primarily of a daily log headed by the date and followed by cryptic comments. There are in addition some working maps, sketches, poems, and copies of official communications. Later, during the period from February 1917 to December 1918, he composed a combat memoir based on his diary.[73] The memoir consists of approximately 313 handwritten pages containing thirty-three chapters. The first two-thirds of the manuscript, from January 1915 to August 1916, are devoted to the time Lécluse spent with his squadron. The remaining third of the manuscript is devoted to personal anecdotes based on events that occurred either in 1914, before the author reached the front, or in 1918, during the German offensive and immediately following the armistice. Lécluse preferred to keep these personal reminiscences not associated with his service in the Third

Fig. 6. Lestrade Château at Badefois d'Ans (Dordogne).

Regiment separate from the rest of the manuscript, an organization reflected in this book.

The individual chapters in the memoir are devoted to descriptions of ruined villages, stately châteaux, desecrated churches, night patrols gone awry, visits to cemeteries, artillery bombardments, encounters with the enemy, frustrations with the military bureaucracy, a winter in Lorraine, and the murder of a pet bull terrier, to name a few. Toward the end of the manuscript, Lécluse describes meeting two black African soldiers from Senegal. Such descriptions are relatively rare in the diaries and memoirs of World War I despite the fact that colonial troops fought with great courage, suffered enormous casualties, and played a critical role in halting the enemy advance in 1914.

The French attitude toward black Africans has been a source of lively debate. Some commentators have seen France as an egalitarian state that is remarkably free of racial prejudice. That, however, is not an opinion shared by all. In fact, many descriptions of black Africans by French politicians, journalists, and colonial administrators in the late-nineteenth and early-twentieth centuries suggested that blacks were lazy, uncivilized, promiscuous, and prone to savagery and cannibalism. A famous work by Onésime Reclus, *Lâchons l'Asie, Prenons l'Afrique,* offered the opinion that

Fig. 7. Interior of the château.

"there is something youthful, childish or infantile about the Negro which we find charming."[74] According to Christopher M. Andrew and A. S. Kanya-Forstner, the French high command had little regard for the fighting capabilities of the *force noir* from sub-Saharan Africa. Similarly, civilian authorities had little regard for the abilities of colonial workers in general: "It takes three or four natives to do the work of one European. . . . [The native] has fewer needs than the European; he is without personal ambition. Capricious as a child, he has a horror of regular working-hours."[75] In view of these widespread racist and pejorative views of black African soldiers and workers, it is interesting to see how a French army officer from a wealthy aristocratic family described two Senegalese soldiers whom he encountered during the war.[76]

Each chapter of the manuscript takes on the form of a short story and might be read independently. However, chapters 1–24 are organized in rough chronological order and closely reflect the entries in the author's combat diary. Lécluse organized his manuscript into a series of subsections based on the region in which he was stationed. The early chapters recount the experiences of Lécluse's squadron, which was part of the Ninth Light Group until May 1916 and the Second Light Group thereafter.

The chapters reveal that Lécluse was a patriot who loved his country, hated the enemy, and believed in Divine Providence. The author's motivation for writing his memoir is clear: He wanted to memorialize those who had fallen in combat, and he needed to tell others about his experiences. With rare exceptions, this is not a story of individual heroism or hand-to-hand combat as much as it is an account of persons, places, and events that had special meaning to the author. As a storyteller and poet, Lécluse might be favorably compared to such celebrated war memoirists such as Marc Bloch, Edmund Blunden, Robert Graves, and Siegfried Sassoon. His memoir is in some ways, however, more personal and passionate than the work of these other, more famous authors.

We have wondered why this beautifully written manuscript was never published. Unfortunately, the letters sent to France from Lécluse and his family between 1920 and 1944 were destroyed in a fire set by the Nazis during World War II at the family château in the Dordogne. Thus, we can only speculate. The threefold losses of his only son, the patronal estate, and the family canning business were traumatic events that closely followed the experience of war. Migration to the United States may also have inhibited publication. Perhaps the author was unable to reconcile in an artistic sense the earlier, more journalistic chapters with the more personal and more intimate reminiscences. In any case, we are not likely to ever know why this manuscript remained unpublished and undiscovered until it was auctioned off by mistake in Grinnell, Iowa, in 1987.

While no one soldier can speak for all his comrades, the combat memoir of Henri de Lécluse is representative of the diaries and memoirs of line officers of his generation, a subject discussed in detail in the conclusion. It also reflects many of the themes identified by Denis Winter and Stéphane Audoin-Rouzeau, especially the author's concern for his men, his love of country, his hatred of the enemy, his deep religiosity, and his ceaseless concern for his wife and family. In the debate between Jean Norton Cru and Tony Ashworth on the one hand and Denis Winter and Stéphane Audoin-Rouzeau on the other, the manuscript of Captain de Lécluse falls clearly into the latter camp and is consistent with the perspective of the revisionists.

Wartime Lécluse Chronology

1914

August	16	Arrived at Nantes
	21	Notified of assignment with Third Regiment
October	30	Assigned to command foot-squadron
November	2	Began organizing squadron
	12	Selected his horse (Gajut)
	14	Received uniforms and equipment for his squadron
	17	Selected second horse (Braise)
	19	Weapons distributed
December	4	Received order to depart to front
	6	Left for front
	8	Reached Dunkerque
	11	Assigned to command fourth squadron
	26	Squadron at full strength
	27	Celebrated forty-seventh birthday
	30	Arrived at front

1915

January	4	Visited front line trenches for first time
	5	Fourth squadron occupied front-line trenches
	6	First man in squadron killed (Detray)
	7	Squadron pulled-back from trenches; basis of Chapter 1: "The Mud"
	15	Planned for a theatrical and musical "Revue of the Light Group"
	19	Received first postcard from his wife since he arrived at the front
	23	Performed in the "revue"

February	4	Received orders to relieve troops at Roye
	7	Headed for trenches at La Berlière (Canny-sur-Matz)
	14	Occupied trenches
	15	Under enemy shell fire
	26	Relieved by Delacour's squadron
March	3	Learned that the squadron will be split between Hill 91 and the "Impenetrable" Woods
	6	Informed that six hundred cavalry officers will be transferred to the infantry
	7	Attended mass; basis for chapter 4: "The Mass of the Catacombs"
	9	Bellot transferred to the infantry
	11	Rescued religious objects; basis for chapter 5: "The Good Thieves"
	12	Notified they will be transferred to the Bois des Loges
	22	Ordered to celebrate noisily the capture of Prunyzl
	23	Saw one thousand dead Germans near edge of woods; basis for chapter 6: "The Sentinels"
April	7	Two men wounded in bombardment (Bolées and Morceau)
	13	Received a visit from General de Frétay
	17	Barale shot himself by accident
	18	Soldier bringing coffee to the trenches slightly wounded by a spent bullet; Couespel asked to be transferred to the infantry
	19	Heard Grandjean was killed in action at the forest of Aprémont
	20	Described apparent attack; basis for chapter 2: "The False Alert"
May	15	General d'Espée visited Lécluse's troops
	28	Couespel was transferred; unit departed for Puchevillers (near Amiens)
June	11	Met Gorce, his "best and first" noncommissioned officer, whom he had not seen in twenty-two years
	30	Learned Couespel has been killed
July	2	Mass for Couespel; unit transferred by train to the Vosges
	12	On leave to St. Malo to join his family
	20	Returned from leave

August	10	One of his men was wounded in the hand by an errant shot
	11	Learned that Bonnet has been killed
	14	Ordered to make a raid that he regarded as very risky
	15	Raid at Ammerzviller; de Goff and d'Ollendon were shot; basis for Chapter 8: "Moment of Anguish"
	20	Peyronnet was transferred to the air corps
	21	Discovered that d'Ollendon died during an operation to remove a bullet
	30	General d'Espée brought the croix de guerre for Lécluse and Delaire
September	2	General de Frétay told Lécluse that seven of his men would receive the croix de guerre for their part in the Ammerzviller raid
	6	Unit received gas masks
	9	Visited the ruins of several villages, including Sermaize and Vassincourt; contributes to chapter 23: "Ruins"
	15	Visited chateau near St Dizier; basis for Chapter 9: "Forgetting About Time"
	28	Arrived at the Trou Bricot
	30	Guyon was slightly wounded
October	6	Twelve men killed and thirty-three wounded in a single shell burst; basis for chapter 11: "The Hole of Death"
	7	Commandant Delaire replaced by Lefevre
	8	Visited Delaire's grave; basis for chapter 13: "In the Field of Crosses"
	10	Assigned to command 350 men at Trou Bricot
	15	Hercé and Moissec killed; Launay, Gentil, and Guiniche wounded
	19	Seven men killed by a shell that hit an ammunition dump
	22	Mentioned Pataud for first time
November	17	Saw a large statue of Christ; basis for chapter 16: "The Heartbroken Christ"
	22	Heard story of Lung and Blanchard; basis for chapter 17: "The Mad Escapade"
December	27	Celebrated forty-eighth birthday

1916

January	9	On leave
	19	Returned from leave
February	12	Under heavy bombardment
	14	Enemy patrol attacked in force
	20	Narrowly escaped injury from three bombs dropped close to him by an airplane
March	14	Visited by Colonel de Teyssières, one of Lécluse's former instructors at Saumur
	18	Captain de Montergon became adjutant to the colonel; Captain Rollin was assigned to the Ninth Light Group
April	3	Pet bull terrier shot and killed; basis for chapter 22: "Pataud"
	21	Lécluse had minor surgery
	23	Personal visit to Lécluse in the hospital by General de l'Espée
	30	On medical leave
May	12	Returned to duty
	22	Colonel received orders to disband the Ninth and Tenth Cavalry Divisions; Light Group of the Third Regiment to be joined with that of the Eighth Regiment to form the Second Light Group
	28	Third Regiment on joint maneuvers with the 51st Infantry Division at Arches; Captain de Maud'huit received regimental citation
	20	Pierre Loti visited Lécluse's sector
	21	Received news that wife Jeanne Bertrande and son Guy had reached Arachon
	30	Learned of the Anglo-French offensive on the Somme
July	7	Visited Gerbéviller; contributes to chapter 23: "Ruins"
	17	Traveled in an old bus; basis for chapter 30: "The Bus"
	22	Notified that they may be sent to the Somme
	23	Orders to leave for the Somme were countermanded
	30	On leave
August	8	Returned from leave
	9	Informed that the Ninth Cavalry Division would be dissolved; General Baratier said good-bye
	16	Said goodby to his troops; basis for chapter 19: "The Farewell"
	24	Left for the reserve depot

Dedication

To my comrades in arms of the 9th and 2d light section

I offer these anecdotes, these thoughts from my war journal, to you my fellow travelers, who shared moments of fatigue as well as of battle, to you my friends in both good and bad times! . . .

This journal describing twenty months on the battle front, of which twelve were spent in the trenches, in different regions, Artois, Picardy, Champagne, Alsace and Lorraine, also belongs to you, for we lived through them together.

The fortunes of war suddenly separated us, but out of this shared experience which we endured with both courage and exultation, emerged a kinship which neither distance nor time can ever destroy!

Alas! Many of us will never see this journal! Some fell gloriously at their combat post, at the very moment when I was writing these entries; others have joined them since I have finished it. It is especially to those men, that, with respect and a heavy heart, I dedicate these pages. . . .

I

The Mud

*[Editor's Note: On 2 January 1915, the squadron received orders to take
positions in the front trenches. The next day Lécluse's men were shelled as
they arrived at the Bertonval farm.[1] This was one of the "quiet sectors,"
where only a few harmless rifle shots were fired from time to time, although the enemy trenches were only one hundred meters away and the
listening posts were only fifty meters away from enemy lines. In fact,
Lécluse tells us that Margraff's squadron was positioned only thirty meters
away from the enemy.*

*This chapter describes the difficulties experienced by Lécluse and his
men as they attempted to exit the front lines during a downpour. The material for the first chapter of the memoir comes from Lécluse's 7 January
1915 diary entry. Both the diary and the memoir contain the same words
and phrases. This is typical of most of the memoir's chapters and, except
in those rare instances where the author deviated from that practice, it
can be assumed that the memoir closely follows the text of the diary.]*

*In memory of Captain Bellot, lieutenant of
the 9th light section, who gave his life for France.[2]*

"In the sector of Arras, in the woods of Berthonval, men had to be
evacuated from some trenches even though they were not under attack,
because they were shoulder deep in mud." — So read a communiqué
written on the 8th of January, 1915.

These were my men and the territorial soldiers who came to relieve
us. Since that day, I can tell you in all sincerity that I know the true
definition of the word "mud." I don't mean that slimy mud where you
slosh around, slip and slide, and sink to your ankles. I am referring to
that treacherous substance which grabs you and paralyzes you, the one
which seems to swallow you slowly, little by little, like a swamp or
quicksand, that horrible mud, "the one which frightens you!"

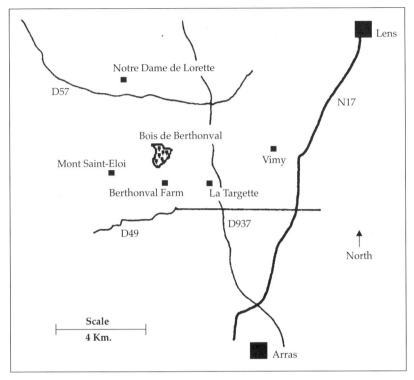

Map 2. Bois de Berthonval

It was our first sector, what a beginning! My squadron was posted at the bottom of a small valley, in a trench dug across heavy fields of plowed clay. It had been pouring rain for fourteen straight hours and the water, running down from the surrounding hills, rushed into the trench as if it were a canal and formed a pool at our feet. In a relatively short time the earth started to slide, the walls of the trench were giving way in places and the shelters were collapsing. My men, shaking from the cold but resigned, wrapped as best they could in the canvas of their tents, were stoically enduring this torrential downpour, up to their knees in the glue-like mud. . . .

I had gone back to look over the sap[3] in the trench which we needed to take in order to return to the rear. I had reached it with great difficulty even though it was daylight and I had not taken my pack. How were we supposed to make the same trip at night, fully packed, in a terrain which was becoming more impassable every minute? I was very worried as I awaited the arrival of the replacement troops. . . .

Could they get to us? By six o'clock, night had already fallen, and the only person who had made it was the captain of an alpine regiment stationed to our right. He told me that his sections were stuck in the communication trenches. Trapped in the mud as they were, it took three men to free one man and as a result he would be unable to relieve his comrades by himself.

I shared the information with those near me while adding a few hollow words of encouragement. I had to make an effort to mask my dejection. I could just see ourselves stuck in this cesspool. Without shelters, with no possibility of receiving supplies, and with at least half of our weapons jammed and useless, how long could we last?

To make matters worse, I was told that we had lost telephone communication, and the rains became diluvial as the storm gained in intensity! We needed to crouch down in the dangerous stream which flowed through the trench in order to avoid the strong gusts of wind. Desperate, I sent a scout to see if the relieving troops were coming, not even thinking about how he was going to get there!

After a few minutes which seemed liked hours, I saw some shadows approaching in the night and I heard the voice of my scout utter words which were music to my ears: "Captain, I am bringing back the troops. . . ." What a brave man! I could have embraced him! I wondered how the men were able to make it but I didn't waste my time asking. Orders to evacuate were given . . . and we began our slow return in the trench. I told each new troop where to go. They would be up to their thighs in mud in no time. I shuddered at the idea that they would be there at least through the night! Like a captain abandoning ship, I was the last one to enter the exit sap. I had asked one of my young officers to remain next to me in order to help me if I got stuck. The horrible trip began. . . .

One by one, along the endless communication trench, under a torrential rain and ferocious wind, we dragged ourselves, tripping at every step, leaning against the collapsing side walls, knee deep and sometimes waist deep in mud. Someone was constantly calling for help to get his legs out of a pot-hole and at times we had to dig by hand at the clay which immobilized our every movement. . . .

After forty-five minutes, a break occurred in the column and the men were split up. . . . The guide had gone ahead with one group, and my men, not knowing which of two trenches to take, could no longer advance. Whatever the cost, we had to get out of there. Since it was impossible for two people to pass each other in the trench, I asked my men to help me get above ground. We had lost our way! I vaguely knew where the Berthonval farm was located; we had to try to get there through the field by crossing the communication trenches which we might encounter. Fortunately for us who were now unprotected, the night was pitch black, the Boches[4] were huddled in their holes, and a few bullets were whistling around us. We had to go. Anything was better than staying in that pot-hole and taking a chance of getting killed! The place where we were was a labyrinth of communication trenches and abandoned firing trenches.

We gathered above the ground only to dive back in the mud when a German flare burst above our heads. Between Couespel[5] and myself, we had approximately a platoon and a half, a poor, demoralized and worn out bunch of men, to whom I addressed a few comforting words which I had to yell to be heard above the raging storm. I took the lead.

With the help of our pocket lamps, we were trying to find our way out of this maze. We tumbled into the communication trenches by sliding in the mud on our backs, we climbed back out by crawling on our stomachs. We kept running into dead ends. . . . I was beginning to lose hope. At one time, I admitted to being afraid, really afraid, lost as we were in the night and in the mud! Would we have to lie face down on the ground, chilled to the bone and drenched in the swampy water while waiting for daylight to come? What would happen then?

Suddenly, I ran into an officer sent by the Berthonval farm to come to the rescue of those poor souls lost in this dreadful night. He indicated to us which communication trench to take and went on to look for other men who had gotten lost. The trench had become a river, but after all the suffering in the mud we were almost glad to be walking in the icy water which came up to our knees. At least we were making ground! Splash! I fell into a pot-hole. While struggling to get out I felt a ladder leaning against the side, an indication that I had to leave the trench again. We climbed out one by one. What a pleasant sight! The outline of the Berthonval farm could be seen in the darkness. Two more trenches to cross and we would be there.

We had been walking for three hours to cover less than a kilometer! I asked to be taken to the commander of the trenches and when I stood in the doorway of his room, he was taken aback. . . . From head to toe I resembled a clay statue. I gave him my name and he told me that my other four officers and the rest of my men had arrived forty-five minutes sooner looking exactly as I did. Thank God! I had not lost any of my men! A sergeant led us to the main road because, in spite of the risk, we didn't want to go back any other way. Only a fence, a small moat, and a trench filled with water into which one of my men took a head-long dive, stood in our way. We felt safe and we arrived exhausted at Mont Saint-Eloi[6] at around eleven o'clock. Our cooks had waited for us and we forgot all about the pot-holes and the mud in front of the best hot soup which I have ever eaten in my life!

Berthonval
(Pas-de-Calais)[7]

Fig. 8. French soldiers in trench. *Copyright SIRPA/ECPA France.*

2

The False Alert

[Editor's Note: Dated 25 February 1915, this chapter concerned events at the quarry of Canny-sur-Matz (Oise). The diary entry indicates that the weather was excellent and that, during the morning, the author watched an aerial combat between two biplanes, one French and one German. During the afternoon, the Germans fired an artillery barrage, including thirteen heavy projectiles on the town of Canny and its environs. There was only one soldier slightly wounded. As they were making preparations for the night relief, just as they were finishing their after-dinner coffee, a few shells burst in the trench right above them. As Lécluse and Couespel de Ménil, his lieutenant, scrambled to find out what was going on, they discovered that their vision was partially obscured by fog. They heard firing along the line to their right.

As he peered out of his trench, with rifle shots passing near his head, Lécluse saw what appeared to be flashes of light caused by rifle fire in the distance. He ordered his men to fire at the barbed wire in front of his position as a precautionary measure. Now that his men were fully ready, he ordered them to cease fire and wait for the attack. Two junior officers, one to the left and one to the right, advanced to the barbed wire and could see nothing, even though the fog had lifted slightly. After ten minutes, he sent his men back to their shelters, leaving only sentries and patrols to guard the trenches. He then described what actually had happened in great detail.

Events such as the ones described in this chapter were commonplace during World War I. They serve to remind us of the psychological trauma of high levels of stress caused by frequent alerts. Here, for instance, the author describes his feelings on a night when he did not expect to survive.]

*To the memory of Second Lieutenant Couespel
du Ménil, of the 9th Light Group, who died for France.*

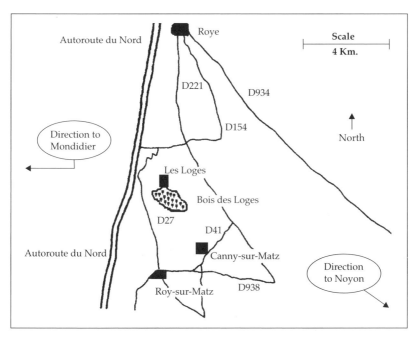

Map 3. Canny-sur-Matz and Bois des Loges

Those who will return home after the war will bring back with them numerous memories. The war will have lasted so long, undergone so many changes, triggered so many unexpected events, led to so many extraordinary inventions, that each one of its participants, no matter how brief his stay at the front, will have had his share of spectacles be they heartrending, bizarre or tragic, enough to animate many fireside conversations at home or with long lost friends.

I believe that among all of these moments which we will want to relive in our minds, there will be, for those who have experienced it, that one unique moment when you thought that your time had come, that you were going to clash with the enemy and that you were going to lose your life in the process. As far as I am concerned, even though nearly two years have gone by, as I am writing this[1] I can see the whole scene as if it were yesterday. Although it turned out to be a false alert, I really thought "this was it."

It was eight o'clock on a cold and humid February evening. The pale light of the moon was dimmed even further by the fog which hovered over the plain. My men and I were finishing dinner in my small shelter built against the wall of the quarry, just below where my trench ran. We were on our last evening of guard duty and all was quiet as it was usually the case at that time of the day. We were talking about the work which had been done, about different things which had occurred during the day, about our impending replacement, and about our plans during our stay away from the front line. The fire was roaring in the stove, the coffee was piping hot in our glasses and the men were lighting up their pipes and cigarettes. It was that moment for rest and relaxation which leads you to forget that you were on guard duty in a trench barely five hundred yards from the Boches.

All of a sudden, as I was speaking, bang! bang! gun fire rang out just above our heads. . . . We jumped outside, bare-headed, in my case still wearing my clogs. . . . The shooting could be heard all along the right side trench and got even worse in the neighboring one, beyond the village. The enemy replied generously, and above our ears it was as if a swarm of bees were buzzing by. Rockets were shooting up everywhere into the sky in a cloud of white lights. Keeping calm, my men came out of their shelter where they had begun their game of manille[2] and looked at me inquisitively. "To your post!" I yelled, and without looking back, I climbed the ramp leading to the trench. What a moment! and how intense life can be then! It is amazing how quickly our minds reacted and went to work.

In an instant, the time needed to take a few steps, my mind was overwhelmed with flashing thoughts of God, of my family, of my impending death, of the eventual battle, of the time which I deemed necessary to get my men to fill the trench, of the machine guns which I had to uncover, of the lack of contact with my comrade to my left,[3] a situation which I deplored, of my lieutenant sent to the Calvary monument and who was above ground.[4]

I quickly signed myself,[5] not having time to say a prayer, and by the time I got to the trench, my mind was as clear and as calm as when I would make my rounds. So much so that later on, I would be surprised at my composure, which was much greater than I would have hoped.

Still my heart stopped beating the moment I jumped on the bench to look around from the top of the parapet. What was going to stare me in the face? Phew! It was not too late! I could clearly see the first rows of barbed wire;[6] the others disappeared behind the fog. I was able to make out numerous short flames which indicated gunshots. Moreover, bullets were whistling by my ear. . . . It was an attack after all but our lines were solid and we would not be caught by surprise! I could see my men running over; they were filling the trench and opened fire on the barbed wire. I was completely at ease. It was time for me to tend to my machine guns. The two I had were hidden in a bombproof shelter in the middle of my line. The Boches would be in for a surprise. I got there in no time and found my territorial gunners tangled up in the dark, and, like the monkey in the fable, they had forgotten to light the lantern. I threw them my box of amber and ordered them to open fire. Next to me, my second lieutenant, still without his helmet and sitting boldly atop a protective shield, called out orders and words of encouragement to his men as they passed by. Reassured by the situation, I needed to tend to my appearance, in anticipation of what was to come, by switching from my clogs to my boots so as to be able to walk and run in the night and the mud. I was now "decked out," as they say in the navy, just as the rat! tat! tat! of my machine guns could be heard mowing down a few inches above the ground the weathering of my defense work. Everything was going fine!

But after a short while, I began to have a few doubts. I noticed that the flames which I had seen a while ago through the fog were caused by the ricochets of our own bullets. The fire of the enemy was much more subdued and could have been coming from a long way. I noticed too that the German cannon had remained inactive. Could this be a false alarm? I just had to be sure. "Cease fire!" We could always determine what to do later. The order was relayed from man to man but was not obeyed very quickly. When men, especially new soldiers, had begun firing, it was almost impossible to get them to stop. Finally our side became quiet and not much out of the ordinary could be heard from the German side. A few men volunteered to crawl as far as the barbed wire to see what was going on. All was still. All right! The attack would come some other day. We just made a lot of noise for nothing. Over to our right, where the shooting had been particularly violent, and where, as we learned later, two patrols had run into each other, calm had returned. The men shook themselves, exchanged a few jokes and returned to their shelters, leaving the usual number of guards at their posts. "Your coffee is going to be cold" said Bellot as he walked in front of me. That was very true. "Let's not forget that good coffee and let's get back to our pipes, and our interrupted conversation as soon as we have called the commander[7] to tell him: 'Excellent alert drill. Nothing new. Good night!'"

There you have it! That's what a false alert is all about. We laughed about it later on, we took some razzing from comrades, but, deep down, we knew very well that when we thought our time had come, we spent a hellish moment, as the "poilus" say.[8]

The Quarry of Canny-sur-Matz
(Oise)
25 February 1915

3

The Lair

[Editor's Note: The text below is drawn from notes in the diary for 4 March 1915. In this chapter, the author describes life in the underground shelters that provided protection from enemy artillery shells at the front. Here Lécluse had relieved Delacour and inherited a small, ill-equipped shelter. He soon adjusted to the constant risks from enemy bombardment and even found a way to play bridge in his tiny quarters. Whereas the first two chapters of the memoir described the physical discomforts and terrors of the trenches, this chapter describes the soldiers' attempts to accommodate themselves to very uncomfortable surroundings and even to steal a moment's pleasure from the war.]

*To Captain Delacour of the 9th Light Group
and of the 2d Light*[1]

I have lived in many underground shelters all along the front lines, from the Artois and Lorraine regions, where it was so humid and muddy that you sometime had to sleep with a hood over your head to avoid having water dripping on to your nose, to the Champagne region, [where the shelter was] carved out of chalk in which any heavy artillery fire, no matter how distant, would leave its occupants covered with a white blanket of dust.

Some I furnished myself, others were left to me by comrades who had brought to them different degrees of refinement. There were also some which had belonged to Boches whom we had dislodged. I must say that the latter were by far the best since the Germans were much more conscious of their own comfort.

Only once did I have to move into what I might call a "lair." I almost said a burrow. I am not referring to holes, or temporary shelters, dug out hastily from the wall of a trench in order to protect oneself from enemy bombs, but rather to "quarters" which your orders require you to occupy over several days and nights. This one was as primitive from the viewpoint of comfort as it was safety.

It was in the trench located east of Canny-sur-Matz which we had baptized rather pompously the "trench of the impenetrable forest," a name which was not without irony since this "impenetrable forest" was only a small copse covering a half hectare, where a few elm trees towered over a tangle of brush. The trench which we occupied ran in front of and on either side of this small wood. Fortunately it was protected by an intricate network of barbed wire. It was rather primitive and shapeless and quite vulnerable to an attack coming from the famous "Bois Triangulaire" or triangle-shaped wood. With its inadequate milling, its poor layout, and its shabby construction, it made it almost impossible to move about without breaking a bone due to the unstable, slippery floor of mud-caked boards. It was difficult to comprehend how an infantry regiment, whose number I will not divulge, could have lived in this chaotic mess, this cesspool, for weeks on end, without making the slightest effort to improve the living conditions or the safety! As we will see later, the shelters were in keeping with the trench.

We were coming to take our post at around 4:00 A.M. one very cold and dark night. On the side of the muddy road I could make out a rectangular shaped light which I took to be the window of a shelter. It was the "door" of my home! Following the invitation of comrade Delacour, whom I was relieving and who looked as if he had fallen into the mud-filled roadside ditch, I worked my way into my new command post. The door was about forty inches high and thirty-two inches wide with an entryway of three descending steps. You first had to put down your gear, and then go down backward, bent over so that your knees were hitting your chin, or you couldn't enter! Of course the procedure was reversed to come out. You should have seen Lieutenant Peyronnet who was just over six feet tall trying to get in and out!

The inside of the shelter was somewhat comparable to its entrance. The quarters had been dug out of the roadside ditch, by making the drainage ditch a little deeper and digging out a little bit more of the terreplein² which extended above. The timber work was rudimentary and of questionable value. The living space was some fifteen by nine feet and anyone over five foot six hit the ceiling with his head. The furniture consisted of a cot with a straw mattress, a table and two chairs. With the two of us in there, there was practically no room left! There was also a small fireplace which had been carved out of the back wall. You had to keep a constant eye on the fire since it was within a couple of feet of the straw and fires were quite a source of worry. In addition to the blaze itself you could expect the fire to draw a downpour of shells from the Boches. The light for the shelter came, as was often the case, from the door opening. It was not very large at that.

Finally, as far as our safety was concerned, the only thing which protected us against the rain was a sheet of corrugated metal which a cobble stone could have caved in. Since the Boches were quite willing to shell our trench line and we were surrounded by rather impressive craters a few feet away from our shelter, it was obvious to us that we had to rely mostly on Providence to bring us peace of mind. But we had become fatalists and I recall one time a card game with Gasté[3] of the Fifth Cavalry, which was not even disturbed although the Germans were doing a nice job of bombing us and even had a direct hit on the machine guns of our comrade Pavy,[4] as well as some other close calls. . . .

I spent many days and nights in my "lair" as I called it and, well, I got used to it. As you can imagine it was easy to heat and there was no humidity. What more can you ask from a "lair?" Peyronnet and I were able to take our meals together in there and his large physique took up all the available space.

We even did one better. We played bridge in it — further proof that the word "impossible" does not exist in French! One day when I was complaining about our tight quarters, Gasté told me: "But Captain, we played bridge in your place!" "Oh, come on," I exclaimed, "I'll believe it when I see it!" "Okay! Give me time to find a fourth and I'll show you!" But, he added, "We have to go through a few contortions which I will guide." A half-hour later, after some tricky moves and some fancy gymnastics, we were four players sitting around my table. One was on the cot, another on the entrance steps, and the other two on the two chairs. To say that we had a lot of elbow room would be an exaggeration, but God did we enjoy ourselves that day in the "lair" of the "impenetrable forest!"

Canny-sur-Matz
(Oise)
March 1915

4

The Mass of the Catacombs

[Editor's Note: This chapter describes a mass held in the subterranean shelters, which originally had been cellars for homes in the town of Canny-sur-Matz. What appeared at first sight to be a deserted village turned out to be a very active, well-organized community of several hundred soldiers living what Lécluse called a "troglodyte existence." It was in these subterranean caves that the author attended a mass, which is the basis for this chapter.

For practicing Catholics, the experience of attending mass at the front, close to the enemy, was often a moving experience.[1] The strong association of Catholicism with faith, family, church, nation, and duty in the prewar period naturally attracted French patriots during the war. Some forty-five thousand Catholic clergy were mobilized during World War I, five thousand of whom were killed. Many served as chaplains, hospital orderlies, stretcher-bearers, or even combatants. Other clergy were taken hostage by the Germans in occupied territory, and many were deported or executed. Cholvy and Hilaire indicate that these chaplains "shared the life of the soldiers, the cold, the work, the suffering, the fear, the risk of death." Regarded with some suspicion at first, these chaplains soon were accepted as equals and friends. In all, the French clergy received 17,715 citations and 18,552 decorations. Fourteen percent of the mobilized clergy were killed during the war, one of the highest percentages for those in the professional categories.[2]

Not all French men and women were practicing Catholics before the war. According to Gibson, rates of male and female church attendance varied widely by region. In Chartres in 1909, male attendance was 2.3 percent while female attendance was 16.9 percent. In Nantes, 91.4 percent of all males and 97.7 percent of all females attended mass in the period 1899–1902. In addition to church attendance, baptism, marriage, and extreme unction are three sacraments that help to define observance of church law and hence provide a quantitative look at the degree to which French men and women were practicing Catholics around the turn of the twentieth century. By 1908, 37.9 percent of all French new-

borns were not baptized in any religion; 39.0 percent of those newly mar-
ried had only a civil ceremony; and 25.7 percent of those who died had
no religious burial. Perhaps the best single indicator of religious practice
for Catholics is Easter communion. Church laws prescribe taking commu-
nion at least once per year. Performing one's "Easter Duty" by attending
mass and receiving communion is also required of practicing Catholics.
Thus, the tendency of French men and women to take Easter commu-
nion is one index of what would be expected as a threshold level of reli-
gious observance. Unfortunately, most statistics on Easter communion
focus on teenagers, not on adult parishioners. By the turn of the twenti-
eth century, the percentages of twenty year olds taking Easter communion
at Bourges in the Cher (1909–13) ranged from 4.1 percent of all males
and 27.5 percent of all females to 92.1 percent of all males and 97.7 per-
cent of all females at Rennes in the Ille-et-Vilaine (1899).[3]]

To Captain de Peyronnet of the 9th Light Group[4]

From dawn to dusk, the hikers who would venture as far as the village of
Canny-sur-Matz would have brought back the impression of a vast,
abandoned ruin. All the houses were more or less destroyed, many of the
roofs had collapsed, and, through the gaping windows, we could see the
pillaged interiors, devoid of furniture, where only a shapeless pile of
debris remained in the middle of each room. In this little Pompeii,
where the main street extended slightly more than a kilometer, all life
seemed extinguished. We could barely see, from a distance, a furtive
prowler crossing a street with hurried steps. You had to wend your way
from one house to the next, hugging the walls.

But as soon as night fell and as the shadows darkened, the scene
changed abruptly. The deserted village transformed itself into a busy bee
hive. In a muffled din, streets filled with soldiers who seemed to come
out of the ground, and who actually did. Some were heading for the
trenches; others were busying themselves with chores of all kinds; others
crowded around the cars which were entering the village, loaded with
food and supplies. It only lasted a few hours, in darkened streets (because all light was forbidden so close to the enemy) crawling with an
intense life, which during all the day had been confined to the basement
of the village. As a matter of fact, each house was inhabited, but only the
cellar, where all furniture had been brought. In such a way, the poor

inhabitants of Canny, if they ever found their houses again in a very bad state, would at least be able to recover a part of their furniture.

There were bedroom cellars, cook cellars, office cellars, infirmary cellars. Hundreds of men, many squadrons at once, who led there a troglodyte existence, had become cave men again, since the day when the daily bombing had rendered life impossible above ground. The village of Canny, which was the center of supply and the headquarters of the reserves for several sectors of trenches, had fortunately lent itself in the most complete manner for that role, thanks to the manufacture of cheese, which flourished there before the war, and which demanded a spacious, vaulted, and perfectly dry cellar under each house, which could be reached by a stone staircase made up of about fifteen steps.

You could live there very comfortably and hardly move during the entire day, venturing out only in the interior courtyards, ready to tumble underground at the first whistling of a shell. Little by little, the fixing up of these underground homes had become almost luxurious.

I lived in one whose walls were almost completely hung with percale. It is true that the drapery was black and white, and that it had a false appearance of a temporary morgue! But we didn't let that bother us! In an other one, which was particularly spacious, we had laid out two rooms separated by portals, and we had installed a parquet floor. One was our bedroom, furnished with four complete beds, dressing table, mirrored armoires, night stands, ceiling lights and appliqués; the other a meeting room with a dining room table, desk, buffet, writing table, couch and armchairs, hanging lamps, mirrors and some paintings on the walls, nic-nacs on the tables, and flowers in bases of artillery shells. The whole was heated by a beautiful stove which we also used for our morning lunch and our five o'clock tea, because in our monotonous existence as moles, it is quite understandable that bridge and teas brought precious relief.

It was in this large cellar that I had the opportunity to witness a sight of a truly unforgettable beauty. It was a "mass in the Catacombs," similar to the ones which, at the time of the primitive Church, brought together persecuted Christians in the depths of the earth, out of the reach of tyrants, who were the Boches of that time.

Religious ceremonies celebrated at the front, at times under enemy fire, were always moving. I saw many of them, in barns, under the shelter of a shack, in the ruins of a church, or even in the middle of a forest under large trees. It was always very beautiful and all the details contributed to creating a profound impression, but this mass replaced all others in my mind!

It was still pitch black, this Sunday in March 1915. We were coming down from the trenches, around 4:00 A.M., to settle ourselves in this new cellar well-regarded for the moment. I had just taken possession of my "home"[5] when I saw a tall dragoon arrive, with the beard of a patriarch, and his legs coated with clay up to the knees, like the rest of us. It was the diocesan missionary, Father Lucas, stretcher-bearer of the Third Dragoons. He told me that he would celebrate mass at my place in a half-hour.

There we were both at work, sweeping, cleaning and tidying everything up as best we could. The humble altar was quickly erected. It was a small table of white wood, covered by a few newspapers and a towel, and placed in front of the access staircase, in order to be seen by everyone. The Father opened his small suitcase, which we called a "portable altar," and we admired the ingenuity which provided all which was necessary to celebrate the mass. It was evident that everything was meant to be multi-functional, and reduced to minimum size: a supple, double-sided ornament, white on one side for all the feasts, black on the other for burials; a chalice as tall as a stemmed glass and collapsible in two pieces, a missal which had the dimensions of a prayer book, a desk where appeared a clapper, chandeliers, candles and cruets from a doll house, and everything was improvised.

At five o'clock, everything was ready, and groups of faithful slowly made their way in the cellar gently illuminated by a lamp hung from its vaulted ceiling. They packed it, leaving barely enough room for the celebrant to turn around. The last arrivals stood on each step of the staircase up into the yard, bare-headed in spite of the biting cold. What an interesting sight, this gathering, silent and collected, whose eyes, shining in the semi-darkness, stared avidly at the little corner of cellar where the God of Armies was about to descend![6]

In the front row, our commander, Colonel de La Tour,[7] officers, doctors, behind them the muddy, the wretched, their features drawn by insomnia and by fatigue caused by the rough guard duty from which they had come, soldiers of all arms and all countries. We were a long way from the customary ceremonies, so pompous and so edifying as they may be! Here, it was truly the Act of Faith in all its sincerity, intense and trusting prayer, the fervent call for the help of God. . . . There were, perhaps, some men who had just escaped death a few minutes before, and not a single one of them was assured of seeing the end of this day which they had begun in prayer, and their presence meant that they were thanking, hoping, and placing themselves in the hands of God! The mass took place piously, in complete silence, because we could not, as usual, sing the Creed out loud; the Boches were too close and their hearing too keen. When, at the solemn moment of the Elevation, the whole gathering of soldiers fell to their knees in one movement, as at maneuvers, we thought about the majesty of the mystery which took place in this wretched setting. More than one heart was heavy and many eyes no longer saw the celebrant except through a veil of tears. . . .

If I have ever felt the inadequacy of words, it is in seeking to describe this sublime ceremony, about which one of those in attendance, expressing our common thoughts, told me upon leaving: "I am happy to have lived to see this, but now I would want to be able to live to remember it!"

Canny-sur-Matz
(Oise)
7 March 1915

5

The Good Thieves

*[Editor's Note: In this chapter, Lécluse and his men rescue religious arti-
facts from a ruined church in Canny-sur-Matz. As the author indicates,
this was the first church in ruins that they encountered. The author had
seen the church before it had been destroyed by bombardment and was
particularly saddened by its loss. The chapter ends with the discovery of a
fallen Christ statue, which seems to the author to command respect for
those buried in the cemetery. In the diary, the author identifies the chaplain, himself, Couespel, Peyronnet, and three enlisted men as the "good
thieves." They take a pushcart to rescue the sacred objects in the church.*

*Little scenes such as this were repeated dozens of times by pious
officers and men in the contested areas along the western front. Churches
were often targets of attack because German soldiers believed that partisans used church towers to direct sniper and artillery fire at occupying
troops or even signaled German troop movements to French army units.]*

To Lieutenant de Durat of the 9th Light Group[1]

We ransacked you but our intentions were good, poor little church of
Canny, sitting so pleasantly in the hollow of a little valley, at the end of
the long row of poplar trees covered with mistletoe, which gave you a
stately appearance, so coquettish with your elegant steeple and your
decorative Louis XV woodwork in white and gold, worthy of the chapel
in a château. You might have been able to escape the rage of the Boches,
because you were some distance from the village which they bombed
daily, useless anger which we mocked as we sat comfortably housed in
deep cellars. But, on the contrary, they seemed to display a particular
hatred toward you, and too often honored you with one of their salvoes,
as if they had been dealing with a cathedral. Too often, some of their
shells hit the mark. They were not always as bad shots as this day of

Mardi Gras 1915, where the only result of a furious cannonade was the toppling of the cock of your steeple, a feat worthy of a shooting gallery!

When I saw you for the first time, you had not suffered much: a few holes in your bell tower, a large opening in the wall of a side chapel, and damage, here and there, on your plaster and your woodwork. You were still standing despite your wounds. We could have prayed in your sanctuary and heard mass at your altar. I remember that, to the great delight of my comrade Grandjean[2] who was nosing-about in the sacristy, I suddenly played some chords on your intact harmonium. But at the following relief, what change, and what desolation! Shells had pierced the little church in twenty places; others had burst in the interior, ruining everything; the main altar had disappeared under a section of the roof, the chapels had been devastated, the harmonium in pieces, statues mutilated, and above all, a vaulted roof full of gaping holes threatened to collapse. . . .

In the middle of this destruction, there were some strange sights: a rather beautiful painting, representing Mary-Magdalene, barely scuffed; a bouquet of artificial flowers under a crystal globe intact at the top of an altar which was broken and three-quarters destroyed. . . .

It was the first church we had seen in ruins, and we stood there with hearts aching in front of this lamentable spectacle. Then we started wandering around in the ruins looking for souvenirs, and in my case I gathered a beautiful bouquet of flowers from the main altar, lily petals in white satin with pistils of gold, which, placed in the pages of missals, now bring, hopefully, my name to the lips of friends during their hour of prayer.

You can not imagine our astonishment when, upon exploring the ruins of the sacristy, and looking in one of the armoires whose doors had been smashed, we noticed that all the items commonly used for mass were still there! The parish priest of Canny, fleeing the Germans when they occupied the village, had had just enough time to save the sacred vessels, leaving the rest of his wealth, which still filled the drawers. There were more than fifteen complete vestments of all colors, copes, stoles, procession banners, some in beautiful, old embroidered silk, the vestments of altar boys, albs of lace, chasubles, all this untouched and complete. What feelings had inspired the Germans? Had this been done out of a type of religious respect? Or, rather were these specialized spoils less tempting than the bottles of wine in the cellars or the clocks of the residents of Canny? Whatever the reason, they had not touched anything. . . . Of course, as time had passed, we had retaken the village, but it was on line with our trenches, shelled on a daily basis, and the poor priest had never ventured to return to get his belongings which he believed had been lost forever.

I quickly proposed to my officers to rescue everything, if there were a lull in the fighting, an offer which was accepted enthusiastically, and which received the blessing and thanks of the curé of Briquebourg, who offered to safeguard the treasures of his colleague. That is how, one morning, without having notified anyone of our project, and taking advantage of the first glow of day, because the Boches were never early risers, we returned with a hand cart pulled by two resourceful poilus.

Within fifteen minutes, everything had disappeared. Professional thieves would not have done a better job! We finished off our looting with a few processional crosses, some wood statues, a large, polychrome, stucco statue of the Virgin, one of Mary-Magdalene, Gospels, some missals, some silver chandeliers, and, our cart straining under the load, my men at the shafts, my officers pushing the wheels, we departed just like thieves, so to speak, to go back to our cellars, happy with our escapade like some university students having just played a prank, and marched proudly under the stunned eyes of the sentry posted behind the barricade.

Before leaving the square, I went into the small cemetery facing the church and on the other side of the road, because I had noticed that the large cross which used to stand over it had disappeared. It had fallen indeed, cut right at the base by a shell, but it had not been broken in its fall, and it was lying lengthwise on the tombs. . . . The Christ, his arms outstretched in a sublime gesture, seemed to be protecting and defending those who had come to sleep at his feet, and his eyes, turned toward the enemy, seemed to say: "Halt your rage at the threshold of this asylum! You can massacre the living, sow ruin and death, demolish my temple, uproot my cross, break my limbs once again, but respect at least the deep sleep of those who are here!"

Canny-sur-Matz
(Oise)
11 March 1915

6

The Sentinels

[*Editor's Note: This is one of the more morbid chapters in the memoir. Originally entitled "The Stars," it describes the bodies of German soldiers strewn about a recent battlefield.*

Lécluse and his men headed off to Conchy-les-Pots[1] on 14 March 1915. On the night of 22 March, the French sang songs, shouted insults at the Germans, made animal noises, and played trumpets. The Germans responded to this harassment with a few ineffective rifle shots and then an artillery salvo. The next day, Lécluse and Peyronnet decided to take a tour of the village and its cemetery after lunch, hoping to see the Germans that had been killed on 1 October 1914. During that battle, the French had taken twelve hundred prisoners and killed one thousand enemy troops just to the north of the village at the edge of the woods. Initially they burned some of the rotting corpses close to their listening posts. But, the rest of the dead were strewn along a front of five hundred to eight hundred meters. In the meantime, the French lines had advanced one hundred meters so that these cadavers were now some five to six meters from the French troops. The macabre sight and foul stench of the rotting corpses were characteristic of life at the front, and similar entries can be found in other war memoirs.[2] In words which bring to mind some of the most hideous images of World War I, Lécluse recreates the ghastliness of this spectacle.]

To Lieutenant de la Villéon, 9th Light group — 2d Light[3]

When we would go to the trenches of Bois des Loges and a new man or an officer from another company out for a stroll joined us from the rear, before showing him our model sector with its well-kept encampment, its wire-covered passages and its small firing trenches with its intricate system of slits — all that was rather new at that time which seems so long ago, we first took him to see the "Boches" to impress him a little.

We would walk close to the "Boar" and the "Panther," the two seventy-five caliber guns which had wiped out so many Germans during their last attack, and which lately had been startling us much too frequently as we lay half-asleep in the shelters along the second line. As we continued on down the road, we saluted the heartrending cemetery which pious hands always kept decorated with fresh cut flowers, and we would arrive at the mines of the village of the Loges, wretched heaps of rubble whose cellars still provided a somewhat precarious shelter for our kitchens.

From there we walked along the only road to the village, trying not to look too closely at the suspicious pools on whose murky, oil-saturated water floated a collection of vile debris. We would go around the barricade, in front of which laid the half-charred, withering carcasses of three horses. Then we would disappear from view into the open trenches in front of the next-to-the-last house to keep from being hit by the fire of the ever-watchful Germans.

A few steps farther on, there was a ladder which had been opportunely placed by the territorial army. We would cordially invite our guest to scale a few rungs in order to peer into the ruins of a house, gutted by one of our shells during our return to Les Loges. We would study his facial expression which always revealed a great feeling of revulsion at what he saw. There was a good reason for it. In the part of the house which had been exposed by the explosion was a bedroom which had been nicely furnished at one time. There lay the bodies of two Germans, in the exact position they were in when death caught them by surprise. One was stretched out on the bed, the other half fallen out of bed, his feet still on the mattress and his head on the floor. . . . Our predecessors evidently hadn't had time to bury them and were content to cover them with quick lime. With the passage of time, they had been forgotten, and the two miserable "Boches" were left to dry up, their bodies being gnawed away little by little, becoming more shapeless and grotesque with each passing day, insignificant remains in the midst of such destruction.

This, however, was only a taste of what was to come. We had our man sufficiently prepared for the sight which was in store for him as we would take him to the trenches on the front line. We would move with great caution since the least carelessness could cost us our lives.

On the plain, dotted with apple trees, which rose slightly toward enemy lines, toward a small cluster of houses which had been given the strange name of "Abbey Street" we could make out innumerable blue-gray patches. They were "Boches."

They had been there for some ten months, tragic witnesses of the last assault where their furious charge had come to a sudden halt, in the very spot where death had struck them down. Most had fallen forward, only a few had fallen on their back, yet all were found as close to cover as the ground could provide: a clump of dirt, a bush, a manure pile. . . . They had been there to provide fire cover for a larger number of their comrades-in-arms who had charged our barbed wire fences from the side. Some were lying amid the tangled wire. One of them, in particular, made quite an impression since we had moved up our firing trenches and now he was only some ten feet away from us.

He was a very tall infantryman, rawboned, the typical Prussian mercenary. He was lying on his back, one knee bent, his arms stretched outward in the shape of a cross, his eyes closed, his upper lip curled up in a sinister sneer. Bad weather, the rain and the sun, had mummified somewhat this oversized corpse and given his hands and face a grayish, sallow color making his hair and reddish beard barely noticeable. With time the faded uniform, the boots, the leather belt had taken on a neutral tint which was both undefinable and grim. It was an eerie sight which one wouldn't soon forget and which produced on the newcomer the effect we had hoped for.

One might wonder why all these bodies had not been given a decent burial. . . . The answer we were given was: the day following the battle all the dead who could be reached without risk of our being shot were buried. However, the fierce Colonel D., who was in charge of the sector he had just taken back and defended successfully, gave the order to leave some of those victims lying there as "an example," as he put it, a sort of salutary warning to those who might be tempted to imitate them! In fact, they created a strange curtain of sentinels to guard our lines. However the surrounding area was rather short on charm, and my comrade Villéon, whose machine guns were in the area, will never forgot the spectacle which awaited him each time he came up to the shooting slit, the horrible odors which the wind carried to him, and the obstacles which caused him to stumble during his night rounds! On one occasion, a shell launched by the Boches landed dead center . . . on one of their countrymen! Needless to say the fragments which rained upon the trench that time were not limited to iron!

Since that time, we had to remove all of these ghastly human wrecks and we no longer took visitors "to see the Boches." Only lookouts who were very much alive were asked to guard the trenches and the German sentinels, after having served for several months on their morbid watch, had finally found rest . . . and oblivion!

Bois des Loges
(Oise)
March 1915

7

In Boche Country

[Editor's Note: This chapter describes events that took place during July and August 1915, when Lécluse and his men were stationed in Mulhouse.[1] Part of Alsace, this territory had been seized by Prussia in 1871. The French regained control of that small territory very briefly early in the war, lost it within a few days, recaptured it again, and held it tenuously in the summer of 1915. In the interim, Lécluse's squadron had suffered from cold, wind, rain, and mud. On 9 April, he complained in his diary of arduous work details assigned to his unit by Colonel Chapez, including repair of a road from Roye-au-Bois[2] to Bois des Loges, a distance of three to four kilometers. (See map 3.) Many soldiers' diaries complain of needless or arduous work details and, in this chapter, Lécluse echoes the complaints of his men.

The author also expresses delight at reentering part of Alsace. Feelings of joy were commonly expressed among French soldiers liberating Alsace, which had been seized by the Germans during the Franco-Prussian war of 1870–71. Lécluse was stationed in a quiet sector where peace was interrupted only by occasional sniper fire. The men were on an eight-day rotation with twenty-four hours at the front, twenty-four hours in reserve barracks, and eight days of rest in the villages of Starneberg, Hecken, and Guildwiller.[3] The diary entry of 6 July 1915 is the basis for this chapter.]

To Lieutenant Destressou of the 9th Light Group 1914–15[4]

There was on the front, a small parcel of land, alas! too small, where we were "in Boche country." But, this expression was not quite accurate, since all we had done was to take back some of our property stolen in 1871.

If we were unable to keep Mulhouse, captured thanks to audacity but which we could not or did not wish to retain, we had been hanging on dearly since the first days of the war to a rather sizable piece of this dear land of Alsace, which had been awaiting for so many years in sublime confidence, the moment of its liberation.

Indeed, it was not very much when compared to the four or five French departments which suffered terribly under the Prussian boot, and compared to Lille, Cambrai, Saint-Quentin, and Laon,[5] we occupied only a few villages and a few, larger Alsacian towns. But, no matter how small it was, this re-annexed parcel of Alsace held a marvelous attraction for French soldiers! The mere fact of having lived there, even for a few days, depending on the hazards of war, left in the heart of those who had that opportunity a certain sweet charm and the burning desire to return there again. . . . We only spent two months there. It's true that it was at the beginning of the summer of 1915, when the Alsatian countryside adorned itself with all its charms, but it remained the best memory of our numerous peregrinations, and since then, each time that we had to move to a different region, among the numerous rumors which circulated, the one mentioning a return to Alsace was always the most popular. Alas! it has not yet been realized![6]

I recall our emotion, when we arrived in this beautiful land, which I knew a little, having gone there on several different occasions before the war, invited to some activities by one of those Strasbourgeois who had remained as French in his customs, language and heart, after forty years of servitude, as he had been the day after that Terrible Year.[7]

We had just been on a rather nice jaunt. We had embarked at Longpré-les-Corps-Saints, west of Amiens, without knowing our destination, and it was only en route that we were apprised that we were going non-stop to Belfort. . . . This small trip reminded me of another similar one, at the time when my squadron was dispatched to the front, from Nantes to Dunkerque![8]

Upon our arrival at nine P.M., while our squadrons were unloading, our commander gathered us on the platform of the station, and announced to us, that after spending a night in villages surrounding Belfort, the following day, we would cross the old border and would camp in Alsace. Higher authorities were even careful to remind us to be polite and how to behave toward Alsatians, a warning we found insulting to our self-esteem!

Right away, this was cause for great joy, and, in the black night through which we filed through the silent streets of Belfort, everybody was chatting excitedly. Just think of the effect it could have on our men — to hear unexpectedly that they were going to step on Alsatian soil, this quasi-legendary country whose beauties, harsh suffering and indomitable hope had been related to them.

Early the next morning, under a radiant sun, we crossed the border, and when we saw the odious black and white pole, topped by the imperial eagle, toppled in the road-side ditch, it drew indeed some cat-calls from the ranks. Among some French troopers, it is to be expected. But, it was followed by a profound silence, suggestive of a type of contemplation. It was true! We had "returned home!" We felt lighter, more alert, as if rid of a deep concern, a heavy remorse, and we kept this feeling during our entire stay there. We looked with as much emotion as curiosity at the large prairies, these flowing and clear waters, these beautiful trees of this dear Alsace, so rich and radiant in its summer costume. Then we saw the first Alsatian houses, with their unique tile roofs and complicated and jagged outlines, their wooden exterior staircases, and the large canopies under which, after harvest, corn stalks hang in tight rows. It is understandable if my low-Bretons were staring, and it was amusing and a bit banal to hear them, so many miles from the native country, exchange their opinions and astonishment in their resonant and guttural dialect.

Once we got to the village of Bretten,[9] where we were supposed to camp, things got even better. There, we really felt like we were "in Boche country." The forges, the saddlers, the grocery stores, the inns had kept their German signs. At the post office, where I was living, the mail box, adorned with the imperial eagle, broken by some vindictive poilu, was still hanging on the wall.

It was a Sunday, and, after the ablutions necessitated by an excursion in motorized trucks along dusty roads, we headed to the church, perched high on a terrace overlooking the road. Needless to say, our entry caused a sensation, particularly among the children and the young Alsatian girls, all the more since this was almost an invasion, since my men, from Brittany and the Vendée, were deeply religious. The priest himself was obviously extremely surprised, and, to begin his sermon, spoken in excellent French, he showered us with compliments, and offered us as models to his parishioners, praises which my brave poilus accepted without flinching!

This radiant summer Sunday was the prelude to two charming months spent for the most part in the shade of a superb beech forest, as you find only in Alsace. Our trenches were just ahead of the edge of the woods, and, at night-fall, on these beautiful summer evenings, we could see the lights of Mulhouse shining in front of us, a dozen kilometers away.

When we would go back to the second line, we lived, in the middle of the forest, in comfortable forest chalets, which were the ideal residence at this time of the year. Naturally, everything, even the locks and their latches, was made out of wood. Our carpenters, in their leisure hours, gave free reign to their talents, and I saw them make some Louis XVI beds by hand which looked as if they had come from the Faubourg Saint-Antoine.

O the beautiful forest! As far as the eye could see, the large white beech trunks climbing majestically, fifty and sixty meters in height, like pillars of an immense cathedral. A thick carpet of moss, sprinkled with small flowers of delicate hues, covered the ground and muffled the noise of footsteps. The dense foliage, which only a few rays of the sun pierced here and there, maintained under the trees, even at high noon, a delicious freshness, and hid us so well from the eyes of the enemy, that we lived in the most complete tranquillity, as if we had been twenty leagues from the lines. We would go horseback riding in the forest; we cooked meals; we ate outside, lamps lighted; my men drilled or indulged in their games, and on Sunday the chaplain came to celebrate mass on an altar of greenery. What a wonderful life we led there! Most of the time, the Boches were not bothersome. Nor were we. And, except for a few rounds of shooting, which were extremely inaccurate, we could forget for hours, sometimes for days, that we were at war.

Twice, however, first as victims of an attack, and then as assailants, we were rudely reminded of the reality of the times, and a few of our brave horsemen stayed behind, to sleep their last sleep in "re-annexed Alsace."

Dear Alsace! Be light and maternal for them! They were granted this favor so rare, alas! to repose in conquered country, and to fall on your twice French soil! Their brothers-in-arms will fight to the death, until the Triumph, to liberate you completely from your odious captivity of nearly a half-century! And we, who had possession of you during these beautiful months of 1915, as long as we live, we will remember these fleeting days, spent under the trees of your forest, to dream of the Victory which we hope will follow, but which will come, as you know, and which will return you forever to your mother, France, this France which also knows how to suffer for you as you have suffered for her!

Forest of Psannestiehl
(High-Alsace)
July–August 1915

8

Moment of Anguish

[Editor's Note: This chapter describes an offensive raid that resulted in several casualties. Of particular interest is the author's ability to depict the apprehension of his men as they faced a very difficult assignment. In what appears to be the response of the High Command to inactivity by French troops at the front, Lécluse received an order on 14 August 1915 detailing the reorganization of the light groups. They were to be divided into units of 180 men—no cyclists, one captain, and three officers, all mounted with two horses each. Each light group would have two sections of machine gunners with two officers. They were told to constantly harass the enemy and, specifically, to raid the enemy trenches the day following a heavy artillery barrage. Lécluse thought this was useless and dangerous. This story is based on the diary entry for 15 August 1915. It is reflective of the attempts of the general staff to force aggressive raids by French troops and to curb informal truces such as those described by Tony Ashworth. Lécluse's reaction is also quite characteristic of those of other officers and enlisted men to orders that put their lives in great jeopardy for no apparent military purpose.]

*To the memory of Corporal d'Ollendon, the first
of my soldiers who died for France.[1]*

In this plain of Alsace where our trench was located, we were about to celebrate August 15 in our own way.[2] Much in the way it was done under the Empire, there would be artillery fire and fireworks; this time, however, the cannons would be spewing death and the rockets would be signaling the different phases of an attack and provide light to the combatants. That was the decision reached by the top brass without ever having to show the real usefulness of the operation involved. Lack of action, even unintentional, was not looked at very favorably at the top, and not understood away from the front. Once in a while, in those areas considered "quiet," it was important to offer "the public," by any means possible, the satisfaction of a misleading press release! Unfortunately more often than not, readers, while judging the actual military action presented to them of meager interest, ignore that it was not done without a price, and that good men, often many of them, lost their lives there!

Military glory and servitude, humble sacrifices, unknown acts of heroism, that was what characterized the everyday life of our "poilus" when not involved in major battles! Thus, at seven o'clock, in front of trenches located in the Psannestiehl forest, the foot squadron of the Fifth Cavalry, under the command of my friend Margraff, was planning a raid on the German structures called "la Cuvette" and "la Lanterne" which were in front of the village of Ammerzviller. My squadron, which had taken position immediately to his left, was ready to provide support if needed. I even went as far as sending one of my platoons, led by Peyron-net, to the wooded area which borders the Speebach,[3] in order to protect their flank.

Our men, carrying only their guns with bayonets, knives and grenades, were to attack the trench under the cover fire provided by our three seventy-five caliber guns. They were to jump into it, do the maximum damage and retreat within a half-hour, taking as many prisoners as possible.

It is easy to see that, though of questionable value, the idea was quite simple. It remained to be seen if it could be carried out as easily! The men had to cover a distance of four or five hundred yards, each way, over a rather barren area, in full daylight, since we were in August. . . . How many of them would be lost along this perilous route? Although no one wanted to say it out loud, that was what everyone pondered and the men's hearts were heavy with anguish. . . .

Mass was held at daybreak, in our small green oratory under the large trees. Attendance was greater than usual and the men were particularly meditative as was often the case prior to a dangerous mission. Some knew that it would be their last mass. Afterwards I went to the edge of the forest to assess the damages caused by our heavy artillery on the outworks to be attacked. The outcome did not appear very satisfactory and I anticipated that evening, my comrades would encounter stiff resistance and a network of barbed wires almost intact. . . . It was up to God!

The day, sunny and clear, could not completely erase a feeling of nervousness which decreased as the moment of truth drew near. At five

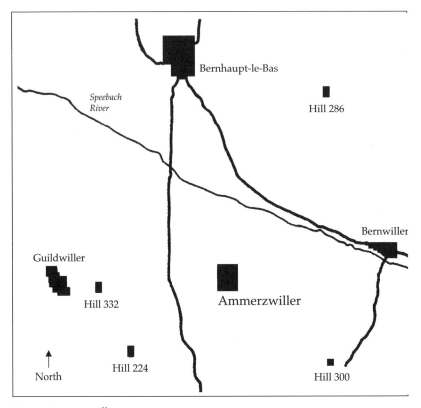

Map 4. Ammerzwiller

o'clock, after a light meal, I went back to my men on the front line, accompanied by my lieutenant, machine gunner Boisfleury.[4] We got there just in time for the start of the celebration. Peyronnet, stretching out his tall body, crawling on his stomach in a furrow, was already out of the trench and ahead of his men who were crawling behind him in order to get to their assigned post. Their movement was done very smoothly and efficiently so as not to draw the attention of the German lookouts. Feeling somewhat reassured I went back to my gabionnade[5] which extended behind my redoubt, the one called "Hill 294," where I had my headquarters. That was where the attack squadron was waiting. Margraff was there, with Cossou,[6] his uniform unbuttoned at the top because the sun was still beating down hard and because in a few moments it was going to get "even warmer." Their men were near by, admirably composed, a spark of courage in their eyes, grenade bags hanging from their shoulders, their trench knives attached to their belts. They were puffing on a last cigarette or on a pipe. The conversations were perhaps a bit more nervous, watches were being glanced at more often, but aside from these barely noticeable signs, no one would suspect that, in a few moments, these men would climb the gabions — and set down in front of them, unprotected, exposing themselves to the canon and machine gun fire. . . .

Quickly we exchanged a few words:

"Is everything O.K.?" — "Great, as you can see!"
"It is two white rockets when you get there and two red when you pull back?"
"Right. Is Peyronnet on his way?"
"He is at his station."
"Great! Then good-bye!"
"And good luck!"

We gave each other a cordial, yet meaningful, hug. Our eyes met and we understood so many things! I had to get back to my post as quickly as I could; the Sabbath was beginning! Our heavy guns had joined in to drench the enemy line with a shower of steel. This time, the Boches who had kept still earlier in the morning, feeling the increasing intensity of the shelling, gladly began to return our fire. In a matter of minutes, a furious exchange of shells and shrapnel was taking place. I even told my men to take cover while we awaited the moment of the attack. The din was getting louder and louder. The Boches had understood what we were up to and were copiously showering the part of the trench where we were presently located, right across from their position. Their fire, coming from three different directions, whistled overhead bursting in gray and yellow clouds. Luckily for us they were shooting "too long" and behind us.

Suddenly, the noise became deafening: in loud bursts, our seventy-fives came into action joining the other guns which were creating a constant rumbling sound. We could hear the sharp and harrowing sounds of the shells leaving, roaring over our heads and the formidable explosions just ahead of us. . . . I looked at my watch: it was six-fifty, the critical moment had almost arrived. . . . The gunfire rattled out, machine guns on both sides joined in as if afraid to miss out on this infernal concert. It was a real cacophony, a collection of indescribable sounds. No one could hear anything and to make myself understood, I had to scream in the ear of Lieutenant Billet, standing next to me behind the protective wall.[7]

We climbed onto the bench seat and looked through a slit. In front of us and to the right the spectacle was truly frightening. Churned by the shells of our seventy-five batteries, loaded with a new more powerful charge, the plain resembled a succession of volcanoes each spewing clumps of dirt and rocks toward enormous black or greenish clouds which darkened the sunlit sky. Bullets whistled or crackled, projectiles roared, screamed, squealed, each making their own music. And what music! All of sudden, in the middle of the wreathes of smoke which the wind was trying to sweep away, our cavalrymen appeared! By God, they were a sight to behold! Determined and in complete unison; now we could hear their voices over the din. . . . "Listen" said Billet, "Can you hear them, captain?" "Yes! They are singing!"

All eyes were focused on them! Bent over, they moved swiftly, following the small spring as they advanced behind a curtain of explosions from our big guns which were lengthening their fire and leading our men toward enemy lines. They disappeared from our sight and then we had to go through agonizing moments. Watch in hand, we counted the minutes . . . ten . . . fifteen . . . a half hour! It was taking forever!

Oblivious of the storm of steel raging around us, unnerved from waiting and having to stay where we were, motionless, so near to our fighting comrades, we exchanged a few "What if . . ." and "What then . . ." with each other, in fractured sentences. Had we only known what was going on there, so close to us, in all that smoke and noise!

Night was setting upon us, increasing our oppressing fear. Time after time, rockets shot up showering an area of the plain with light. Everywhere, in front of us, behind us, exploding projectiles streaked the darkness with reddish bolts of light. Our large batteries had started a fire in the direction of Ammerzwiller and we watched with morbid satisfaction the flames climbing toward the sky and the thick smoke swirling about.

Suddenly, a man jumped into the trench right next to where we were:

"We have two wounded soldiers, Captain."

"Who are they? What happened?"

"Sergeant Le Goff has been hit in the arm and Corporal d'Ollendon in the jaw . . ."

"Besides that, is there anything else new?"

"The cavalrymen are coming back, captain . . . The lieutenant is calling for two stretchers . . ."

Incredible! I didn't even have time to give the order. . . . Before I could say anything, five or six of the men who had rushed over to inquire about the news were already running toward the stretchers, and, ignoring the whistling bullets, had jumped over the protective wall to rescue their comrades. What brave men!

All of a sudden, in the trench, we could hear a tumultuous roar followed by cheers! It was a group of cavalrymen, covered with dirt and sweat, their clothing all messed up. . . . One of them was brandishing a German helmet, another, covered with blood from a shoulder wound and leaning on the arm of another, was swearing and shaking his fist with his good arm toward an enemy which was no longer in front of him. . . . Voices cried out, men were calling out to each other. Some were telling their stories, each trying to speak louder than the other. It was a deafening sound which increased every time another man came from the connecting trenches. I was finally able to bring a bit of calm to the situation and noticing the arrival of a young member of the corps of engineers who was coming back from the attack, I asked him for some details related to the action. Thank God! Our comrades had come out pretty well and luck had been on their side. Thanks to the fortunate idea of Margraff, who had begun the attack five minutes before it was scheduled, the men were able to get to the German trench at the same time as the fire barrage of the seventy-five, therefore before the Germans would dare to come out of their shelters. There, they ran into a network of wires which was still intact. One of the platoons was able to find the chicane.[8] Some twenty men slid through it, jumped into the trench and fanned out in both directions, throwing grenades in the shelters, capturing or killing with their bayonets the few Boches they encountered. We destroyed a lot of material, including the telephone. When it came time to get out, things went sour. The Germans filled the trenches behind our men and started to shoot at them. Fortunately nightfall and a ground fog spreading from the Speebach bog impaired their accuracy. Still, quite a few of my men were left behind.

We brought back a dozen or so prisoners. We had to shoot one who refused to move. Margraff and Cosson were fine, the young Second-Lieutenant Ehrmann[9] was wounded in the foot.

I tried, unsuccessfully, to contact our commanding officer by phone. The wires had been cut for a while by all the fireworks. My communications men were trying their best to find the breaks in order to reestablish the line. What unselfishness and courage!

Now it was Peyronnet's turn to come back with his two wounded men. It was over. That courageous Le Goff, from lower-Brittany, perhaps the most gallant of my NCO's, greeted me proudly in spite of his pain: "Oh! I am not dead yet, captain!" A bullet had pierced his side and then his arm, fortunately the bone was not broken. Poor Ollendon, his head wrapped with a blood-covered handkerchief, forced a small smile. When I leaned over to him to shake his hand, he mumbled something which I believed to be a thank-you. I led them both through the side trenches to my gabion, straddling the Burnhaupt road, from which they could be evacuated to the first aid station as soon as the Boches ceased or at least lessened their raging barrage aimed at the rear of our front line. Phew! It was over! We congratulated each other and I went about taking our customary safety precautions, with perhaps increased care that night, including flares every fifteen minutes, out of fear of an eventual though unlikely counter attack since the moon was presently bathing the area with its light. Slowly, calm returned to the area. One by one the canons became still. Gun shots were farther and farther apart. Within an hour all was quiet, except for one Boche who persisted in firing a shot every five minutes. His bullets slammed just above my shelter. You should have heard the swearing and the bad jokes aimed at him!

The only thing left for us to do was to chain smoke in order to avoid falling asleep. We could breathe a little easier, a big burden off our chests, and the men were chatting away, their conversation interspersed with laughter. Still, when additional information reached us, the final human cost of the operation was somewhat less palatable: eight cavalry men were dead or missing, twenty-five were wounded, some mortally, two of my men had been hit, Ehrmann and an other officer, seven sappers killed, twelve wounded, fifty troopers and two officers out of commission. All of this to inflict some damage on the enemy line, kill or wound an unknown number of Germans, and to take nine prisoners!

You must admit, you who, as a stern critic, is sitting in your comfortable armchair and who sneered scornfully upon reading the two lines of the communiqué informing you of "the bit of help at Ammerzwiller," that, had you known the cost, you might have said, as we did: "That turned out to be a rather costly endeavor!"

Ammerzwiller
(High-Alsace)
15 August 1915

9

Forgetting About Time

[Editor's Note: Two days after the costly raid at Ammerzwiller, Lécluse nominated several of his dead and wounded for the croix de guerre. But they were refused. On 30 August, Lécluse learned that he was going to receive the croix de guerre at the divisional level for his actions at Ammerzwiller. In his diary Lécluse comments that he composed and read a satirical piece based on La Fontaine's "The City Rat and the Country Rat," substituting the names of Commandant Delaire and Commandant Guinebault of the First Dragoons. Apparently, that rendition of La Fontaine's famous tale spread quickly throughout the division.

Soldiers' diaries and memoirs often contained lengthy descriptions of unusual meals, trips to nearby towns, and encounters with local inhabitants. These interludes between moments of violence had special meaning and intensity for many of these men. This chapter of the memoir concerns a brief visit into the forest near Chamouilley, a period filled with serenity.[1]]

To Lieutenant C. de Lorgeril—9th Light Group[2]

This is a pleasurable recollection of the countryside, saved preciously on the eve of those horrible days which we experienced during the offensive of September 1915. During one's life, even during its worst moments, there are oases of freshness and serenity like these whose charm we like to recall at a later date.

We were on the road, two comrades and I, crossing the Forest of the Three Fountains.[3] We indulged in this short side trip because our absence would be brief and we had to make the best of the remaining hours of rest we had been enjoying for the past month in the peaceful village of Chamouilley. The next day, perhaps that evening, we would be getting on the road, not for an unknown land this time, but for a destination, alas! we knew too well, that horrible, despicable Champagne where we were going to attempt the big attack, the great clash which, we hoped, would burst the German line.

The forest was beautiful. Late that September, it had put on its wonderful autumn garb. Its still thick foliage was speckled with all the tones of green and gold. The sun shone discretely through its branches over the thick and grassy underbrush. The car took us through this winding road, across that enchanting landscape, quickly and smoothly toward a marvelous surprise. . . .

There it was, all of a sudden, at a turn in the road, so strange and unexpected, that we let out a gasp. In the large clearing where we had arrived, it was as if a magician, with a touch of his wand, had created this fairy-like scenery, throwing us suddenly back into the past and away from ordinary sights and occurrences!

In front of our startled eyes, a large Louis XIV château presented its imposing and sumptuous architecture. Beyond a paved esplanade, there were two symmetrical buildings connected by a high, cloister wall, and crowned with vases sculptured in stone. In the middle of it, there was a monumental door framed with coats-of-arms. The forged iron gate was wide open, and we could see, at the back of the interior court yard, the greenhouse and the colonnade which connected again the two main buildings. Still farther, beyond the columns and the windows of the greenhouse, we could see the classic green carpet and the French garden. The whole thing was most distinguished and pure in style. And all around, silence and solitude reigned. . . .

To tell the truth, we would have expected to see a gilded coach or a sedan chair escorted by noblemen in full costume emerge from under the arch. . . . What were we doing there, and what must we have looked like with our car, our azure blue uniforms and our police helmets?

But, like a link between the dull reality which we represented and the magnificent past so strangely revived in front of us, a noble lady approached with white hair, dressed in a less-than-fashionable costume, even a trifle dated. She walked proudly with the exquisite grace of an Eighteenth Century marquise. Without a doubt, those two bull-terriers which cavorted around her were a bit too modern and did not replace the classic greyhounds very well, but still she was truly the worthy lady of a beautiful residence, the inheritor and guardian of the traditions and customs of a by-gone era, and the spell was not broken when, with a smile, she returned our greeting and welcomed us. Following her, we crossed the threshold and entered the sumptuous home which she wanted to share with us. The enchantment continued. In succession, we visited the large rooms of the main floor, the greenhouse, the French garden, with its large, framed yard and flower beds, the oval ornamental pond, and, way in the back, a raised terrace with three steps, surrounded by a short wall adorned with bushes and statues. All in perfect taste, perfect in style, not one anachronism interrupted the dream in which we found ourselves. . . .

But, in this enchanted setting, another marvel awaited us. There was, at the end of the park, in the shade of the high maple trees, the ruins of a Cistercian church, contemporary, we were told, with Saint-Bernard, and destroyed during the Revolution. Two-thirds of it remained, exterior walls, Gothic vault, massive pillars and slender columns, with capitals chiseled like fine lace. Here and there, large blocks of masonry had collapsed, but it was still in one piece, so strong was the construction. The reddish cast of the stones mixed its warm tones with the green color of the ivy, vine and weeds which were slowly taking them over. We could see that pious care had been taken to preserve and to decorate discretely these venerable ruins. The ground had been raked and covered with sand; green plants, beds of petunias with delicate hues fringed the foot of the walls and encircled the pillars. At the apse of the church, a large cross spread its white marble arms over the sanctified ground where a large number of the companions of Saint Bernard have been sleeping for centuries.

Large trees spread their branches across the gaps in the walls; others had grown into the inside of the building and had created a roof with their foliage. No landscaper, no decorator could envision such a masterpiece, this admirable jumble which was like a hymn of stone and greenery!

But time flies . . . Alas! we had forgotten about time! Far from the noise of the canon, whose rumblings did not reach us, far from the harsh realities, the vulgarity of daily tasks, far from what the next day might bring, we had escaped time . . . and life! We had to return to it and say farewell to these marvels, in the same way you turn the page holding the beautiful picture which you have been admiring, so splendid that it remains forever in the back of your mind.

But as we bowed before the old, smiling woman, she was surprised by the effusion of our thanks: "You say it is nothing, madam!" one of us answered. "We beg to disagree. . . . Thanks to you, thanks to this exquisite vision of the past, so engaging and pure, in this serene and collected atmosphere, we have had the priceless happiness to savor fully, for a few minutes, an escape from the present."

Chamouilley, near Saint-Dizier[4]
(Marne)
15 September 1915

10

In Chalkland

[Editor's Note: This chapter was written soon after the preceding chapter. The author's location was given as Trou Bricot, Maison Forestière,[1] and Butte de Souain. Located near hill 193, some three kilometers to the south-southeast of the Butte de Souain, the Trou Bricot had already become famous, as the author explains, because of the number of enemy troops captured there two days earlier. (See maps 5 and 6.) This chapter is particularly important because it provides the general setting for the horrendous slaughter of his men that occurred on 6 October 1915.

On 2 September, General Frétay announced that seven of Lécluse's men would be awarded the croix de guerre for their efforts to rescue wounded men. That ceremony took place two days later, and the general gave Lécluse one hundred francs to buy wine for his men. On 6 September, new gas masks arrived as did two machine guns. The next day, a mass was held at 8:00 A.M. for the three men killed earlier: Bornet, Dervudinger, and d'Ollendon. On 9 September, the author visited the ruins of Revigny and said that the whole region had been "devastated with a frightening savagery." He also visited Sermaize and Vassincourt[2] and commented, "The only sentiment one senses . . . in oneself is a sort of cold rage." These visits were apparently the basis for chapter 23, "Ruins."]

This was desolate country, the naked and immense plain, undulating slightly here and there, strewn with small woods, with scrubby and puny firs, ungrateful countryside where, on the compact mass of chalk beds, a few wretched centimeters of poor earth exhausted themselves to nourish rare fields of rye. . . . It was the chalky or "dry" Champagne as you wish! a country already quite lacking in beauty in time of peace, and which the war had not improved, demolishing more or less miserable and wretched villages, cutting down here and there the few firs and birches which broke somewhat, the monotony of the scenery, and unwinding from here to infinity its whitish ribbons of communications trenches, saps and firing trenches. . . .

It was in this awful country where, as so many others, we spent some rather lively weeks, at the moment of the famous offensive of Champagne of 1915 which crumbled our hope, this glorious charge from which we expected such beautiful things, the breakthrough, free reign to our squadrons so long useless, the retreat of the Boches, who knows? perhaps the next Victory, beautiful dreams which crashed on the successive barriers the Germans had spread out in depth!

We arrived on the field of struggle in full battle, managing to clear a passage for ourselves across the incessant coming and going of the wounded, of prisoners, or pieces conquered from the Boches ebbing to the rear, ammunitions and reinforcement convoys hastening towards the line of fire. Otherwise, the disorder was only apparent, so much happened without noise and without a hitch, we felt that we had a carefully laid-out plan, with men tested and hardened, with a methodically-functioning machine and without surprises.

From on high, from one of the rare promontories which dominated the immense plain, we had contemplated the impressive spectacle of this cannonade of which, for nearly a week, we heard the stunning din, night and day, several kilometers away. On all the front, and everywhere you looked, explosions were occurring. Ones produced by the heavy shells of 150-mm and 220-mm raised white chalk clouds which mixed with the black smoke of the powder climbing in the sky in spiral curls of thick smoke much as unchained volcanoes.

Then, we proceeded toward the line of fire by following the large communications trenches prepared for the recent attack, and by which assault troops had reached the attack trenches. The approaches had been dug in a soil already well-churned by combat, as one could see, in gruesome fashion from the unfortunate remains, across which the territorials stoically had to continue their tasks, working as one of them said cynically, "in cadaver!" From place to place, it was necessary to turn sideways so as not to be snagged in passing by a clenched and blackish hand or a withered foot, still shod with military boots, sticking out of the wall of the sap.[3]

We emerged finally in one of these nightmarish landscapes, one of those "lunar" sites, as someone has justly called them, this space between opposing trenches baptized by the English as "no man's land." There, the spectacle was fantastic, and the appearance of the terrain, after seventy-two hours of uninterrupted heavy shelling which had literally pulverized the German trenches, escaped all description. Just picture an infinity of shell holes overlapping each other, strewn with the debris of stakes, pieces of iron wires, shell fragments, lumps of cast metal, parcels of equipment and fragments of arms, torpedoes and unexploded grenades, all of that sprinkled with this whitish dust characteristic of the Chalkland. In some places, the avalanche of iron had been so dense, the projectiles so numerous and repeated that the earth no longer was only turned over, but worked as if by "the pickax" of millions of diggers. . . . That is where the German trenches had been. . . We guessed their location from a few bulges in the ground, some holes where debris from some timbering survived, and some entries to shelters three-quarters obstructed, which had become transformed into tombs.

We could not avoid feeling a sort of mental terror at the thought that these men had to stay there, huddled and confined in their holes until death, for seventy-two hours, without possible communication with the rear, deprived of help, supplies and water, the dead and the wounded piled up pell-mell with the rare survivors, without being able even to lift their heads under the hurricane of iron which bit by bit crumbled and swept away their last defenses!

We crossed this frightening upheaval, and we felt as we had a short time ago in Alsace, but more sadly this time, because of the desolation which surrounded us, a sentiment of satisfaction at the idea that we had "entered among the Boches," or rather that we had "returned home." But you had to see the condition of this ground re-conquered at the price of so much blood!

We had as our destination the Trou Bricot, that corner of Champagne which had become famous two days before by the capture of four to five thousand Boches, who, encircled on all sides, had put down their arms after a brief show of resistance, which quickly vanished at the announcement that we were going to release our terrible colonials on them. It was there at night fall, under a gloomy and penetrating haze, that we set up camp in our miserable bivouac.

We spent several days there, without being exposed to much danger. The German mortars tried hard to find us, but without great success, because the poor firs of Champagne, whose paltry vegetation we had often mocked, were sufficient however to conceal us, and our airplanes were keeping sharp watch, scattering the indiscreet tanks. The only victims of our sojourn were the numerous rabbits which Germans had respected, and which our men, undoubtedly more inclined to poach, and certainly less disciplined, had ferreted out in the twinkling of an eye.

The main distraction was going to visit installations of the "Hasse-bourg Trench," at the Trou Bricot, where our soldiers had replaced the Germans. Some corpses, which the territorials had not yet had the time to bury, were the lone reminders of the occupants of the preceding day. I remember a particularly impressive one. It was undoubtedly a wounded man who had dragged himself into a shell hole to shelter himself and to await help. He was fully stretched out on his side, along the wall of the excavation, his head resting on his left arm. Death had surprised him in this posture, and eyes closed, his face relaxed, he appeared to sleep in a most peaceful manner!

There were a series of officers' huts luxuriously arranged, because Messieurs the Boches were as skilled in creating comfortable quarters as they were in razing a village! The rooms had parquet floors, ceilings, covered with woodwork embellished with moldings, or hung with flowered cretonnes, well-appointed with perfectly made furniture, armchairs, angled sofas, or rocking-chairs.

At the back of the main room, a sliding door exposed a staircase of twelve to fifteen steps leading to the underground shelter allocated to each hut. Outside, some kiosks, some arbors allowed us to enjoy the cool night air.

At some distance there was a large military cemetery. How different from ours, that one at the Maison Forestière, for example! Here bad German taste was displayed in all its hideousness: heavy and pretentious mausoleums, overly-elaborate crosses, misshapen rocks, and everywhere, even at the edge of the paths, mosaics made of flakes of chalk with the German colors, red, white and black. How much more moving were our French cemeteries with their uniform tombs, aligned as on parade, their simple black or white crosses, their modest, wooden cloister walls, and adorned with bouquets or crowns laid down by comrades and sent by families.

Our sad October days followed with our squadrons decimated at the Camp de l'Aiguille, the death of our dear commander, and of so many brave comrades and brave cavalrymen, and finally our hard tour of duty across from the Butte de Souain which marked the extent of our advance, in improvised trenches dug in full chalk, giving the illusion, especially at night in the moonlight, of living and circulating in a landscape of snow. There we were also among the Boches, and we made the best possible use of the installations and shelters from where we had dislodged them. The drawback was that they knew the location and the layout so much better, and, day and night, balls, shells and torpedoes persisted in rendering the position difficult, if not untenable, for us. Happily the nature of the ground came to assist us, and our men hastily dug some cave-shelters in the chalk where safety was a bit more secure.

It was with this painful test, the halt of our offensive, the loss of so many brave men uselessly mowed down, the return to this horrible war of holes which might last for a while, that we ended our sojourn in the "country of the chalk" where we, a month before, had arrived full of enthusiasm and hope! The beautiful dreams had vanished, the splenetic landscape where we lived became more horrible to us each day, and it was with shouts of joy that we greeted the news of our departure. Indeed, little did our new destination matter to us! We were leaving Champagne, and did not ask more . . . and on the evening when we regained the rear, oblivious of the last Boche shells which escorted us, it seemed that we were walking out of a tomb on the day of reincarnation. And, without regret other than for our dear companions who remained behind, we left without looking back at this horrible "Country of Chalk" where we had spent the worst days of our existence at the front.

Dry Champagne
(Trou Bricot. Maison
Forestière. Butte de Souain)
September–October 1915

II

The Hole of Death

[Editor's Note: This event was the most traumatic for Lécluse in the war. He tells of this "abominable day," the memory of which will haunt his days and nights to the end of his life. He adds, "the heart is not in me and my hand hesitates to write the story of these twelve hours spent in the face of death, and what death!" The fog, he states, was so thick that they could not see five meters in front of them. Meanwhile, German artillery shells were falling nearby. The captains in charge of the attack were convinced that they were together for the last time and that few, if any, would survive the attack planned for that day.

The enemy opened fire on their position which, Lécluse indicates in his diary, had been called "the hole of death" by colonial troops who occupied it previously. As they moved forward, the colonial troops told Lécluse's men to take positions anywhere but in the trench. However, as Lécluse indicates, he had been given explicit orders and they had no choice.

For twelve hours, especially from 5:30 A.M. to 10:30 A.M., they suffered from heavy bombardment by guns of 105 mm and larger. The enemy knew their position well and had them bracketed. Shells fell in front of them, behind them, to their left, and to their right. The precise location where an artillery shell landed, killing twelve men and wounding thirty-three others, was marked in pen by Lécluse on a battlefield map published by Le Matin *and has been reproduced in this chapter.]*

To the memory of my men who gave their lives for France

In one of his books, Georges d'Esparbes, in his own distinct style, has one of his "grognards" say: "I have been face to face with death some forty times, we were so close sometimes that we could have shaken hands."[1]

Some people might find this metaphor quite outrageous, but on 6

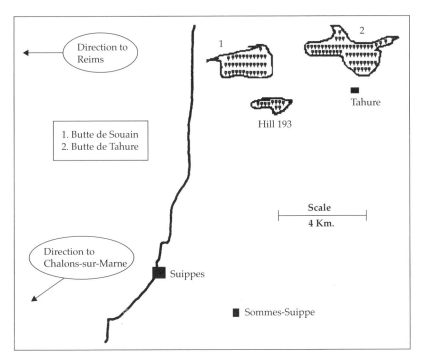

Map 5. Butte de Tahure

October 1915—I am asking my comrades-in-arms who were with me in the trench of the Camp de l'Aiguille to bear me out—we learned to understand and appreciate its meaning. Twelve hours like those we spent there have a special place in my memory and stand out in tragic fashion above everything one has seen or done in one's lifetime, no matter how old he is.

The following day, when I was back to our camp with one third of my men missing, I tried to write in my war journal my impressions of what had taken place. I thought that I would have difficulty finding the words to describe the hellish nightmare from which we had escaped. . . . Nevertheless, as I read over these pages scribbled in haste, I was able to relive that sinister day in "the Hole of Death" in all of its gory detail.

I dedicate these notes, which I am transcribing at this time with barely any changes, to the memory of those brave men for which this day was their last on this earth.

We left our camp at Maison Forestière at a half past midnight along with the two other light groups of the C. C. [Cavalry Corps]. Last night we were called suddenly by our commander, who wanted to inform us of the orders which he had just received. We had to be in the Camp de l'Aiguille, a former German position by five in the morning, behind the assault column whose goal was to take the trench of the Butte de Souain. As soon as we had taken it, we were to occupy it and face the enemy. . . . A very delicate and risky mission! As our commander said, "we are given a difficult and dangerous assignment!" He added with melancholy: "I fear that by tomorrow at this time we will have lost a lot of men!" But I don't want to get ahead of myself. . . .

Walking was extremely slow and difficult, even though the night was not pitch black. We had to make our way through numerous detachments of all kinds of arms, convoys, artillery pieces moving quietly in all directions. We encountered many delays, forcing us to run to catch up with the column and not lose that precious contact. In spite of the coolness of the night, it wasn't long before we were soaked [with sweat] and exhausted under our heavy load. It was with great satisfaction that, after crossing a large encampment where hundreds of poilus were eating their soup around large campfires, we were able to pause for the first time. We were in a clump of trees near our old Trou Bricot where we had camped just eight days before. All of this took place in the midst of an infernal din. Hundreds of batteries were hammering relentlessly the positions which we were to attack at dawn. Huge red flashes streaked the sky above us and projectiles of all calibers zoomed over our heads in bursts. We felt as tiny and insignificant as a piece of straw in a windstorm.

After catching our breath, we picked up our packs and resumed our journey. The second leg took us to Elberfeld which used to be a German post. We had just gotten there when a dense fog descended upon us. The feeling was eerie: we could see no more than a few feet in front of us; our men were lying on their stomachs, their arms wrapped around their heads, because the Boches were firing back. We could hear their heavy shells whistling and exploding in the fog closer and closer to our position. . . . It was quite ominous!

Montergon, the commander's aide, had been sent ahead to scout the position to which we had been assigned. He must have gotten lost in the fog; time was going by and he had not made it back. . . . Our poor dear commander was fidgeting and getting impatient; he was afraid of not being able to make it to our position or of getting there late. He was surrounded by his captains who had stayed up with him to reassure him as best they could, without realizing of course that it was the last meeting they would ever have with him. . . . Battle weary, we decided that we would go due North, using a compass, which should lead us somewhere along the trench line which we were to man. We took off in platoon columns keeping in contact with each other thanks to men serving as markers by holding hands and forming a line, allowing us to make our way through the frigid and dense fog. We were constantly falling: we tumbled in shell holes; we tripped over bodies; we got snagged by the barbed wire. I found myself caught in some wires as if it were a trap. Finally, luck took us right to our combat post.

It was a rather shapeless trench, which had already collapsed in places. Colonial soldiers were swarming in it while getting ready to begin their assault. As one of them left, one of us took his place in this rather precarious shelter, too small to accommodate all of us. Even though we were piled on the top of each other, the squadron from the Twenty-fourth had to lie down on the terreplein above the trench, behind a small dirt wall barely sufficient to protect it from the wind. That was also where our commander and his small staff decided to stay.

Our fate was in the hands of God! Those were the words which came to mind because the critical moment had arrived. The attack had begun and the German fire was directed right at us! It was not totally unexpected since the enemy was very familiar with our position. The colonial troops who had learned this harsh lesson first hand told us when they left: "Anywhere but here, guys! Don't you know the name of this place?" — "The Camp de l'Aiguille." — "Sure, on the map! Here we call it the Hole of Death!" But you can't argue with orders, this was our assignment. . . . As I said before: our fate was in the hands of God!

We stayed at this post twelve hours, twelve centuries! from five thirty in the morning to five thirty at night, under a constant barrage of fire which was particularly heavy in the morning hours. At one time, seeing that we were being decimated without being able to fight back and noticing that one area of land seemed not to be bombarded, inasmuch as work crews of the territorial army could walk through it at will, we asked if we could move forward to escape the risk of complete annihilation. The reply we received: "You are to remain at your position" was inexorable and totally unsympathetic, furthermore subsequently no one ever took responsibility for issuing it.

Thus we remained, stoic and resigned . . . and miserably useless! German shells, including some containing tear gas, pounded us without

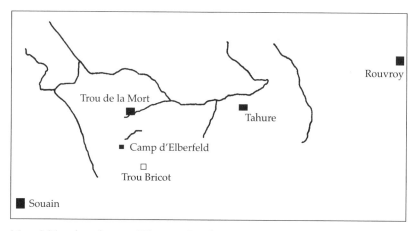

Map 6. Trenchworks near Tahure, 6 October 1915

interruption. Many were large caliber, at least 105mm. They fell right on the top of us, sometimes they landed near us, in front or behind us. We were huddled next to the wall, silent, resigned to death, our faces hardened by anguish. Surrounded by the cries for help, the cries of pain from the wounded and by the groans of those mortally hit, we were being showered by fragments of stones and chunks of dirt thrown up by each projectile and blinded by the burning and suffocating smoke. Each time we heard the ominous whistling of an oncoming large shell, we told ourselves: "That is the one!" Then after it had missed us we added: "Not yet."

Those are the hours which count for something; they are unforgettable. Do you know of any others which compare with them? Hours where you can feel yourself living with great intensity, almost painfully, because each minute appears to be your last one, and as a poilu talking about them said so well: "Life is just passing through!"

Right away the situation had become desperate. At the entrance to the trench located a few feet from the one I was standing in, a large caliber shell hit dead on, right in the middle of my cavalry men who had huddled together because of the overcrowding! I saw a heavy cloud of black dust rise and fall back to the ground followed by cries, men running in every direction, screaming through the smoke-filled air. Suddenly there was silence! As a result fifteen of my men were dead and some thirty others wounded.[2] They brought me one of the latter; it was poor Samson. His face was ashen, he looked near death. . . . He implored me in a weak voice: "Captain, have them take me back. . . ." Alas!

Such a feeling of helplessness! In a matter of a few moments all of the stretchers had been put to work, there was nothing that we could do!

By then, the bad news was becoming more frequent. A voice called out: "The chaplain for our commander!" We could not hold back a cry of anger. Was it possible? Our dear commander, our friend, a father to all of us even more than a commanding officer, had already been hit!

Then, all of a sudden, we heard someone crying out from our left: "Lieutenant de Béjarry is dead!" "Lieutenant Levylier has been mortally wounded, his leg has been crushed and he is half buried!" My comrade Delacour was left with only one of his three officers. Poor Levylier! When I think that only three days ago, I rebuffed him for saying with a touch of snobbism, that he found war to be quite "sporting." What an ironic turn of events!

The fireworks were far from over. . . . Ragilly and du Plessis, from the Twenty-fourth, came to me. The latter was covered with the blood of the wounded who fell on the top of him. Even his helmet was red. He was hideous. Ragilly had just lost his NCO who was decapitated by shrapnel as he stood at his side. It came so close to getting him too that it made a cut in the blanket roll which he carried on his pack.

Without thinking, we ate a piece of dry bread, washing it down with a swallow of cold coffee. We were so dazed that we fell asleep, yes we slept! In spite of the deafening noise, and not knowing if they would ever wake up, some men were leaning against the sides of the trench, others were all hunched up in shapeless holes, the size of coffins, hastily dug at ground level in this chalky soil which made us look like plasterers, white as we were from head to toe. The hours went by . . . slowly? . . . rapidly? I was incapable of judging. To tell the truth the situation was so exceptional "that time didn't exist!" You lived "a minute at a time!" You waited! And you waited!

At around twelve o'clock, taking advantage of a lull in the action, I went out on the terreplein and entered the other trench where the hecatomb had begun. . . . What a nightmare! There was a pile of shredded corpses, heaped one on top of the other like so many discarded puppets. . . . One of them could only be identified with the aid of his dog tag; this bloody mess, which no longer resembled a human being, had a name, Viard, just a few hours ago! One man's skull had been completely crushed, his head pushed into his shoulders. Another displayed, where his legs had been, a pile of chopped flesh which resembled sausage meat. A third had taken on the air of a macabre carnival: a shell seemed to have lifted his face, and it now laid flat, like a grimacing Mardi-Gras mask!

In the middle of this mass grave, my men, undaunted, had dug individual holes where they stoically sat as if indifferent, with the passive resignation of men from Brittany. Not a complaint, not a question came out of their mouths but what expressions on those faces, pale from fatigue and anguish. Their stares turned toward me told me everything I needed to know!

At the entrance to the gallery, Ragilly's non-commissioned officer remained seated in the very place and posture where death struck him down. His hands hanging between his legs, his helmet tipped forward over his face, you would swear that it was someone taking a nap while lazing in the sun. However, as you drew near and you leaned down, you noticed that, under the helmet, there was no head.

With their customary devotion, the stretcher-bearers cleared out this scene of carnage. One by one, under my watchful eye, they removed the mutilated remains of their comrades and gently, piously, they laid them out in front of the trench as if they were only wounded. Poor fellows! At least these didn't have to suffer!

The order to pull back finally arrived. It was about time! You could feel that the officers and men were all "at the end of their rope." My! How quickly word of the order spread and was carried out! The Boches' infernal bombardment was not yet over but who cared? In an orderly fashion, we quickly scaled the trench wall and moved out of range. Then, no longer phased by fatigue or the weight of our packs, with a feeling of walking out of hell and of being reborn, we returned to the camp which we had left that morning. Alas! When we counted ourselves off, so many were missing! Three officers were dead, including our commander; two others had been wounded, one of them mortally, and more than a hundred men were out of commission! My poor squadron, which had been quite lucky up to that time, held the record for losses with one-third of its troops grounded: forty-five men, twelve of them dead! All of this took place without our making one move, without seeing the enemy without firing or hearing a single shot! You might think that it was all for nothing. No! No! Not that! There are no useless sacrifices! You did not die in vain, you the men we left over there, in the Hole of Death, and to whom I gave a last farewell when we pulled out!

Rest gloriously in peace, oh humble victims! All deaths incurred in this war will contribute to Victory and weigh equally on the scale of

Supreme Justice; all are equally worthy in the eyes of the God of Armies! As for us, to comfort and strengthen our souls, let us not forget the words of self-sacrifice spoken by the painter Le Mordant, the young and brilliant artist blinded by a shell fragment: "What does it matter! As long as it had a purpose!"

The Hole of Death
(Camp de l'Aiguille)
(Champagne)
6 October 1915

12

Brothers-in-Arms

[Editor's Note: This chapter is dedicated to Lieutenants Béjarry and Levylier as well as soldiers Hercé and Moissec, all killed in the war. According to the author, the diary entries were written between the 7th and the 15th of October 1915 at the Butte de Souaine. Commandant Delaire and the two lieutenants were buried on the 7th, while Hercé and Moissec were killed on the 15th and buried that same day. The chapter in the memoir combines the diary entries for those two days but is slightly more detailed. Despite the somber mood of this chapter, the author tries to find some inspiration in the sacrifice of these men's lives for the sake of their country.

The author also tells of his visit to Delaire's grave on 8 October. He describes the explosion that took the men's lives, their wounds, the situation at the aide station, and then the procession to the cemetery as well as the burial of all four men.]

To the memory of my comrades, Lieutenants de Béjarry and Levylier of the 9th Light Group, and my men Hercé and Moissec who died for France.[1]

How soundly you were sleeping, my comrades, when I saw you for the first time, and how handsome you were! The night before, at the dawn of this horrible day of 6 October, you had fallen heroically at your post, you, Béjarry, without a whimper, felled by a single shot, you, Levylier, mortally wounded, but still having the strength to utter these beautiful words: "Tell my father that I am happy to die for France!"

Now, to bid you good-bye, they had opened the folds of your shrouds, the bloody and torn garments which enveloped you at the bottom of your crude coffins. Death, brutal as it was, while breaking your limbs, had respected your features, and, your eyes, so calm, almost smiling, closed to the sorrows where you left us, but open doubtlessly to eternal beauties, you seemed to have succumbed to a peaceful sleep. We studied your faces for a long time, trying to read the great lesson of sacrifice which you gave us, and to keep your features permanently fixed in our minds. Then, they shut the coffins, and we headed off to make with you the ultimate leg of your journey as soldiers.

Oh! the magnificent cortege! No hearse, no flowers, no hymns, no priests in opulent vestments, no pompous ceremony, no funeral decorations, no glittering lights, no clouds of incense, but with your coffins made of ill-jointed boards, carried by your own men, the crude crown of ivy and moss, the soldier-priest, who had been at your sides the night before, under machine gun fire, and who preceded you in his combat uniform, his stole worn over his heavily-soiled fatigue jacket. The compact group of your friends and your soldiers, huddled around you for the last time, and the murmur of heart-felt prayers raised to our lips, with the blue sky for a canopy and the thundering voice of the canon for music!

We descended the slope which, a few hours earlier, we had followed in column, in the night broken up by the furious cannonade, illuminated by the flashes of lightning from the big cannons, a tragic march toward the battle, from which so many of us would never return! We crossed the innumerable crush of these soldiers carrying all sorts of weapons, teeming with life so intense in bivouacs hidden in the shade of the trees. From as far away as one could see, all these men faced the road, halting their horse or setting down their tools, and, heads bare, many kneeled in the chalky dust, paying honor to these two officers who were going to their final resting place, to this admirable cemetery of soldiers at Maison Forestière, framed by firs, bristling with hundreds of crosses, compact as the sheaves of a wheat field, a harvest of martyrs and heroes, ripe for the granaries of God!

It is there that we left you, my comrades, in the middle of so many others who had preceded you in glory, saying, not a good-bye, but the "adieu" of the Christian and the soldier who knows that he will rejoin you soon perhaps, happy friends during calm moments, faithful companions in hard times, sorrows and combat, brothers-in-arms who have become our models, and whose example we must follow, and whose deaths we must avenge!

You also, more humble brothers in arms, Hercé, Moissec, brave boys of Brittany who were part of the cortege, your turn came a few days later. In the camp at the Butte de Souain where we had replaced the enemy, at the limit of our advance in Champagne, we had been dug in for an hour under a terrible bombardment, some in the underground rooms, others surprised at work, crouched at the bottom of the narrow communications trenches waiting for the storm to pass. Large shells came down in waves, with a thunderous din, without respite, in salvoes, making the ground tremble, splitting eardrums, raising geysers of white chalk, and my officers and I, seated at the table where we were finishing lunch, exchanged a silent nod of the head from time to time which spoke volumes. . . .

Suddenly, someone came running. . . .

"Let's go! there's trouble!" one of us said. . . .

Alas! it was only too true!

"Hercé dead, his throat torn open, Moissec dead, hit in the stomach, a leg crushed, one killed in the trench, the other at the entrance to his shelter. . . ."

"Where are they?"

"Hercé at the aid station of the chasseurs,[2] Moissec at ours. . . ."

"Let's go!"

And we left running. Rouxel and I weaved our way along the communications trenches, bending our backs under squalls of projectiles which rained down constantly.[3]

Here we were at the chasseurs. I pushed open the door. . . . What a sight! In front of me, laid out on a stretcher, Hercé looked at me with his eyes fixed and wide open. From his throat, his blood had streamed in waves, from head to feet, to his puttees.[4] It was as if he were dressed in crimson. Behind him, impassive and straight, the chaplain-stretcher-bearer of the chasseurs, his helmet on his head, his jacket thrown on his shoulders, his shirt splattered with blood stains, was looking at him, his arms crossed. . . . Nobody seemed to notice our entry, because who knows where their thoughts were? And it was in this profound silence, where the sound of my voice seemed strange, that a word of anger and sarcasm rose to my lips in face of this butchery: "Ah! they sure are taking good care of my men!" A rapid good-bye, a sign of the cross, it was on to the other unfortunate one!

Poor Moissec! He had been laid out on the terrace, near the entrance to our aid station. His arms were still raised and crossed over his forehead, the instinctive gesture of one who saw the blow coming . . .

the death blow, alas! His stomach was slit open down to his thigh; his right foot hanged on the end of a scrap of flesh. It was awful! Another one they had fixed for me!

By a bizarre coincidence, it was the first time that we found ourselves in front of the new doctor who had arrived the night before,[5] and, as we were no longer easily disturbed by those sights, any of us, the presentations were made in front of the mutilated corpses, according to the rules, as correctly as in a drill yard, but the phrases exchanged contained only the usual banalities. . . .

At five o'clock, we were gathered here in the small cemetery improvised in a somewhat protected corner, and which filled rapidly with people. My two soldiers were there, wrapped in their shrouds, spread at the edge of the hastily dug pit where they were going to sleep side by side, comrades in bed, for eternity. . . . The short ceremony had an impressive grandeur, and emotion took us by the throat! My officers and I, the stretcher-bearer gravediggers, some cyclists reunited by chance, listened, bare-headed, to the prayers which the brave abbot Mabrilet, the soldier-priest of the First Dragoons,[6] recited rapidly, because it would have been imprudent to linger outside of the communications trenches, as the canon fire and the thud of bullets kept in brutal rhythm with the sacred words. To our side, the bloody bodies of two infantrymen from the 22d waited for someone to finish digging their tomb. The gray evening was already descending on the plain and cast a pale hue on the landscape of desolation which surrounded us. . . . A last benediction, and then it was finished! The shovels of dirt fell dully, covering bodies still warm, burying strength, youth, hopes, and dreams of the future.

Good-bye! my boys, your task is finished, we are going to ours, on the hard path where we walked together, forward always, towards Victory!

In Front of the Butte de Souain
(Champagne)
7-15 October 1915

13

In the Field of Crosses

[Editor's Note: Dedicated to Commandant Delaire, who died during the bombardment of 6 October, this chapter is, in essence, a eulogy based on the notes for 8 October, when Lécluse and his men went in search of the commandant's grave. This chapter is particularly touching for the profound expression of affection and the deep sense of loss expressed by the author.]

To the memory of Commandant Delaire commandant of the 9th Light Group, who died for France.[1]

The field of crosses covered all the plain. Everywhere we looked, we saw only crosses, innumerable and bunched like the sheaves of a wheat field. . . . And their arms were raised to the sky in a gesture which was both a protest and a prayer. . . .

It is in the field of crosses that I took leave of you, my commander, and said good-bye. . . . You were already under the earth, this earth which you had bathed with your blood, but your image was still so alive in our eyes, your soul invisible and nevertheless present, I could feel it so clearly at my side. I knew that you were hearing my words, and our last chat was as intimate as those of the past. Here today, in evoking this painful time, I want to dedicate this in memory of you. . . . You are still here, I believe it firmly, leaning over my shoulder, approving smilingly the words which I write, and it seems to me that on my hand which trembles at times from emotion I am going to feel the affectionate pressure of your guiding hand!

O the awful anguish felt by all of us, at the dawn of that day of 6 October, when this cry was heard in the trench: "They are calling for the chaplain for the commander!" I remember that this event appeared so cruel, so unjust to us that, instead of a complaint or a prayer, it was an exclamation of rage which rose to my lips! Hardly a few minutes ago, I had heard you ask me, your voice tranquil as always, as the barrage was beginning: "Lécluse, have you been able to place all your men?" because your ever-present concern led you to ask if all your men had found shelter, while you were doing without one, bravely posted unprotected on the terrace where death was about to strike you. . . . Alas! these were the last words which I heard from your mouth! A half-hour later, you fell, one of the first, fatally wounded in the head by a shell fragment. . . . A hurricane of death crashed down at this moment on the trench where we were huddled, twelve of my men were crushed by a single shell, our comrades de Béjarry and Levylier killed, Laroche[2] struck dead, Montergon wounded beside you! In spite of it all, under this deluge of iron, we took you to the aid station, and from there to the Somme-Suippe ambulance, and, that evening, when we returned to our bivouac, all still panting from the infernal hours which we had just experienced, we learned that all was finished! The best of us went first, we lost, not our commander, but our friend, who joined to the qualities of a true leader, whom we would have followed to the end of the world, the extreme kindness, the affectionate solicitude of an elder brother!

There again, what a pious and respectful crowd came to escort you the following day, to your last rest, a simple yet poignant funeral, obsequies of a soldier, as you would have wished them! Alas! I could not be present there, because at the same hour, we were burying our two comrades killed the night before at Maison Forestière, and it had been necessary to divide the painful task. . . . Rouxel and I therefore remained, but, then early the following day we said, as if talking about the departure of a friend: "We must go to say good-bye to the commandant. . . ." And then we left on horseback, on a day resplendent with sun.

As soon as we exited from the woods where we had bivouacked, the spectacle was extraordinary. All the Champagne countryside seemed to be an anthill in motion. On all roads, it was an unceasing coming and going of isolated soldiers, troops in step, trucks, automobiles, artillery pieces. In each dip in the terrain, huts, tents, horses at the stake, unhitched wagons, and finally in the plain itself endless columns of horses converging from all points of the horizon to the unique drinking trough of Somme-Suippe. . . .

We passed one these columns, and, upon arriving at the village, we took up the "search for our commander." The humble church, whose

steeple alone bore damage from shells, and which has since been artisti-
cally camouflaged to avoid others, had been transformed into a field
hospital, but the small cemetery scattered around it has been filled for a
long time, and our search there was in vain. . . . On the other hand,
through a painful bit of chance, the first tomb which I encountered was
that of one of my friends, of whose death I was unaware![3] We needed to
go farther, to the big military cemetery. . . .

There, it was indeed the "Field of Crosses," so impressive because of
their prodigious number and also their uniform aspect — only a few were
flowered and decorated with a tri-colored ribbon — because no longer
were there either chiefs or soldiers, but comrades and martyrs!

In the chalky ground, graves seemed to have been carved out "with
a knife," exactly to the dimensions of the body or the coarse coffin
which they would receive. They could prepare a large number in advance, leaving only a thin partition of chalk to separate them, and these
gaping tombs, arranged in parallel rows much as those of the catacombs
of Rome are by floors, resembled somewhat the cells of a bee hive.

Disconcerted at first by this forest of crosses where we had to find
without any indication the one which interested us, we set out bravely in
quest, each on our own side. At the end of a quarter of an hour, I called
my companion. I had found the tomb, on the edge of the cemetery, in
the middle of a row of excavations still empty, but not for long! Neigh-
bors would soon be coming! And there we were, both of us, on our
knees in front of the little, white, wooden cross. . . .

My commander, we come to take leave of you. As you showed us
the path of duty, you preceded us on the one of sacrifice. . . . May God
allow us to follow that path as fearlessly as you! Here ends brutally our
ten months in the countryside lived side by side, under so many skies!
finished also our good chats, when we strolled together in the great
forest of Alsace, or when you dropped in on me unannounced, that
morning, at the Bois des Loges, in my underground shelter cave. . . . All
that was yesterday, and it is over! Still, your memory will never die! You
had an encouraging openness, a comforting demeanor, a sustaining
strength; you had above all this virtue which supersedes all others: Kindness! On a day when misfortune struck you cruelly,[4] you said again:
"Think of those who are more unfortunate than we are!" Think also of
us, my commander, whose struggle, suffering and troubles remain! Protect from on High those whom you commanded, those who loved you,
and may your soul reside with us until the end of the test! Good-bye! my

commander, remain here in the Field of Crosses until the day when we will return to tell you: "You can now go and sleep next to your people, because we have finished your task, avenged your death, and brought the sacred cause for which you have given your life to a triumphal ending!"

And we went through the forest of crosses by the paths traced between lines of glorious tombs, our hearts full of emotion, pride and hope and it seemed to us that through its branches passed already the breath of Victory, rustling its branches, gently rocking to sleep those who had died for it!

Cemetery of Somme-Suippe
(Champagne)
8 October 1915

14

Accompaniment in Music

[Editor's Note: This chapter is the inverse of chapter 1 in the sense that Lécluse and his men are headed into the front line, rather than to the rear areas. At 1:00 A.M., the men marched in single file to the shelters that supported the trenches. The process took two hours. The trenches were relatively deep (two meters) but quite narrow. The men had great difficulty moving past the narrower places in the trenches with all their equipment and had to turn sideways to make any progress. When they arrived, they were jammed together as the Germans fired a volley of shells at them. This chapter describes the difficulties experienced in so simple a task as moving up to the front on an otherwise quiet night.]

To Lieutenant Bellot — 9th Light Group — 2d Light[1]

One o'clock in the morning. It was quite dark, the moon was veiled by large clouds, as we left our bivouac at the Hamburg trench. It was without much regret, because truly we were housed there in too rudimentary a fashion. Our comrades, who, two hundred meters farther, occupied the former German dugouts which we used to visit when we were at the Trou Bricot, lived like kings, while we resided on the edge of a communication trench barely sufficient to shelter us somewhat in case of a bombardment, in some shacks consisting of a relatively large, rectangular pit, dug in that ever-present chalk, and covered by a picturesque melange of boards, corrugated iron, branches of firs and tent cloth, a true camp of Bohemians or even of savages. For bunks, we had a pile of twigs of firs, and for a seat, the most fortunate had an old wooden crate. . . . We still spent two or three good days there, because a Frenchman, especially on a beautiful day, can make do with anything and can laugh about it. . . .

We finally took off, Indian file, to reach our new positions on the Butte de Souain, through the communications trenches dug by the Germans, the principal one of which is still called the Meimingen Trench. My squadron followed behind me, like a long snake, unwinding slowly and ponderously its hundred fifty coils. We had been doing that for two or three hours. Fortunately, the bottom of the trenches, two meters deep, was perfectly dry, and as level as one might expect, and our march would have been only dreadfully monotonous, if it were not rendered more arduous by the heavy packs which we were carrying on our backs, and especially because of the multiple accessories hanging around us: musettes, cans, water bottles, map cases, binoculars, gas masks, etc. . . . We constantly bumped into the walls of the trench and had to walk sideways, a nearly impossible task, or come up with some other way of progressing, which consisted of turning alternatively a quarter turn to the right or left, depending on which way you got hung up, while continuing to advance. This could have been somewhat amusing to see, when done by others, but when one applied the procedure himself, it was simply exhausting. Others obstacles were equally difficult. There were the numerous poilus, stretched full length, and against whom we stumbled. They had no right to be there, because the communications trenches were reserved exclusively for circulation and liaison between the lines, and we could have stepped on them without scruple, but this would only have led us to painful tumbles. It was better to yield to a rather tiresome gymnastic of jumping and stepping over them, because it was impossible to make a poilu, who was sleeping or pretended to be, move over.

So we marched, on and on. . . . Perchance, the orders which gave us our itinerary were clear and respected, and we did not collide with another column coming the other way, an occurrence which caused great despair for troops engaged in the communications trenches. Despite everything you could do, the meeting of another unit was one of the most painful, if not impossible, things to do.

We passed the Souain-Tahure road, and, a little later, emerged in a small, brushy woods which we crossed using as a point of reference a railway track to Decauville abandoned by the Boches. Little by little, the moon had emerged, and the walk was rendered easier, more perilous also, because of the blue uniforms, especially when, instead of being darkened by mud, they were, as ours, covered with chalky dust, white in the moonlight, and we had to fear being seen by a tank only too happy to signal us to its artillery. Thus, we hastened to climb back down to a new succession of communications trenches which brought us finally near the former Boche camp where we had to set ourselves up in the second line, behind the squadrons of cuirassiers.[2] At this moment, a small bottleneck occurred: the comrades whom we replaced had not finished evacuating their shelters. We were obliged to halt, catch our breath and smoke a cigarette, when suddenly, without a warning to take cover, a volley of projectiles, the kind of which the Boches were so fond, came down upon us at the time of probable relief. Had they gotten wind of something? Had their lookouts heard some peculiar noise? This was not impossible, because although my men had already spent many months in the front and in trenches, they were unfortunately too care-free in this regard, and it was difficult to make them maintain silence which, in relief operations, is the first and the most elementary of pre-cautions.

In any case, exposed or not, we were welcomed in beautiful fashion! "God damn! What a downpour!" murmured a somewhat philosophical poilu squatted beside me, because instantly, each man had crouched down and humped over to let the storm pass. Mortars arrived by salvoes, howling and whistling a few meters above our heads, and the earth trembled from the din of the explosions.

Fortunately, the German fire was a bit long, and since it was very unlikely that they would correct it, it was probable that we would make it. Nevertheless, the end of the combat or the possibility of resuming our march were equally awaited with an impatience which, although not expressed loudly, was still shared by everyone. The order to move for-ward arrived first, and, with an undisguised eagerness, each platoon, properly guided by the markers which our predecessors left us, reached its underground home. Behind us, the Boches could continue to spit their grapeshot; here, we were once again out of the range of their fire, and sheltered from their spitefulness.

The shelter which I entered was occupied three weeks ago by some officer of the Kaiser. It was comfortable enough, as was the case of those these gentlemen built for their personal use. The bedroom was spacious and healthy, the camp bed sufficiently padded: it was time to quietly put an end to an action-packed night, after having assured myself that all my men were under cover. It seemed that the small pause under the shell fire lasted only some ten minutes. . . . I confess that it had appeared a bit longer to me! Bah! it was just another memory to be added to the others!

And as the French trooper is always joking, especially when nothing comes to disturb his good humor: "But, captain," one of my men said to me, "you did not tell us that relief would be made to the accompaniment of music!"

Butte de Souain
(Champagne)
13 October 1915

15

The Croix de Guerre

[*Editor's Note: Nearly two weeks after the incident at the Hole of Death, Lécluse and his men were back at the front. The sector was relatively quiet. On 18 October, General de Frétay and Lécluse inspected troops in the front lines, some thirty meters from the German trenches. The Germans fired two slow-moving "torpedoes" that were seen by sentries in time to be avoided. The French replied with three volleys of seventy-five-millimeter artillery and heard an enormous explosion beyond the crest of the hill.*

On the 19th, Commandant Lefevre, his aide, de Maud'huit, and Lécluse returned to the front lines at 8:00 A.M. to distribute the croix de guerre to men who had been cited prior to their departure from Alsace. The men received their decorations some 150 meters from the Germans as artillery shells passed overhead. Then, at 9:00 A.M., Lécluse reported back to the command post to see Colonel Geoffroy distribute medals to men who had been cited for their conduct on 6 October. In the midst of the ceremony, an enemy shell exploded thirty meters away, killing one man. Lécluse tells us that, following the ceremony, he returned to the front line where he declared, "except for the horrible torpedoes, it is decidedly better." He indicates that the Germans regularly fired torpedoes at 4:00 P.M., suggesting ritualized fire characteristic of a quiet sector. One of these torpedoes exploded ten meters from his communications trench, extinguishing his lights and covering the interior of the subterranean shelters with dirt while shaking them ferociously.]

*To Commandant Lefevre commandant of the 9th
Light Group, and 3d Battalion of the 2d Light*[1]

From our sojourn in Champagne, so short, and yet so full of bitterness, one single image remained which I like to recall: it was a very modest, austere scene, but it offers at the same time a simple yet poignant impression.

Fig. 9. *(from left)* Captain de
Lécluse, Captain Maud'huit,
and Second-Lieutenant Billet,
31 October 1915.

A telephone call brought me out of my bunk, at the bottom of my
German P.C. [command post], dug down some four meters under earth
where I was half-dozing after a sleepless night spent at the watch posts.
Our commander informed me that he had just received the croix de
guerre awarded to ten of our men for the exemplary way they had
handled themselves at the Hole of Death, hardly two weeks ago, and,
that he was going to come to award them in the front line without
further delay.

I dispatched a cyclist to warn the newly-decorated, and to set up a
meeting in the firing trench at the opening of the main communications
trench. In that way, the small ceremony would take place under the
noses of the Boches, some hundred fifty meters from their firing posts. I
believed that this would be rather original, and rather classy!

I quickly washed up, with the light of two candles held in holders
which my men sculpted right from the pieces of chalk coming from our
digging. Once more, with large brush strokes, I struggled to make disappear as best I could this unbearable white dust, which penetrated our
clothing, and, somewhat presentable, I went out to meet the commander.

It was a hazy, depressing and cold day and the sky seemed to weigh

heavily on the lunar landscape and the labyrinth of the various trenches
and saps which surrounded us. Behind us, the woods of the Trou Bricot
spread their somber shadows. Ahead, beyond the slopes which ascended to
the north from the German lines and which appeared to be snow-covered
because of the chalk, our heavy batteries had set a blaze whose large clouds
of black smoke my men contemplated with evident satisfaction. Moreover,
the atmosphere was calm, on this side at least. The canons hushed, as if out
of breath from their nocturnal din, and the silence was interrupted from
time to time only by the gunshot of a sentry, who amused himself by
"trying for a bull's eye." It was most often quiet at this time of the morning, and we knew, except for unforeseen events naturally, the habits of
messieurs the artillerymen, ours as well as the Boches. Starting at eleven
o'clock—it was an axiom for the poilu that gunners are late risers—the
little artillery duels would resume, more or less lively, and at around four
o'clock especially there would be a dreadful moment to pass, when the
Boches regularly sent us a half-a-dozen torpedoes, the dirtiest gadget that I
knew.[2] Unfortunately, our mortars were still not very well-equipped to
respond appropriately to them.

But here was our new squadron chief, who had arrived some two
weeks ago to replace our poor Commandant Delaire, in rather less than
enticing conditions, housed in a command post which served as target
for bullets, for shells and for torpedoes from morning to night and from
night to morning. He did not seem to be affected at all by the situation.
First, we made a tour of the sector together, and I was pleased to show
him the improvements which my men and I had been able to make,
thanks to the zeal of our brave cavalrymen. You could no longer recognize the crudely outlined trenches which my predecessors had occupied
two weeks ago. Our men, taking advantage of the ease with which one
had to work in strips of chalk on which we were situated, were finishing
digging underground shelters which could be accessed by a flight of
twelve steps, and which would be connected by underground corridors.
Parapets had been raised, the trenches and the saps deepened and sani-
tized. The revetments of sand bags insured everywhere an efficient protection;[3] from place to place, armored shelters allowed us to limit the
number of lookouts. Ahead of the line, coils of iron wire had been
strung with the cleverness of Apaches, because the enemy was very close,
so close that one of our listening posts was shared and sentries there were
separated only by a heap of sand bags, ten meters wide. Yesterday, General du Frétay, came to visit me, and always curious, felt obliged to go

lean his back against this barricade, next to the lookouts, to "hear the Boches stir." And it was not at all amusing to see him curl up his tall frame, and the brave Parisot, his ordinance officer, losing his monocle from despair, raise his arms to the sky in response to these imprudences to which he has not been able to get accustomed![4]

But here we were at the point fixed for the ceremony. The commander leaned back against the shooting parapet, I stood at his left, and on the other side of Maud'huit, who handed him the medals.[5] Some of the lookouts grouped around us as we passed some of the medals to the men in the trench. One by one, the newly decorated, as their name was called, came out of the entrance of the trench directly across from us, and halted, arms in hand, before the commander. That sufficed to fill the available space, and put them almost chest to chest. To each he read the citation, then he pinned the medal on the uniform jacket, and, eye-to-eye, with affectionate words, like a father speaking to his son, he congratulated and thanked the man who was either trembling with emotion or blushing with pleasure. I can assure you that the spectators, too, were deeply moved, and did not try to hide it. This glorification without any obscure grandiloquence, among comrades-in-arms, among family, at a combat post, under German guns, was truly a very simple sight, but such a beautiful one!

Little Croix de Guerre, in subdued colors, with dark shadows, you who are the best reward and the most envied, by all soldiers of the Great War, because you will perpetuate its memory, because you will decorate only the chests of those who have participated in it, and your green and red ribbon will later be the rallying sign which will allow two men to say: "And I too, I was part of it as you were!" Little Croix de Guerre, it was on this day that I understood the grandeur of your symbol and found it to be most beautiful!

I have seen you given out in all sorts of circumstances, often with solemnity, with emotion as well, when you were placed in the hands of a widow, an orphan or an old man in tears, but there, it was exactly the right setting, this landscape of war and desolation, the front line trench, with the wretched, muddy and magnificent poilus as honor guard, the rumbling voice of the canon to open the proclamation, and Death hovering above our heads!

Butte de Souain
(Champagne)
19 October 1915

16

The Heartbroken Christ

[Editor's Note: Nearly a month had passed since the simple ceremony in the trenches. Lécluse and his men were now in the town of Arracourt, on the border of Lorraine.[1] As a young officer, Lécluse had been stationed eight kilometers away at Lunéville and knew this region well. His return occasioned a series of notes in his diary concerning places he had visited some twenty-two years before as well as the people and places he visited in 1915. His diary for 17 November 1915 indicate that he met with Captain Mignot of the First Dragoons, Commandant Bastrun, and a lieutenant in the machine-gun corps before heading off toward Arracourt, a village with some twelve hundred inhabitants. That town had been severely damaged by both the Germans and the French. Upon their arrival, Lécluse and his companions were greeted by Captain d'Aumale, the commandant of that sector. Shown the local defenses, Lécluse describes the system in great detail since it varied considerably from the defensive fortifications encountered elsewhere.

On this tour of the area, Lécluse saw a large, "beautiful, modern church" that had been completely destroyed. He saw a large statue, still intact, of the Sacred Heart and describes its impact on him. This sort of description is commonly found in many diaries and memoirs written by combat line officers during World War I.

Unlike both the diary and other published works, however, Lécluse transposes the scene from historical narrative to what might be called "faction," a combination of fact and fiction. This chapter seems to be a combination of literature and historical narrative. What is important to the author is the impression this scene had on him and his reflections at the time. Lécluse takes poetic license and conveys a sense of the Christ statue speaking to the visitors. This gives a better conclusion to the story than the one contained in the diary, yet it is consistent with the feelings expressed in the diary itself.]

To Captain Viot of the 9th Light Group, and 2d Light[2]

On that day, I believed that I saw a vision! It was in Lorraine, at the village of Arracourt, where I had been sent, with other officers from my division, to reconnoiter a sector. Arracourt was a large village, deserted and half in ruin, situated in that small portion of our territory where the hazards of war had hardly altered the outline of the border. After the various swings of the battle of Lorraine, we were facing the Boches in about the same place as during peace time, until the day when the final Victory will return to us our dear provinces, lost forty-six years ago![3]

The snow covered the earth, that cold November morning, and we were congratulating ourselves for having been able to make the trip in a comfortable automobile, which had dropped us off some five hundred meters from Arracourt. There, we had to take, for prudence sake or rather to follow orders, the traditional, ever-muddy and slippery communications trench to approach the village.

Whether as the host or the visitor, a visit to a sector is always an interesting thing. Whatever the rank of the visitor, one feels that whoever receives him is the "master of his own home." It is the castle owner who invites you to tour his estate, the ship commander who invites you on board, happy to show you the details of his domain, to bring out some interesting points, the improvements he has made, to which he devotes all his cares and all his spare time.

The same was true at Arracourt, and under the escort of Captain d'Aumale, of the Seventeenth Dragoons, we came to appreciate as connoisseurs the admirable defensive organization of the village. It was the work of an artist, who, with the assistance of intelligent and energetic workers, made the best of circumstances, which allowed him to give free reign to his ingenuity, taking advantage of a long period of calm.

Thus, Arracourt had become a veritable fortress, divided into five sectors of resistance, capable of holding on alone and without outside help, forcing the assailant into street fighting, step by step and meter by meter.

Everywhere, impeccable trenches, with double and triple firing steps, mutually flanking each other served by communications trenches themselves transformable into firing trenches, equipped sometimes by small cubby-holes separated and protected for each rifleman, interspersed with machine-gun nests buried under earth, armored, cemented, concrete reinforced. Close by, there were reinforced cellars covered by a thick layer of dirt to shelter the garrison. Ahead spread vast networks of barbed wire, in two or three rows, each one twenty or thirty meters deep!

Finally, underneath it all, as was the case with the Boches, two subterranean passages ran from one end of the village to the other.

We were coming back from our hike while showering our guide with compliments, when the latter, arriving in front of the church, burst out: "Now I am going to show you something extraordinary, something you have never seen!" We stepped forward under the portal, and stopped, astonished. . . .

Of the once-beautiful church, there remained only the four walls, the bell tower, deprived of its spire, and the arcade which enclosed the choir. The altar was no more than a heap of rubble, we walked on pieces of the three bronze bells, on the debris of the stained glass windows and the Way of the Cross. . . . But, in this desolate solitude, in the middle of these ruins leveled bit by bit, upright on its cracked pedestal, held together only by a miracle, the back against the left column of the large arcade, alone, all alone, but perfectly intact, stood a statue of the Sacred Heart, nearly life-sized! And the Christ, towering over the debris because of his great height, was watching us come!

We moved forward in silence, as if drawn by his look which fascinated us and our emotion grew more and more, because we then noticed the expression of the face of this Christ! Truly, he was there standing like a living reproach, making his protest in a sovereign way. . . . Little by little, the rain had tarnished the somewhat gaudy colors and covered them with a beautiful patina, and the sad and pious expression of the sacred face had taken on a poignant despair. . . . The pose of the hands was classic, the left hand showing the bloody heart, the right lowered and extended in a gesture of welcome, but now this gesture was pointing to the ruins!

As if to further amplify the intensity of the effect, chance — was this really chance? — had determined that one or two light splinters of brick should scuff the forehead of the Savior, and that gave the impression of drops of blood!

And this Christ seemed to say to us, he was really telling us, with unbounded bitterness, with an infinite despair:

> Look! This is what men have done to the House of God! Here
> was a place of Prayer, the asylum of the humble, those who suffer
> and who cry, the refuge of those who no longer have hope! Over
> the ages, the storms of time, revolutions and wars have respected
> this Sanctuary, but it found no mercy from you who claim to be

so civilized! And nevertheless, for two thousand years, men heard this word which summarizes my Gospel, all the sum of its virtues, all the Wisdom of the world: 'Love one another!' And here is what they have done!

Certainly, some of us were not easily moved, those whose souls the spectacles of war had armored and whose sensitivity had been blunted, but in front of this Christ we felt motionless and speechless, similar to those Napoleonic veterans whom Coppée shows us at the entrance of the church of Saragossa:

". . . nailed to the ground, speechless, almost cowardly!"

And we left without saying anything, furtively and as if ashamed, and without daring to look back, from fear of meeting the eyes of the heartbroken Christ full of pain and reproach!

Arracourt
(Meurthe-et-Moselle)
17 November 1915

17

The Mad Escapade

[*Editor's Note: This is one of the few chapters where the treatment or tone of the memoir is substantially different from that of the diary. The story of "The Mad Escapade," as told by Lécluse, is far more light-hearted and entertaining than the actual diary entry, losing none of its basic information in the process of transforming it into a short story.*

On 27 November 1915, two of Lécluse's men, Branchard and Lung, wandered off from their listening post, not with the intention of desert-ing, but to reconnoiter on their own. This was contrary to standing orders, and both would be punished for their transgression, which was a very serious matter. Vincent Suard tells us that the abandonment of one's post at the front was the most frequent cause of convictions and execu-tions in the French army during World War I.[1] However, since the obvious intention of the men was not to abandon their post, their punishment would be much less severe.

Five days earlier, the squadron had been repositioned near the vil-lage of Bures.[2] The enemy was reportedly some fifteen hundred to two thousand meters away, separated by marsh and a pond. This secondhand story, one of two in the memoir, was told to Lécluse by soldier named Blin on the morning of the 27th. Lécluse describes Branchard and his friend Lung as "dirty dogs" who became bored at their listening post and set off in the night, headed the wrong way. Challenged by a German sen-try, they ran in panic under small arms fire, losing Branchard's rifle in the process. Captain de Lécluse was inclined to be merciful toward Lung, whom he regarded as a good soldier led astray by his "madcap" comrade. Only Branchard was punished "with a good dose of prison," according to the author. In the French text, the author gave Lung a heavy, Alsatian accent, which has been preserved in the translation.]

*To the memory of Lieutenant Rouxel — 9th
Light Group — 2d Light who died for France.*

"Say! We are becoming mildewed here! My feet are like ice! What if we got the hell out of here?"

"Are you krazy? Where vill ve go?"

"My God, look what is in front of us!"

"You know very vell it is forbidden!"

"Ah! Well! They are not going to hold it against us if we go on patrol on the German side! The hell with it! Stay here if you want. I am getting out of here."

Those words were exchanged with hushed voices between two poilus, the Breton Branchard, and the Alsatian Lung, huddled together, in the dark and cold night, at the bottom of a listening post more or less transformed into a sitz bath. Branchard, a scatterbrain, good-hearted but a whimsical character, the amateur soldier, tried vainly to lead his companion astray, a brave carpenter of Altkirch, who escaped from Germany to enlist under our flag. Lung was just the opposite of Branchard. He had, as did the German soldiers, a thick head, a certain coolness and nerves of steel, and blind respect for discipline, a respect which was vigorously inculcated in him, previously, during years of service in the German navy. He was alarmed at his comrade's proposal, which he considered simply as an act of madness. But since the stubborn Branchard had jumped out the hole and already distanced himself in the shadows, the poor Lung decided that he could not really leave a buddy to take that sort of risk towards the enemy, all alone in the treacherous night. He knew him to be imprudent, daredevil, courageous but incapable of getting out of trouble in a critical circumstance, and, after a short struggle between friendship and a sense of duty, his heart won out. He hoisted himself in turn onto the terrace, and, while cursing Branchard, he joined him in a few strides. . . .

God! It was black, wet and cold! They went bent over, feeling the ground with their feet, holding their guns in front of them to protect themselves from obstacles. The terrain where they ventured was the tail end of a pond,[3] swampy, bristling with rushes and thin willows, cut with small streams and puddles of water. . . . Lung grumbled:

"Vat makes sense to vander about in such mess!"

"So what! At least my feet aren't any wetter and at least I am moving them!"

And they went on, probing the haze with their eyes, ears on alert, but not too worried however, because they knew that the German trenches were far away, some twelve hundred meters.

Still, a half-hour later, even Branchard had had enough. Walking was too difficult. He went sprawling several times in the slimy marsh. Also the night was too black; they couldn't see anything. It was really not much fun; and, above all they had to think about getting back and about the change of the sentries. Lung shuddered at the idea of the corporal finding the listening post abandoned!

"Let's go! Ve must go back."

Alas! it was easier said than done. . . . They had taken off without noting any land marks, without marking their route. Unbeknownst to them, the obstacles of the terrain, the network of iron wire which they had to avoid, had forced them to make innumerable detours, and at the end of a few steps they stopped, because they no longer knew whether to turn to the left or right, to advance or retrace their steps. . . . There was no getting around it, they were lost!

"God damn it!" Branchard swore.

"Vhy you svear?" replied Lung coolly. . . . "Bedder to tink."

"That's a good one! It is all thought out. We are done for!"

"Not yet! All ve need is find de shtreet. . . ."

"The street! Are you crazy? You think you're in a city?"

"De shtreet vitch runs in front of de trench five hundret meters avay, de lieutenant said."

"Ah! The road! It's called a road, you fool."

"It makes no difference," Lung said sententiously. "But there are schmall paths vitch lead to de drench. Ve are betveen de drench and de shtreet. Ve vill find one or de oder by marching schraight ahead."

"Ah! That's great!" replied Branchard. "Lung, my old pal, if you were a chubby blonde, I would kiss you!"

"Keep on valking! It's not vorth talking schtupid. It is no use!"

"Ah! Shut up" replied Branchard, vexed. "This stroll is not going to kill us!"

"Berhaps, but it not tanks to you."

As a result, Branchard, muzzled, no longer said anything, and there they were on their way again, as fast as they could, since they knew that they would get either to the road or the trench. In fact, a quarter of an hour later, which seemed much longer to them, they did come to the road. There, a new hesitation. Should they go left or right? They had wandered so much in all directions that they no longer knew if they were looking at their own trenches or if they had turned their backs to them. The night was black as ink with not a star to guide them. Lung thought for a second. Branchard, convinced of the superiority of his comrade, awaited his decision without saying a word, and fell obediently into step with him as soon as he had made up his mind. At the first crossing, Lung turned to the right; Branchard followed. And, a hundred meters farther, o joy! There was iron wire! They were saved! They followed the network, found the chicane, entered there, and ahead of them they could barely make out the parapet of the trench. . . . They were about to hail their comrades and be recognized, when suddenly. . . . "Wer da?" shouted a hoarse voice. . . . "Gott dam!" howled the phlegmatic Lung. "Ve have turned de vrong vay! Ve are vit de Boches!"

What a helter-skelter flight! Lung, who always kept his presence of mind, crossed the narrow chicane by leaping from side to side, but Branchard got caught by the barbed wire and fell forward head first. At the noise, the Boche sentry shot and sounded the alarm. . . . Branchard got up, managed to leave the network, but his comrade was already far away, and now they were separated and who knew what was ahead? As soon as he had gotten away, Lung, always helpful, thought of his companion, for whom he had a slightly scornful pity: "Damn Branchard! what is he going to do?!" — and, as the Boches began to shoot steadily (which meant that they had not understood what had taken place), he knelt down in a shell hole and boldly discharged his magazine at the Boche trenches. "Dat make dem tink!" He mumbled and chuckled silently. . . .

Minutes passed, long as centuries, the fire ceased, and, the Alsatian, his ears alert to the least sound, realized that an enemy patrol was coming out of the iron wire. As a result, he had to get away and fast! He worked his way by crawling, then started running, rejoined the famous "street," turned correctly this time, and, without any problem, arrived panting at the French wire network. Chance had returned him precisely to his trench, where the junior officer, worried about the shooting which had just occurred, called him abruptly. But Lung interrupted him:

"And Brantchard?"
"What do you mean, Branchard? He is not with you?"
"Brantchard not back?"

"But no! Damned Idiot!"

"Gott dam!" howled Lung, and making an about-face, he ran off again. The junior officer raised his arms to the sky: "He is mad!"

No, Lung was not mad! He was simply amazing, that's all! He left with Branchard. He was his elder. He let him do something stupid. He decided which way to go. He considered himself responsible for Branchard, and, quietly he was going to get him!

Do you grasp what is heroic about this simple gesture of the brave Alsatian? He knew that the Boches were now on alert. He could have asked for help from the trench, but no! He had made a mistake. He would make amends. He would return to the Boches' iron wire, if necessary, but he would bring back his comrade, or, if it was too late, he would stay with him. But, as far as he was concerned, they would not get him alive!

And the terrible journey began anew! Lung found the road, the oblique path which led to the Boches. He moved quickly, but prudently, his gun ready, and, every ten steps, he stopped, listened, then called softly: "Brantchard! . . . Brantchard?" And all at once, he nearly passed out with joy, because, fifty meters ahead, a muffled voice responded: "Hey! Here!" Lung crawled over to him very carefully, because he was not a child, he knew the Boches—he was one of them—they did not hesitate to use any trick. But no! It was truly Branchard, crouched along a hedge-row, dead tired, muddy, miserable. . . . Ah! what an meeting!

But, after congratulations and explanations, Lung's brow darkened.

"Unt your gun?" he said.

"Lost when I fell down in the barbed wire."

"Gott dam!" swore Lung for the third time, and, out of politeness, he finished "in German" because it was no compliment he aimed at Branchard.

The return took place without incident, but the two characters very sheepishly wondered what kind of welcome to expect. As a matter of fact, the explanation was stormy, in spite of the happy ending of this mad escapade.

Thereafter, the authorities got involved. The specter of a court-martial was raised, but the captain intervened and, out of consideration for the brave Lung, succeeded in hushing the affair. The only outcome, and

who would have believed it?, was a coolness between the two companions who took part in this adventure. "But, captain," as Lung said
gravely, "I am no longer Brantchard's friend! A man who lost his gun is
not a man!"

This story is real. It happened to two men in my squadron in
Lorraine on 27 November 1915, and their names are true to the letter.

Trench of Bures
(Lorraine)
27 November 1915

18

A Winter in Lorraine

[Editor's Note: In this chapter, Lécluse drew together a substantial amount of material from various places in his diary and organized it into a coherent narrative. Relevant diary entries include the end of November 1915 through the end of May 1916.

Lécluse and his men were stationed near the village of Crion (see map 7), some five kilometers north of Lunéville for much of the winter and spring of 1916.[1] He had been stationed there in 1894 when first out of military school. The first several weeks were uneventful, except for one incident on 20 February 1916 when the author narrowly escaped serious injury. A German airplane dropped a bomb very close to Lécluse and his horse, who were in the middle of a street. Then, on 26 February, the men heard cannon fire from Verdun for the first time.

In 1894, as a young lieutenant, Lécluse had hunted and fished in the Parroy Forest where his men were now stationed. He describes the defenses employed in that area, including both blockhouses and conventional trench systems. At times, they were close enough to the enemy to hear their movements and their conversation but were unable to see them. The real risk was not so much from artillery fire as from sniper fire, as the chapter indicates. Although this was another supposedly "quiet sector," the author's perception of that sector was very different from what one might expect.

By this time, Lécluse's attitude toward Germany and German culture had become more hostile. When he comments on the German army's behavior, he complains bitterly about the "Boches" and their "atrocities." But when he sees German corpses or prisoners at close range, he tends to be sympathetic and even compassionate.]

To General Haln du Frétay.

The village of Crion, five kilometers north of Lunéville, bordered the Parroy forest. It was one of those Lorraine villages about which it can be

Fig. 10. An artillery unit in winter. *Copyright SIRPA/ECPA France.*

said once you have seen one you have seen them all. The long and solitary street, formed by the main road, was bordered by rather ugly, low houses, covered with blackish tiles. Normally, you gained entrance through a large coach door, giving access to a passageway which served as a threshing floor and where the main entrance to the house was located. The entrance to the cellars took place by outside staircases covered by bulkhead doors, as long as the residents had not forgotten to close them, in which case unwarned passers-by could take some dangerous spills. In front of the windows, even in the case of the most comfortable homes, rose up the inevitable heaps of dung, and the large Lorraine wagons were aligned, riding high on their skinny, narrow, rickety and wobbling wheels. All these streets gave the villages an unfortunate appearance of disorder and filth, despite the numerous fountains and drinking troughs, where pipes full of running and clear water gushed day and night.

The village of Crion, which, like all its counterparts, conformed to this description, was our rest camp during the winter and the spring of 1915-16. If someone would have told me previously, when I was garrisoned at Lunéville, that I would live in Crion, intermittently but regularly for six months, I would have been greatly surprised, and even more so if

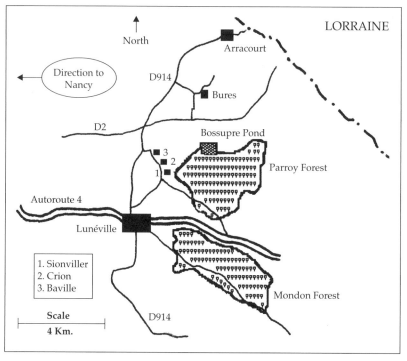

Map 7. Parroy Forest

told that I would be vacationing even longer in this Parroy forest which I knew as a second-lieutenant only for hunting, horseback riding, and fishing outings in the Bossupré pond![12] Now the poor forest, fallen into the hands of the Boches, to the pickaxes of the poilu and to the ingenuity of the disciples of Vauban which we were trying to become, was lined with footpaths from Decauville, lumber roads, telegraph and telephone lines and innumerable networks of barbed wire, bristling with blockhouses and Adrian huts, dug with shelters, communications trenches, saps and cave-shelters. The only thing it would have gained from this occupation was an impressive road built and maintained relentlessly by hundreds of territorials, and which ran from one end of the forest to the other. But this improvement was far from sufficient to compensate for the many serious wounds from which Parroy, as well as its neighbor Mondon,[3] was not going to be able to recover for a long time.

After nearly a year of being a sort of unclaimed zone where opposing patrols used to exchange gunshots daily, we finally had taken possession of the forest and chased away the Boches, except for a small area, situated at the north-east horn, where the enemy had clung. We had taken over, in this region, a system of continuous trenches, used almost everywhere else, and we occupied a few isolated blockhouses, bastions surrounded by fortified walls, enclosed at the gorge by drawbridges or spiked barriers, and in which everything was planned to be able to hold off, even under siege, for twenty hours, enough time to mount a serious counterattack.

These blockhouses, called "small outposts," were shadowed, two or three hundred meters farther back, by a second line of more important works, called "centers of resistance." Farther yet were sites of the reserves for the sector, divided in turn in two tiers. All these lines of successive defenses, served by communications trenches or the lumber roads, covered by the networks of iron wire, were tied together perpendicularly by other networks which were meant to compartmentalize and channel attacks. The result of this enormous system of defensive works, continually reinforced and perfected, had been to make the Parroy forest a nearly impregnable fortress, forcing the enemy, fearful of disproportionate losses, to avoid it and go around it, to go toward Lunéville on their way to Nancy.

I had always thought of Parroy as a somber, thick and damp forest, and that's the way I found it again. Our first stay there was rather rigorous, from January to April. During the first three months, we waded and mildewed there in the muddy swamps.

Our light group was posted in the part of the forest still held by the Boches. The underbrush was so tight and so bushy we found ourselves "nose to nose" there, reduced to hearing each other walking and talking without being able to see each other! Thus, we had nothing to fear from the enemy artillery which could not adjust its fire and would have risked bombing its own lines. On the other hand, you had to be wary of isolated fire as soon as you arrived in first line, because you could be shot like game by some Boches on the look-out behind a tree trunk or perched in its branches. That's the way two of our comrades of the Twenty-fifth Dragoons sadly met their end one day some fifty meters ahead of us for having carelessly shown themselves at the edge of a clearing.

But, deep down, our greatest enemies, those which we feared the most, those about which we can not truly say "we got the best of them!" were mud and boredom! Thus it was with great impatience we counted the days which separated us from our return to the third line, and how great was our depression when, as a result of an unfortunate course of events at headquarters, we had to spend, as happened to me twice, thirty days in a row without coming out of the forest, singing, as would William Tell, but in a tone of lament: "Dark forest! Savage and sad Desert!" Ah!, yes! sad and savage! which made our six days' rest in the modest village of Crion appear enchanting!

Crion was also just a short ride from Lunéville, which we considered like a capital. The shops, the cotton damask establishments, the pastry shops, the messes of the two fortunate regiments which were quartered in town, the dining room of the restaurant of the Hotel des Vosges, the railroad to Nancy, so many attractions which only woodsmen like ourselves could appreciate at their true value. To sum up, I will mention one home with a profound gratitude shared by all of my comrades who have been the guests of Mme Géhin. There, this exquisite lady of the house, as artistic as she was gracious, invited each evening, for five o'clock tea, all the stars whom we indicated to her, brought together to the area by the hazards of war. [We assume these "stars" are talented singers and musicians serving as soldiers in the area.] I saw there gatherings of wonderful artists and savored musical programs which only some capital cities can offer. Outstanding singers, piano or violin virtuosos, whose ranks were increased by talented amateurs, dressed in a great variety of uniforms, followed each other with charming grace, for the great pleasure of the listeners. Ah! the great hours of relaxation, the wonderful rest which we could savor there, rocked gently by the divine music!

But let's get back to Crion, antechamber of these wonders. Crion, like Sionviller, like Baville,[4] like so many other neighboring towns, was within the reach of the heavy German cannons, and, for months, had never been bombarded. Why? These were inexplicable mysteries, because the enemy knew very well that all these villages were inhabited by soldiers. Moreover, as if they had wanted to prove to us that they were not the ones who decided to shell us, on one occasion they sent us some of their largest caliber shells behind the village, on the road to Lunéville. At the time, we were in the forest, and we had expressed our intent to run the risks of a mortar rather than deprive ourselves of our sole entertainment, but the Boches never did it again. Once again, there was no use trying to figure it out.[5]

There was in the cemetery of Crion, as is typical in the region, even in the Parroy forest, at the post at the Maison Brulée,[6] a small corner of tombs reserved for soldiers. Little by little the number of crosses was growing, because, even though the sector was "quiet," there was from time to time what we called an "accident." It was an unlucky shell or aerial bomb fragment, a "lost bullet" as the French say which was not completely so, and a poor cavalryman or a brave old territorial grandpa came to rest in Lorraine soil, far from his village and far from his people. I often went, while taking a stroll, into that small cemetery, to reassure myself that the tombs were being maintained and to read names of the latest arrivals, and, each time, I felt the same way as I had on my first visit. There were some thirty crosses, — I said that it was a quiet sector — aligned as at maneuvers, covered with bouquets and wreaths decorated with ribbons, and in the corner of the enclosure, where the cloister walls met, one stood, similar to the others, but desolate and without a flower! This somber spot, at the back of this colorful flower bed, drew your attention and gripped your heart. I had come near, wanting to know the name of the poor forsaken or the poor unknown, having decided that, if it was necessary, I would take some flowers from a neighboring tomb to atone for this neglect; and I had read, tragic response to my wondering: "Unter-Officer Schimmelmans." It was a Boche! He was there, all alone, tucked in his corner, as an outcast, with all these dead Frenchmen grouped around him, against him. . . . It evoked the idea of an evil beast, cornered by the pack which was going to tear his throat, the idea of the evil-doer tracked down by the howling crowd, who leaned against the wall, grimacing and livid, to face them one last time and to make them pay dearly for his life! It was ominous and poignant at the same time, and I could not stop myself, in front of this spectacle, from feeling both fright and sympathy! Another Boche tomb, in the middle of all those which strewed the countryside, mixed in with the others, also caught my attention and evoked pity. It was at the edge of the main road which crossed the forest, a little bit before you arrive at the barracks of Grand Taille. Not even a name on the black cross, nothing but the dry inscription: "Prussian soldier" and the tomb dug in the ditch of the road. The grave diggers, in a hurry, had not bothered to remove the corpse from the ditch where they had found it, and the unfortunate one laid there, in the mud, buried under the dead leaves and the muddy backwaters of the brook which tumbles down the slope. . . . Poor Devil! I have often walked by his tomb, and each time, I had melancholy thoughts of his pitiful destiny! You were full of enthusiasm, "Nach-Paris!," as your chiefs whispered to you. But, on this road so completely clear, you fell in your first steps, having barely crossed the frontier. . . . And those who await your return will never know your final resting place. It is better this way, because undoubtedly they keep hope that it is in a suitable sepulcher, next to other companions-in-arms, perhaps even in consecrated ground. . . . Poor people! What would they say if they could see your misery! Abandoned by all, thrown there like a discarded object, until the day when, your humble cross overturned by the storm, you no longer will draw even a look!

You seemed to me, o Boche who has elicited my pity, to represent the punishment which Divine Justice has reserved for your master! With you, he left for the "happy war," for "his war," as he said. But the prey slips away from the claws of the predatory eagle, the death blow has already been struck by a poilu, the beast has been struck, the death knell is going to ring! Soon, your execrable Kaiser, crushed under the weight of his crimes and the curse of the world, will crumble in turn, and will end up, like you, in a ditch!

Crion-Parroy Forest
(Meurthe and Moselle)
January-May 1916

19

The Farewell

[*Editor's Note: Throughout the month of June 1916, little happened in Lécluse's sector. The weather was cold and wet throughout the first half of the month. There were few casualties, except for a small number of soldiers wounded by artillery fire and one soldier who was shot as he worked on his commandant's roof in full view of the enemy.*

This chapter, contains growing signs that the author has become more cynical toward the war. On 2 June he commented in his diary that "The sector is much more calm than formerly. . . . [but] our good comrades in the cavalry with their usual behavior will make it agitated and dangerous, all in doing nothing useful." He criticized the Germans for wounding a dozen men in an artillery barrage—all for nothing, in his opinion.[1]

On 22 July, he mentioned two tanks that attacked his position. On the 23d, German tanks attacked again and Lécluse and his men were ordered to Blainville, some nine kilometers away, at 2:30 A.M. He commented that he "directed the departure of the third battalion at 3:30 A.M., the commandant having passed me the command as the most senior of his four captains." On 25 July, his battalion was attached to the Sixty-ninth Division. Lécluse spent 30 July to 8 August 1916 on leave. On 9 August, upon his return to Vigneuilles, he discovered that the Eighth Cavalry Division had been dissolved. He anticipated being sent back to the depot at Gray-la-ville (Haute-Saône) and then possibly being reassigned.[2] He said ironically, "For me, it is probably the end of my brilliant career and my great achievements in active duty." On 10 August, General Baratier said good-bye to the officers of the Second Light. The next day, Lécluse noted that he composed a verse on the dissolution of the Second Light, probably a reference to the poem in chapter 33. He arrived at Gray on 13 August and said good-bye to La Rochefordière, Epitalou, Grévin, Gautron, and de Borde on the 14th. On the 16th, he said good-bye to the rest of the squadron for the last time. He commented that they lost seventeen of their men and spent twelve of the twenty months at the front in the trenches. He shook hands with each of his men, who then left at 8:45 A.M. for new assignments.]

To the memory of General Baratier who died for France.[3]

".... And until the final good-bye, it is one's own soul which we
sow, which we sow in each good-bye! ..."

How well I understood the lines of this poem, the day when I said
good-bye to my dear men! It was the ultimate farewell, and I left a bit of
my soul there!

No matter what the separation, no matter how far the trip, we can
always hope to see one another again. Even death, in the case of believ-
ers, is only a temporary separation, which will end in eternal reunion.
. . . But, in this case, it was a departure without any possible return, the
final end to a common existence and also of a beautiful dream! The
disbanding of a regiment is a death after which there is no resurrection!

A few days before, we were, as our colonel[4] put it, stunned by this
thunderbolt! Our beautiful Second Light, this elite regiment, which had
been in operation for only three months, promoted to the first line,
formed in May 1916, from the light groups of two cavalry divisions,
already hardened units, proven under fire, from one end of the front to
the other, honored by flattering eulogies from all the chiefs who had had
them under their command. It was a superb group of twelve foot squadrons, composed half of young soldiers, half of reservists, and, a unique
situation at this point in the war, commanded from the colonel to the
sergeants, by career officers and junior-officers, whom I would describe
as being from the old school, having had years of rank and experience.
They had just organized us, rearmed us and outfitted us with new equipment. We had been trained for combat by virtuosi, a brigade of "blue
devils." In short, we felt ourselves in tip-top shape and burning with the
desire to inscribe as quickly as possible the names of victories on the
virgin folds of our standard. . . .

At that very moment, "Mr. Bureaucrat," this anonymous, all powerful and pernicious being, decreed, since our division was dissolved,
that the Second Light, which was one component of it, no longer had
any reason to exist, and that it would also be disbanded and scattered to
the four corners of France, the officers at random to available places, the
men in various regiments of artillery.

In vain did we point out that this regiment had an exceptional
worth, that it could handle many tasks, capable of filling many roles,

either alone, or paired off with a regiment of infantry or a group of chasseurs. In vain, we were told, the general commanding the cavalry corps[5] went as far as proposing another foot regiment to be sacrificed to satisfy the destructive rage of Mr. Bureaucrat! All was useless! Mr. Bureaucrat sneered at objections which he did not understand! For him, a soldier was just a number, and a regiment was just manpower. . . . Moreover, what good was it to discuss it? Mr. Bureaucrat was infallible, and his decisions were without appeal! And thus died the Second Light, not on the field of honor, as it was its right and its ambition, but from a heart-rending and inglorious death. . . .

During the days which witnessed this senseless destruction, we had the opportunity to taste all of the bitterness. First, it had been through the farewell of our divisionnaire.[6] On a gray morning, as sad as our thoughts, from the various villages where we had been quartered, we had answered his call, and there, with an emotion which made his voice quiver, and a pain which sent shivers down his spine, he shared with us a few words which he found to praise Marchand, his chief and his friend. We were motionless, aligned in front of him, a lump in our throats, incapable of holding back the tears which were coming to our eyes. We were listening to those words which tolled the end of our joys and our hopes:

> I come, to say farewell to your great regiment. . . . I loved it and had faith in it. . . . It was born in the midst of war, in the breath of battle. . . . It had a vibrant and magnificent soul. . . . It was made up of strength and beauty. . . And now it is dead. . . and all is over. . . . As difficult as our tests have been, never again were we asked to make a similar sacrifice. . . . Let's accept it, for France!

And the warm and harmonious voice fell abruptly, broken, in a sob. . . . Most of us were crying and did not hide it. Then, in a moment of silence, our general walked up to us, hugged our colonel, then passed through our ranks, shaking the hand of each one of us, as one does at funerals, and it was indeed a funeral! After that came the dispersion, during which everyone was trying to numb themselves in the hubbub of decisions to make, orders to give, a type of false fever when we avoided reflection and thought. One by one the officers left, brought back to the rear, as assignments were made. Then, in turn, the squadrons made their way as a group to various garrisons, to learn there their new trade of gunners. All of a sudden it was my turn to say good-bye to my men. A last time, I had them line up front of me. It seemed to me that, as so many times before, we were going to proceed toward some sector of trenches or on a dangerous mission. . . . Alas!

I was looking at them, my Bretons, my Vendéens, for a last time, intensely. . . . Most of them had been with me since our arrival at the front, some twenty months ago! I had equipped them, armed them, trained them, and marched them afterwards, always sharp, always courageous, from one end of the front to the other. Others had come to me to fill the voids as they were created. There were forty-year-old reservists and nineteen-year-old young greenhorns. They were all my friends, my children. I could see pass before my eyes all we had experienced together, the countryside we had covered together, the foundries of the Artois, the forest at Mulhouse, the desolate plains of Champagne, the hard winter of Lorraine, and all of the tests endured with a smile, the rain, the snow, the mud, the bullets, the shells, the good and the bad days, the misery and the glory! As I walked through the ranks, I alluded to the men who had stood on that very spot and whose names I still had called out during general assembly, men who had lost their lives at their combat posts. . . .

My men were also looking at me! I could no longer see in their eyes this silent question and this offering of themselves which I had seen there so often, when, in a moment of the danger, the soldier, looking at his leader, expresses silently, his confidence and his devotion, the sublime exchange of two souls one of which commands and the other which obeys, but which share in the same cause! This time it was in addition both a time of sadness and of pride. I understood that these men, had they been allowed to speak, would have said to me:

> "Now that we are about to leave, isn't it true that you were happy with our work?"

Ah! Yes! my boys! And I remember that I was not able to say anything else! I thanked you, almost humbly, you simple soldiers, but the true artisans of Victory, in the name of your officers, in the name of France, for your self-denial, your courage, your Faith! I thanked you for it, and did not praise you, because you do not congratulate a French soldier, even less a Vendéen or a Breton for being resigned, brave, or a believer! I expressed to you how constantly proud I was to have commanded you, that this would be the pride of my life, and also my inconsolable sorrow to have had to give up my command there, when we could have done so many beautiful things together! I asked you to remain what you were, everywhere where fate led you, in the service of the Country. . . . And then, in order to partake of the noble sacrifice which was imposed on us, we shouted: "Long live France!" this phrase which, in the hours which we lived, summarized all of our duty, soothed all of our injuries, and consoled all of our sorrows! After that, we made our final leg together and that proved to be the hardest part.

It is as if, during cruel separations, we refuse to think about it, to pay attention to it, until the last moment. Likewise, it is only when you had boarded the train which took you far from me forever, that I fully realized the heartbreak of this good-bye. . . . I too began my sad procession. Standing at the door of each compartment, I shook the hand of each of my men, addressing to them a word of friendship, of gratitude, of encouragement. That went well at first, then emotion took over, words became stuck in my throat, tears clouded my eyes. I had to finish shaking hands without saying anything, and, in the case of the last one, I had no more strength and I just waved my hand to say good-bye. . . . Painful minutes, which I would not want to relive! The train started up as my brave boys shouted a last hurrah in my honor. I saw a mass of kepis being waved out of the doors.[7] I lifted mine automatically to respond and to salute one last time. . . and found myself on the platform of the station, in the presence of the only one of my officers [Lieutenant Billet] who would remain with me for a few more days, the two of us mute and extremely sad, poor officers without a troop, poor bodies without a soul!

O my dear soldiers, what has become of you? How many of you have already lengthened the list of our dead? And you who remain, still brash, I am sure, and eager for any task, do you sometimes remember your captain? He is with you in his thoughts, without knowing where you are. He suffers your pain and shares in your joys. He applauds your success as he sympathizes with your miseries! May God watch over you and lead you to Victory, which we were not able to know together!

And then, my General, you were right! A regiment is a living being, and possesses a soul! The Second Light is not completely dead! Its memory is present in our thoughts and in our hearts. It left its imprint on us.

It lives in us everywhere where the hazards of war have dispersed those who composed it. . . . Later, this will be the sacred tie which will reunite them forever, those who were before and who will always remain companions of struggle and glory. Its undying soul will always be part of them, just as it floated in the folds of our standard!

Camp Saffais
(Lorraine) — Gray
10 August-16 August 1916

20

The Woodsmen

[Editor's Note: This is part of a series of chapters grouped originally by Lécluse under the title "The Luck of the Road." These character sketches and personal reminiscences are not directly supported by the diary but appear to be recollections of persons, places, and events that were composed in 1918. Whereas the first nineteen chapters are directly based on entries in Lécluse's diary and represent the shared experiences of his squadron, the last fourteen chapters are less closely tied to the author's diary and seem to be personal reminiscences. These later chapters, very different from the ones that precede them, seem driven by a more lyrical impulse and stand in sharp contrast to the journalistic spirit of the earlier chapters.]

To Lieutenant de Mont of the 9th Light Group.[1]

Among the guardians of the immense trench which bars the route to the invaders, from the North Sea down to Switzerland, across mountains, plains and forests, those whom we will call "The Woodsmen" were the privileged ones.

While their comrades from the plain, the "Cave Men," roasted during the summer, drowned during the winter, bombarded at all hours of the day and the night, remained confined like moles at the bottom of their holes, unable to move about except within the walls of a communications trench, and who saw only the sky directly over their heads, the Woodsmen led a peaceful existence, quite pleasant during nice weather, and went about in these picturesque sites at will, without running any sort of risk.

For them the forest was like a mother. Under its cover, especially when the buds had completely opened, they were hidden from the indiscreet eyes of airplanes. It was impossible to direct an efficient fire at this ocean of greenery where shells burst blindly. Thus, the enemy was content to vent its anger by sending a few projectiles haphazardly which were quite often noisy but harmless.

Under the cover of the forest, we could get organized at a leisurely pace. We put a finishing touch on the construction of the shelters which did not have to be underground, except at the edge of the forest and in the front line. Often, we lived in comfortable wooden huts, veritable forest cabins, sometimes even in rather sharp chalets where the ingenuity of carpenters and cabinet-makers was given free reign. Best of all, the communications trench, that horrible trench, more or less transformed into a muddy brook during six months of the year, was not needed in the forest. We went about with dry feet, on logging roads which little by little covered the terrain like the cords of a large net.

The forest was generous. It provided all the wood which we needed, for our lodging, for our heating, for defending ourselves: those beautiful fire-logs and the stacks of wood which brought to the most humble home the joy and light of the flame, the large timbers which created above the homes the mattress where shells would burst harmlessly, the planks for fixing up the interior, the posts from which we would make the fence for the blockhouse, the logs for the transportation of lumber, the pickets used to stretch out networks of iron wire. It increased twofold the value of the secondary defenses: the trees left standing, the brush, the piles of cut trees created along with the barbs an impenetrable jumble, impossible to locate and destroy, and which even a dog would not dare to enter.

The forest held some treasures for gourmands. It provided different types of mushrooms: fine girolles, succulent cepes, the savory morels. In the springtime, the wild strawberries and raspberries scented the thicket. We picked black currants, wild berries, and hazelnuts. Game abounded there, and, if the pheasants had left the area at the arrival of the cannons, rabbits and hares had remained to their great misfortune, and poaching, a trait found in more than one poilu, often embellished our menu with a leg of venison or wild boar.

Finally the forest was coquettish, because nature ignored the horrors of the war. Flowers, as in the past, covered the moss carpet, and the officers' table was decorated, according to the seasons, with lilies of the valley, honeysuckle, wild roses or snowdrops.

In order to please its residents, the forest clad itself with the most varied attire. In the spring, its green dress took on a great variety of shades. Upon the arrival of fall, the infinite range of gold highlighted the dark background of the pines. Finally, in winter, the forest wrapped itself in diamonds of frost and a large coat of snow before going to sleep.

How beautiful were the walks we made in the woods, what marvelous aspects they took on at the various hours of the day, be it at the first light of dawn which gilded the tops of trees and shaded with a thousand tints the diaphanous haze which hovered in the clearings, be it the setting sun which set it ablaze, or moonlight which rummaged the undergrowth with its silver rays.

Generous and beautiful forests of France, which have sheltered and protected me during eight months of war, you, in Alsace, where the large, straight beeches stood like columns of a gigantic temple, you, in Lorraine, with your underbrush so thick that we heard the Boches talk without being able to see them, and you, in Picardy, where I began my life as a woodsman. How pleasant and peaceful it was under your branches, and how well we slept there, once the angry voice of the cannon had become silent, and nothing more disturbed the majestic silence of the night!

What invigorating and healthy air we breathed there, far from the dust, the mud and the noxious fumes of the plain, far from the tumult and ugliness of the war, the war you so often helped us forget!

[No date or location]

21

The Tombs

[Editor's Note: Dedicated to his friend Madame Géhin, who received Lécluse into her home on numerous occasions while he was in Lunéville, this chapter was dated June 1916, but there is no corresponding reference to a cemetery visit in the author's diary for the period. However, there are many references to cemeteries and to individual graves visited by the author during his twenty months at the front. The text of this chapter appears to correspond most closely to a diary entry from Narroy on 23 October 1915, following the offensive in Champagne, which began on 25 September.]

To Madame Géhin.

I have seen tombs of soldiers, touching in their humility, so glorious nevertheless! Vigilant sentries mounting their last guard duty to protect the native soil, and covering the earth with a forest of crosses which those who fell defending it seem to have wanted to insure its eternal possession!

Some of them with their mounds covered with flowers, gave a puffy appearance to the plain where the battle raged. They were grouped here and there, randomly in a fold in the terrain, a hollow, a ditch where a handful of men huddled together to hold the enemy at bay, or more simply perhaps where some wounded dragged themselves off to die together. Sometimes it was a veritable mausoleum improvised right in the midst of a field by the pious ingenuity of comrades, rustic mounds of rocks, a Calvary of logs where the whiteness of the birches created a mood of mourning.

Others tragically alone, appeared at the edge of a grove, along a canal, at the back of a spring under the branches. It looked as if those sleeping there had the pride to hide their agony, the desire to rest alone in the serene peace of nature. . . .

In certain regions, witnesses of great battles, tombs populated the countryside as far as the eye could see, and, when tall crops did not hide them from our eyes, they seemed to reveal the layout of the battle. It was possible to follow lines of the riflemen in their forward advance, to notice points of resistance and the collision of the combatants, to specify the place where the ultimate shock took place, to accompany the wave of attack in its different phases, until the last advance, where the fastest and the bravest of the pursuers fell.

I had this very clear impression one October day in 1915. We were at Narroy,[1] at rest, after the hard offensive of Champagne, and I had gotten on my way with one of my officers [Second Lieutenant Rouxel], on a clear sunny morning, to go to see some comrades bivouacked a few kilometers away. The countryside we were crossing marked the limit of the immense battlefield of the Marne, as the lamentable ruins of villages where we passed attested eloquently, and, immediately, to the right and to the left of the road, we saw "The Tombs."

At first, they were sparse, scattered here and there — the ones first struck at the moment of the offensive — so I began to count them. But, alas, I soon had to give that up, because very quickly it was by tens that white and black crosses began to rise up from all sides! Full of emotion, quiet and collected, we contemplated this sublime blossoming! It lined the march of our soldiers, bringing to life isolated combats in the great battle, the approach to the canal line vehemently defended, the assault on the lock and the bridge, the decisive effort, the final pursuit. O dead! you had signed your work, you had drawn with your torn bodies the map of your Victory!

But the most beautiful, the most touching of these tombs, were the isolated ones, their names already half-erased, or their identification number on the tricolor shield, and the crude adornments such as a kepi deformed and washed out by the rain, a steel helmet hammered out, or simply a canteen hanging on an arm of a white wooden cross. Too often, alas! Not even a name! the sublime anonymity of the last sacrifice! "Here lies a captain of the chasseurs"; "Here rest fifteen French soldiers"; or, more briefly still, with a curtness which was a sort of final bitterness, "a German."

When I was at the trenches of the Bois des Loges, there were several of these anonymous tombs laid out along our communications trenches. The dead and the living held the trench together. One day, near my cell, when we were digging an ammunition shelter, one of my men ran up filled with emotion: "Captain, we have just come in contact with a corpse." I went and looked. You could barely make out a gold braid at the end of a sleeve, that was all! We resealed the hole, my Bretons rapidly dug a suitable tomb, surrounded by switches, a border of moss, a cross made of two boards, with these simple words: "Here lies an infantry officer," and we began digging again farther away. . . . I spent weeks next to this unknown comrade. . . . Often, at night, when the sound of a suspicious gunfire made me come out and listen, I spent a little time pondering about this missing person, and never did I walk by this small corner where he awaited the great day of Victory without saluting him and murmuring a prayer.

A few steps away, a large tomb, more beautiful, but just as anonymous, dominated the terrace where we had arranged a shelter for my men. They rested there next to their dead comrade, separated from him by a slim thickness of earth, sleeping the same trustful sleep, in the same serenity of duty accomplished, under the same eyes of God!

O those who died for my country! You have shown us the road to the supreme sacrifice! You have fallen, a smile on your lips, coloring with your blood the native earth which you were defending! May the earth be light for you! More fortunate than many others, you are sleeping for the last time in ground which has remained French thanks to your heroism, and which, faithful to your example, we will maintain inviolate! We now have something else to defend besides our fields, our cities, our homes and our cathedrals. It is a treasure more precious again, your innumerable tombs, o dead of the Great War! May your sleep be untroubled, your comrades are guarding them!

Later, after the Victory, when the hour of Justice has arrived,[2] she will also come for you, and the grateful living will spread out across the plains, scouring the woods and ravines, everywhere where the Great Reaper struck, until they have found all the scattered tombs in all the battlefields. Then, leaving the discrete shelter of the forest, from the sunken road, from the wheat field, your glorified remains will be going to rest forever in the grandiose ossuairies. . . . But, as far as we are concerned, we will always remember with emotion, even with some regret, the still greater majesty, the mysterious beauty of these modest tombs where you will have awaited so patiently the magnificent dawn of Triumph!

Lunéville
June 1916

22

Pataud

[Editor's Note: Many war diaries contain chapters about a unit mascot, often a dog, adopted by the men. The chapter dedicated to Pataud is one such story. The dog belonged to Second Lieutenant de La Rochefordière and loved to hunt rats. On this particular day, the dog was shot and killed by a German sniper. Although the story is dated January 1917, it is a recollection based on an incident that occurred 3 April 1916, according to Lécluse's diary.]

To Second Lieutenant de la Rochefordière—
9th Light group, 2d Light[1]

Pataud was, like his master, Second Lieutenant de La Rochefordière, a member of the headquarters' staff of my squadron. They had both joined us in Alsace, and he had immediately become a comrade, or more accurately, a friend.

Like all bull terriers, he had an appealing countenance. His stare was deep and sedate, his upper lip slightly turned-up and somewhat mocking. He possessed a calm and disenchanted demeanor devoid of skepticism, a fact which explains why this breed of dog produces such valued companions in times of loneliness and boredom.

His coat was black with red streaks, with very little white. His ears stood straight up, his back and muscles were as hard as steel. He was neither jealous, nor demanding, nor noisy. While he did not lavish his friendship on everyone, he chose his friends well and never wavered. Perhaps his only fault, one shared by all members of his breed, was his staunch independence. The different regions which we crossed together must still be hearing the echoes of voices calling out his name, cursing at him. Pataud was notorious for turning a deaf ear and, while he didn't

Fig. 11. A Poilu and his dog. *Copyright SIRPA/ECPA France.*

systematically run away when called, he came back only when it suited him. He would accept his subsequent punishment stoically, taking the brunt of the blows on his back, and undaunted would do it again the following day. As a matter of fact, this fault ended up being the cause of his death.

Pataud's disposition did not lead to outgoing or violent behavior. He did have one intense dislike, one passion, and one incurable mania. Like all bull terriers, he had this great aversion to cats and to all rodents, and he was driven by this inherited hatred. He would have climbed a tree just to get to a cat. To catch a field mouse or a rat, he would dig a tunnel through shelving or a foot path made of small logs. In the winter time, he would come to us through the mud-lined trenches in unspeakable condition, a block of hardened dirt, which barely revealed the wrinkles around his snout, and where you could discern two mischievous eyes, still glowing from the satisfaction of his latest kill. As far as the other canines were concerned, and God knows they were numerous around our camp, Pataud, while not being arrogant, was less than friendly, and ignored them totally.

Pataud's passion was quite extraordinary in a dog of this breed. He loved water even more than a water spaniel or a Newfoundland. No matter what the weather was, in spite of snow or even ice, he would instinctively run to it, much like a duck, but not just to get his paws wet or walk in it a bit. He would jump into it and swim around like a fish, chasing rats along the river bank, diving after them, and fetching anything and everything we threw for him.

Finally Pataud had this mania: he loved to jump after a stick or any piece of wood. To get to it, he would not hesitate to climb walls much like a police dog, to overcome any kind of obstacle, and we would have killed him from sheer exhaustion had we not stopped the game. Once his jaws were clamped tightly on the object, you could carry him on your back or spin him around like a rock at the end of a sling. You can imagine that this type of play was not the best thing for his teeth.

Now that I have painted an accurate portrait of our wonderful dog, I will tell you a few words about his background. His master had picked him up in Compiègne and had adopted him as his inseparable companion. Pataud came with him and joined our squadron for seven months of the campaign. He became familiar with the tall beech trees, found in Alsace which had been recently taken back from the Germans, the chalets in the woods where he chased rats hiding under the floors, the eerie plains of the Champagne region with its shelters dug out of the chalky soil, from which Pataud, like his masters, would come out all white. Like them, he did not enjoy this very much, for, while not a coward, deep down he was not a warrior and he hated the sound of gunfire. The time spent in Champagne with its never ending cannonade must have been among the most painful of his existence.

After that we headed toward Lorraine, spending the long winter months in another forest. This one was more depressing, however, because of the continuous rain, the downpours, and especially the mud, where our poor dog would get stuck up to his shoulders. This is where, one spring day when the sun was out warming up the earth and enticing Pataud to frolic on the moss and run through thickets, he committed the imprudence which cost him his life. How he got out of the blockhouse still remains a mystery, but suddenly his master heard a gun shot followed by cries of pain. His poor companion had just been hit by a German bullet. The yelps continued a few moments, weakening little by little, then ceasing all together. The only sound which could be heard then was the snickering of these stupid killers, boasting of their feat. Think of it! causing pain to a Frenchman by killing his dog, what a godsend. What we wouldn't have given to be able to put an end to that laughter even though it was over a poor animal.

So that is the way Pataud died. Like a true soldier, felled by the enemy. His corpse remained between the two front lines, because they were only one hundred yards apart and it would have been foolish to risk the life of a man to retrieve a dead dog.

Poor Pataud! humble and faithful friend, through good times and bad times, we would have liked to bury you at the foot of a large oak tree. We would have written: "Here lies Pataud, of the Twenty-fourth Squadron, killed in action!"

At least, I wanted to tell your simple story, as I would have for any of my companion of arms, in memory of your kindness. Dog lovers will understand. I hope that others will also show some interest, no matter how brief, in the modest adventures of our small friend, one of those beings which rank below humans, but who are so dedicated, who love us as we love them, which society bestowed on us to console us, and whose death can almost bring tears to our eyes. . . .

January 1917

23

Ruins

[Editor's Note: Dated May 1918, this chapter is based on the author's visit to the town of Gerbéviller on 7 July 1916.[1] Written toward the end of the war, it reflects the author's patriotism, his animosity toward Germany, and his desire to memorialize the suffering of the community.

Early in 1914, advancing German troops killed some fifty people in Gerbéviller, burning the homes of inhabitants who had taken refuge in their cellars. Lécluse regards Gerbéviller as an example of wanton destruction that must be remembered by future generations. His response to this event is similar to the reaction of many Frenchmen in August 1914 who were horrified by the stories of rape, pillage, arson, and murder that supposedly occurred in German-occupied France.[2] This artful narrative was apparently written from memory, since there were only very sparse notes about Gerbéviller contained in the author's diary for 7 July.]

To Captain de Montergon of the 9th light section[3]

Ruins, propped up toward the sky like an everlasting protest, crying out for justice and revenge through their gaping wounds, disheveled and tragic specters of past happiness, of peaceful farmsteads presently destroyed, of everything which stood for beauty, gentleness and hard work, they stand as accusing witnesses to the crimes of the cursed race.

At times, when the sitting sun cast a reddish glow on their wounds, or when the white light of the moon covered them, they appeared to come to life and scream their hurt, to shout their curses.

Some were imposing and grandiose, others humble and heartbreaking. There were the majestic throes of castles and cathedrals, the resigned moans of cottages and villages. Still all of them exuded a poignant feeling of despair which caused one's heart to hasten and one's fists to clench.

Fig. 12. A French town in ruins. *Copyright SIRPA/ECPA France.*

You walked through them silently, respectfully, afraid of stumbling over the many memories which still haunted the site. Here was the room where the couple lived, dreamed and suffered, where their parents died, where the children came into this world; the hallway which was always filled with shouts of happiness; the large room where the family gathered; a little farther, there was the church where generations knelt to pray; the cemetery where they would go to their final resting place. Now, all that remained were collapsed walls, piles of stones, ashes and mud! And little by little it was as if the weeds were trying to hide this dreadful devastation.

I walked through some of these well-known ruins, for now, it is unfortunate to say, some have acquired a dreary celebrity. When the opportunity arose, I opted to make a pilgrimage, not out of curiosity, but rather out of a desire to engrave in my mind and in my heart the hatred, the holy hatred, since in this case it is fair to use these two words together, the hatred which we must always feel for the perpetrators of such hideous deeds.

After the war, when euphoria has replaced the nightmare and the anguish, and people have become more inclined to forgive, even to forget, and especially later, when time, that great destroyer of memories, has softened the rancor and appeased the anger, I would like to see our children and those who never witnessed or endured directly the horrors of the war be taken on such a pilgrimage.

Of course, you might say that we shouldn't get bogged down in desolation and death! Our devastated cities and countrysides will flourish again. . . . A great people like us must get back on its feet, and, without forgetting the past, walk at the same calm and confident pace toward a future ever more sublime. . . . Life will spring from these ruins. Those who lived there will be the first ones to return, eager to rebuild their destroyed homes, to work again their ravaged fields. They would not accept a land other than the one where they were born, where their parents are at rest, where they want to be buried some day! Still some of these ruins must be left standing to educate future generations!

It is imperative, following the first excuse or hypocritical protest from a despised German, or when a pacifist preaches pardon and forgiveness, that we can answer by showing them the great martyrs of our time: Ypres, Louvain, Arras, Reims, Gerbéviller and Sermaize! Because these cities were not the victims of the war but rather of the unforgettable felony! Because they did not fall victims to soldiers but were rather assassinated by cowards.

Every day, in the heat of battle, cities are destroyed, some even disappear, as if carried away by a hurricane of steel and fire. The rage of combatants has led to the discovery of ever more destructive means and it is no longer possible to say "there remains only stones upon stones," because the stones don't even exist any more, only a shapeless and colorless dust blended with the upturned earth making it necessary to consult a map to be able to locate a missing village! That, however, is what war is about. As far as we are concerned, we are taking part in this frightening destruction, since as soldiers we must, with a heavy heart but with great anticipation of our final goal! The unceasing, calculated, deliberate bombing of defenseless cities, without any military justification, using incendiary bombs, burning them with kerosene or by other means invented by the infernal German Kultur, under ridiculous pretexts, or no pretexts at all, with the sole purpose of inspiring fear or obtaining revenge for a defeat, that can no longer be call war, it is murder. It is a despicable act which must be answerable to justice, the pillory or prison!

And some would like to see these ruins disappear? No! No! We must keep these undeniable exhibits for future generations, for those who were not involved, even for the Germans, from whom we can not escape! We must continue to nurture our hatred in your devastated streets, you, whom we have baptized with a name both ominous and beautiful, Gerbéviller-the-Martyr!

It was there that the lunacy, the sadism of the "Boches" was given free reign. Orgies, rapes, executions, arson, nothing was missing at these monstrous Bacchanalia. Even God was not spared by these men who blasphemed his name every day to the face of the world! They entered the church of Gerbéviller and emptied their guns into the tabernacle, a dreadful sacrilege unseen since the Terror of the revolution! Then, armed with torches, they set ablaze this unfortunate little town, peacefully located on the side of a hill. Think of it! Someone had dared to refuse them access to the town! That was a job well done! Worthy of the "Boches." In a matter of a few moments, the destruction of the town was cleverly organized, everything was destroyed, except for a few houses around the church which were defended bravely by the humble and magnificent heroine, Sister Julie. For once, the "Boches" actually backed off in front of a woman!

Now, it is total annihilation, it is the tragic silence of death. . . . In its desolation, this modern Pompeii, which man's furor ravaged faster and more thoroughly than the lava of a volcano, has a certain aura of awe and beauty. Laid out like a vast amphitheater, the charred ruins reach up majestically toward the sky like jagged lace. Since few of the houses collapsed, Gerbéviller-the-Martyr, gutted by flames and condemned to death, is still standing, facing the enemy, and addressing its cry for revenge to God. The sight of the village conveys to you a mixture of pity and veneration.

The impression created by other ruins which I was fortunate to see was totally different: Vassincourt, Pargny[4] and especially Sermaize. . . . Here the scene was no longer grandiose but rather distressing! In Gerbéviller, the destroyed homes still retained their silhouette and their character; in Sermaize, it was a desert. It was as if the town had been leveled by a hurricane. On the one hand you have ruins, but dignified ruins, on the other nothing, utter destruction. That was even more impressive. We must not forget that crime has its degrees of refinement like everything else. When you stare at what is left of Sermaize, you cannot help but recognize the evil hand of this executioner, of this vanished killer, of this disgusting being, as ferocious as he is cowardly, who seems to have been resuscitated from the times of Nero and Julius Caesar, the hand of the one who dared to tell the American ambassador that

"He would take part in the war if only for the enjoyment of it," the Kronprinz of Germany! The grass no longer grows under the path of Attila; the furor of the Kronprinz has visited Sermaize and nothing remains! Lining the streets, houses were left in piles of rubbish, each designating its former location. All that remained to catch your eye amid this stony desert where the old city of Sermaize once thrived was an occasional section of wall, a chimney-stack or an old balcony railing twisted by fire.

There again the hand of the barbarians was guided by spite and rage. Their triumphant march across France, toward a Paris which was almost in the grasp was suddenly halted and followed by a disorderly retreat. . . . Our fleeing soldiers, responding to the call of Joffre, were unexpectedly marching toward the enemy. . . . Thus seeing that they could not reach their coveted prize, the invading horde was over-whelmed with a bitter rage, with an inhuman desire to at least annihilate what they could not keep, and leave behind nothing but a desert. So across the battle front of the Marne, villages were burned to the ground.

Fellow countrymen, let us not forget![5] Let us show respect for these ruins! Rather than attempting to bring back to life these glorious victims, let us surround them with a pious reverence, much like we do with the relics of martyrs, and let them forever serve as a condemnation of the executioners and as a lesson to the centuries to come. "Outlined against the sky as an eternal protest and screaming for revenge and justice through their gaping wounds, these ruins will always stand as a reminder of the crimes of the cursed race!"

May 1918

24

Missing-in-Action

[Editor's Note: Dated simply 1918, this chapter compares soldiers who were missing in action to fishermen lost at sea. The tone is elevated; the mood is somber. The entire chapter is based on heroic allegory. In this case, Lécluse mourns the loss of a dispatch runner, Yvon, who disappeared one night, and two grenadiers, Hervé and Jean-Marie, who never returned from an attack.]

To Captain Rollin — 9th Light Group — 2d Light[1]

In some cemeteries on the coast of Brittany, you will find some small corner without gravestones where you cannot walk without a shudder. It is there that widows and orphans come to kneel and express their ultimate grief, that of not being able to cry on the remains of their loved ones. . . . It is called "the wall of the missing." Small crosses neatly line the large granite stone. Below each one, you can read the name and the age of a sailor followed by the short heading "Dead at sea" or "Missing." Beyond the low wall which encloses the cemetery, beyond the yellow gorse bushes and the pink brier, you can see, glittering in the sunshine, flecked with whitecaps, the vast ocean which captured the man, the father, the fiancé, the son and keeps them to himself. It is there that the missing men, forever rocked by the waves in the depth of the sea, have found their final resting place. . . . As a poet from Brittany once expressed:

> The sea, which rocked them for so many years,
> The sea, fierce nanny,
> Has chosen them to be her fiancé,
> And has brought them to her bed . . ."
>
> —A. Le Bras, "Chanson de Bretagne"

Before leaving the cemetery, the women stare deeply at the mysterious ocean which swallowed their loved ones who had left one morning, like every other morning, hale and hearty, a song on their lips, a bag on their shoulders and who never returned. More often than not, the bitterness of this disappearance was made even worse by the mystery surrounding it. The time, the place, the circumstances which accompanied this tragic death, all remained unknown. Did the "missing one" even have enough time to realize what was happening, to address his loved ones a final prayer, a final farewell? Was his death quick and peaceful or did he have to struggle with all his might? How long did his death take, hours on end, following a doomed burst of energy, and only after his strength had been sapped? Only God, who witnessed his agony, knows. . . .

Yvon, from Paimpol,[2] was on his four-hour watch near the cat-head of the Saint Anne. The night was pitch dark and the sea swollen. The schooner was having a rough go of it, bouncing around like a buoy, and struggling to reach the top of the next swell. From time to time waves as tall as mountains crashed down onto the front of the ship, sweeping it from one end to the other. One of them must have washed away the sailor before he could grab on to something or utter a sound, for, the next morning, the crew looked everywhere for him when they came up to the deck. It was all for naught. His name was added to the "Missing."

Hervé and Jean-Marie, from Cancale,[3] left in their dory, at the same time as other crew members, for a forty-eight hour period to stretch out lines along a reef. Shortly thereafter, the weather turned cold, and the fog, that treacherous fog common to the coast of Newfoundland, fell on the sea like a frozen shroud. Two days later, as fishing came to an end, all the dories came back to the ship save one. That day the captain, in a straightforward fashion, wrote in his log: "Hervé and Jean-Marie, presumed dead at sea, between the fifth and seventh of April." That was it . . . Missing! Oh! the inexpressible grief caused by these mysterious deaths! It explains somewhat the melancholy, the stern appearance of perpetual mourning found in those regions where so many tears have been shed!

I have often made allusions to these tragic deaths, with God as their only witness, between the ocean and the heavens, while thinking of you, the "missing" of World War I! The same mystery shrouds your death, our memory of you is still tainted by the same suffering.

The telephone lines having been knocked out by gunfire, Yvon, a liaison officer, left to carry an order to battery post seventy-five, over there, where the pine forest bulges out. It was very dark that night, the barrage of fire from the Germans was hammering our positions. "Big blackies" were plowing the ground around us and playing havoc with our galleries and our defenses. The order did reach the battery post, and Yvon, stoically tried to return by the same dangerous path. . . . That is all we know. We have tried in vain to find him since. . . . Missing!

Hervé and Jean-Marie were both grenadiers with the assault troops. They were seen for the last time by their army mates, to the right of the platoon, just when we were nearing the German trench. The fight was ferocious. In spite of their prowess, our poilus, who had gained the upper hand at first, were pushed back when the enemy counter attacked. . . . Back at our base, when we called roll, besides the wounded and the bodies which we could identify, Hervé and Jean-Marie were not there. . . . Missing!

Is it not the same story? Is it not the same ending? Like their brothers from the coast of Brittany, the soldiers were swept away in the great storm and mowed down by a hail of bullets. . . . They too went down, all alone, helpless and without glory, in the dark abyss! Death, like a traitor, struck them from behind. Perhaps they put up a savage struggle, called for help, reached out desperately for aid, only to lie down and die when their strength had abandoned them. . . . Visions from their past as well as the faces of the loved ones which gave meaning, hope and strength to their lives, and which they would never see again, flashed in front of their eyes, like a whirlwind. A final cry rose up in a form of the ultimate prayer from their gasping throat, half choked by Death, followed by the sad and yet sublime word which crosses the lips of those who die, specially those who die alone: "Mother! Mother!" As the poet Henri Bataille wrote in one of his most beautiful poems: "And then it was all over. . . . Silence took back its dead like it drank life. . . . And it is atrocious."[4]

In the same way no one knew of their agony, no one will ever know where they lie! Anonymous casualties, hastily buried on the battlefield by strangers or by the enemy, when the morbid task was not performed by a shell, churning the soil. Pitiful dead, left without a name, without a flower, perhaps without a makeshift cross on your tomb! O sublime dead, who have endured the sacrifice and drank the chalice of bitterness to the last drop! I only wish that there would be, in the cemetery of the village which you will never see again, a wall dedicated to the "Missing." I praise the deputy who came up with the idea of exhuming the body of an unidentified soldier in order to honor all unknown soldiers and to have his remains taken to the Panthéon where an engraving would read: "To all of the unknown martyrs of the war!" At the foot of this wall, in front of the mausoleum, pious and sympathetic crowds will come, kneel down and bring flowers in memory of the past, and the soul of France will fly away, riding the wings of prayers, toward the battlefields where lie hundred of these sublime unknown soldiers, these "missing" for whom my comrade-in-arms Rollin wrote these beautiful lines:

> Nature, be gentle when they die!
> Place their bugle in your echo!
> And you lilies, bluebells, and poppies,
> A flag on their burial place . . .
>
> In order to recognize them as they pass by,
> All mighty God of metempsychosis,
> Make roses from their heart burst,
> Whose crimson will be their blood . . .
>
> —Captain Rollin,
> "Prayer for the Missing Correspondent"

November 1918

25

Settling a Score

[Editor's Note: This chapter, dated January 1916, is dedicated to the author's wife. The author was on leave from 9–19 January that year. Typically, he spent his leaves with his family at the military hospital at Paramé where Lécluse's wife, Jeanne Bertrande, and his daughter, Odette, worked as volunteers during the war. Lécluse deliberated between two titles, "An Eye for An Eye" and "Settling a Score." We prefer the latter.

This is one of the few secondhand stories told by the author. It is typical of those grisly tales of atrocity and revenge that emerge from all wars. To that extent, it suggests something stylized and perhaps fictional. Yet, the details surrounding the story, especially the sergeant's reluctance to tell it and the author's strong emotional reaction, suggest that Lécluse believed it to be true.

Ruth Harris tells us that "the history of First World War atrocities is now receiving attention from historians who have been able to confirm many of the claims made against the German army." She cites several incidents, including the account of a fourteen-year-old girl named Emma P. who testified at the Cour d'appel in Amiens that she had been raped twice by German soldiers at Château-Thierry (Aisne), and the story of a widow named Marie B., who testified at the Cour d'appel in Agen on 2 May 1915 that the Germans entered her house, "seized the baby, skewered it on their bayonets, then they made it twist around in the air in the presence of its unfortunate mother."[2] This powerful but disturbing chapter is consistent with that testimony.]

> *To Bertrande de Le. . . . who took care of*
> *the hero of this story as she did many others.*[3]

"You will see," said my friend. "What will be particularly hard is when someone has to settle a score!"

Fig. 13. War veterans with amputated limbs. *Copyright SIRPA/ECPA France.*

"I am sure," I said. "But whose fault is it that the scores have gotten so high? Eventually they will have to be settled no matter what the cost!"

"Well spoken, Captain!" yelled a voice behind us.

We turned around. The man who had just spoken was a sergeant of the Colonial Infantry. He was decorated with the military medal and the croix de guerre with a bar. The poor devil had earned both of them since they had cost him his right leg. At first glance I knew what kind a man he was. He was one of those strange and unsettling men whom you rarely see outside of the Colonial Infantry or the Foreign Legion.[4] His appearance was at the same time intriguing and unpleasant. The look in his eyes made you say to yourself: "He must be some tough guy under fire," and "I wouldn't want to meet this character alone, some night, in some deserted place!" He was tall, built like a lumberjack with broad shoulders. You couldn't hold back a feeling of grief at the sight of such a well-built man standing on his one leg knowing that he would forever be crippled. His face, angular and dark colored, was striking in an unpleasant way. His eyes, very black, were shifty and scary. With his bluish, clean-shaven face, he reminded you of a defrocked priest or even, let's be honest, of a convict.

Already the sergeant, taking a step forward on his crutches, was excusing himself for having disturbed us, speaking with a strong Paris suburban accent which only served to finalize my opinion of him:

"Of course" I said, "I understand why you think like we do. It is obvious that you have a score to settle with the Boches."

"Oh no, Captain, it has nothing to do with me or my ruined leg. . . . After all, that is what war is all about and that is why we were there, wasn't it? In my case they just damaged me some, but I know that I destroyed a bunch of them and they are no longer around! No, the scores which I am thinking about, the ones which they will have to pay for with their money⁵ and their blood are for the hostages whom they shot, the women they raped, the children they massacred, the villages they burned, the factories they destroyed, for no reason, just for the sake of evil, war against those who were not in it, war against infants, the weak, the innocent, war by criminals and cowards! Those are the horrible and unforgivable scores to which I am referring! As far as I am concerned, I am just glad that I was able to settle one of them before they put me out of action. I can proudly say that they paid dearly for it."

The eyes of the colonial sparkled with a sinister glow, a murderous light, which revealed his arrogance and his hatred. He was frightening and magnificent at the same time. . . .

"Oh, I see, a tooth for a tooth, then!" I said.
"You are right there, Captain. A head for a head!"

My friend nudged me with his elbow. I knew what he meant.

Well, Sergeant, can we ask you to recount this story to us?"

He bent his head sideways and looked at us, without answering. It was obvious that he had second thoughts. I pressed him on right away.

"Come on, to please us! It is most likely that we will approve. Anyway we don't have to pass judgment on what you have done. Here, the chairs are arranged just right for you to tell your story. Be a good sport!"

He looked at us for a few more seconds, then, probably favorably impressed by our countenance, he quickly made up his mind and began, sitting in front of us:

"Well, you must realize that I don't tell this story to everybody. . . . A few people, who didn't blame me too much for what I did, looked at me in a strange way when I told it to them. So, enough is enough! I don't want to be given a hard time about what I have done because it was pretty hard. There is no doubt about it. If I had to do it over, I would do it again, even if, at times, it prevents me from sleeping. Yes a guy like me, I have seen and done about everything there is to do! I swear I would do it again and without batting an eye!

"It took place in Lorraine at the beginning of the war, before the Boches started burying themselves in their holes like the stinking beasts that they are. We were still fighting out in the open, and there were, in between the rows of farms, some villages which we fought over and which went back and forth from one side to the other without anyone knowing for sure who had control over them at any one time. So, one night I was chosen to go with four of my men to see if a village, which had been hammered by our artillery, was free of enemy soldiers. Darkness had fallen and there was just enough light to see. A fine rain was coming down. A perfect night to go on patrol. We started off, each one of us carrying our bayonet and a loaded Browning. We followed the roadside ditches or hid behind the shoulders of the road.

"Once we got near the first houses, we walked around them, our ears open. Nothing was moving, not a light, not a fire, not a sound. . . . Since I was quite suspicious of those damned Boches and I wanted to carry out my mission, I quietly told my men that I wanted to go to the village and search it carefully. Our escape route was clear behind us and we could always scramble back if need be. We immediately took off, pistol in one hand, bayonet in the other. Three men were following me while the fourth one was leading the way some twenty feet ahead of us. We proceeded through the main street, then the side streets, the alleys, the farmyards, still there was nothing. . . .

"There was only one place left to inspect, a kind of isolated country house sitting behind a little garden. Just as we got close to it, I saw my lead man hit the ground and remain motionless.

. . . I stopped the other three and crawled to him. 'Listen!', he whispered to me. I listened. . . . Undoubtedly there was the sound of voices coming from the distance muffled as if they came from underground. . . . There was no mistaking it. People were talking in the basement of the house. . . . I moved ahead on all fours, sometimes dragging on my stomach. It was just what I thought. The house, dark and gloomy from top to bottom, appeared abandoned like the others. The door was partly opened as were some of the windows whose shutters had been broken. Shells had made several large holes in the walls. Still I noticed a fine shaft of light coming out of a basement window three-fourths obstructed. That was where the voices were coming. Upon listening carefully, I recognized that it was in German. I could distinguish a half-dozen harsh, guttural voices slurred under the effects of wine. I surmised that these were looters who were celebrating. In a blink of an eye I decided what to do. The celebration would be total and the captain very happy. In addition to giving him an answer regarding the status of the village I was going to bring in some Boches![6] I quietly called my men over and explained my plan to them. I told them that some Germans were celebrating in the cellar. No one else was around in the house or nearby. There couldn't be too many of them, and in their condition they wouldn't offer much resistance, if any. They would surrender by saying 'Kamarades!' I instructed my men to tuck the sheaths of their bayonets in their trousers to avoid any noise, to remove their shoes, and that we would go inside, our shoes hanging around our necks. Once inside the house, I was to light up the lantern which I had brought along. We would find the cellar door and barge in on them. It was decided that, if something unexpected happened, we were to hightail it back to camp.

"Everything went as planned. We went up the three steps leading to the broken entrance and stepped inside the dark and quiet house. I lit my lantern and then, God damn! When I think about what we saw, all of a sudden, my hair stands on my head. Even though I told you that I am not easily impressed and that we had been exposed to a lot of horrible things, this was too much! Here we were in a large tiled room, with an alcove in the back of it. The whole house had been turned upside down, ransacked, the furniture broken. The walls were splattered with blood, the floor tiles had turned red from it. In the middle of the room there were the bodies of seven children, yes, seven: four boys and three young girls, the oldest was perhaps twelve years old, massacred, mutilated, maimed! A head of one of the boys was completely detached from his body, two of the young girls had their stomachs slit open. The smallest one of the group, a nursing baby, was nailed to the floor with a bayonet. . . . A real carnage! I leaned down to touch one of those poor children. He was barely cold. . . . It had to be those revelers below who had performed such a deed! As we stood there stunned, our teeth chattering, frozen in horror and shock, one of my men pointed toward the alcove. A woman's two feet were sticking out from under the mattress! Now, there was the mother! We went and looked. . . . Oh my, I will not try to describe the condition in which we found her! All I can say is that we couldn't even tell if she had been ugly or beautiful! Oh, those bastards! After that I pointed out to my men the cellar door from which the noise was becoming increasingly louder and told them: 'No prisoners, understand?' The four hostile faces nodded as one. We quickly found the stairs which led to the cellar and went down quietly, although caution was no longer really needed due to the inebriated state of the men who were beginning to become rowdy. I looked inside the room through a slit in the door. It was great, there were seven of them, the same number as the kids upstairs. Seven hearty fellows with their big square heads, real roughneck Prussian soldiers. One of them, lying on the ground, was drinking straight out of a cask. The others were seated around a table made up of two planks laying across two barrels. It was lit up by candles and covered by numerous bottles, most of them empty. The men were all sloppily dressed, pipes in their mouths, their faces flushed from the wine and the heat of the cellar.

"Their guns were standing in the corner of the room, no other weapons were near them. They were ours! I looked at my men to make sure that they were ready and then I gave the signal. I opened the door wide and we burst out together in the cellar, our five Brownings aimed at the drunks. Oh, what a dramatic turn of events! In any other circumstance, it would have been enough to die of laughter! If you could have only seen the Boches. Unable to stand up, they already had their hands in the air, and had sobered up in a hurry as they yelled 'Kamarades! Kamarades! Don't kill us!'

"We told them to be quiet and I gestured for them to line up against the wall. While my men had them covered, I looked at the Germans' bayonets. Just as I thought, one was missing: the one which had nailed the small boy, like a little red butterfly, to the floor of the bedroom above. The others were covered with blood, in fact almost all of the Boches had blood on their hands. Then I asked: 'Does one of you speak French?' Almost all of them answered: 'yes' and one of them added: 'We prisoners. Not hurt us.' 'Shut-up', I screamed. 'You are neither prisoners nor soldiers but bandits unworthy of pity! You have murdered a poor woman and seven small children. There is no use denying it! Well, we are going to mete out justice and you are going to die!' You have to believe that they all understood for they all dropped to their knees, screaming, begging and crying. Ugh, it was repulsive! One of them, a huge, red-headed man with a fierce looking face, crawled toward me, his hands crossed, moaning 'Spare me! Spare me! I have five little ones in Germany!' Ha! That was too much, I lost it. I pounced on that animal and grabbed him by the throat as I screamed in his face: 'Scum! You think that it is going to in-spire pity for you, you who butchers other people's children? You have had it! You are going to pay for the mother's death' and I stuck my bayonet into his chest up to the hilt. . . . I will not tell you what followed. . . . I don't know anymore. . . . We were crazy with rage and it didn't take us very long! We killed all of them with our bayonets since the guns would have been too noisy and there would have been a risk of ricochets. Moreover they didn't put up much resistance, they were just like rags. When we were done, we wiped our weapons on the Boches' uniforms, broke their guns, and we left after blowing out the lights. I remember when we crossed the room where those innocent victims, whose deaths we had avenged, were lying in their blood, one of us grabbed a piece of charcoal and wrote on the wall. 'Justice has been done!'

"Then we left and returned to our lines without any problems after swearing that none of us would talk about this event. But you see, this bothered me, this secret was weighing on me! So, one day, I just had to tell what happened to my captain. He was an old military man who had re-enlisted for the war. He had been exposed to a lot of things in the past. When I had finished my story, he just said: 'I should scold you and remind you that you should not take justice in your own hands, but I too have grand-children, I can't blame you!'

"And then he shook my hand. . . . So there you have it! In your case I don't want to know what you think, my conscience is satisfied and so is my old captain, and that is good enough for me. . . ."

So, as the old sergeant was getting his crutches to leave, I did like his old captain and without saying a word I extended my hand to him. He took it, a sad smile on his face, shrugged his shoulders, and slowly, his head tilted forward as if under the weight of this horrible memory, he walked away.

Paramé
January 1916[7]

26

Mama Pleya, Rifleman

[Editor's Note: This chapter is dedicated to the author's daughter, Odette. Then age twelve, she is described as the good friend of a Senegalese soldier in the military hospital at Paramé. The presence of nonwhite soldiers offers an interesting opportunity to examine racial attitudes in France. Estimates vary, but there appear to have been some 361,000 black troops who served on the western front in World War I. Of these, 161,000 were African. Perhaps another two hundred thousand were African Americans.[1] In both cases, the overwhelming majority of these troops were used as laborers. As best we can determine, thirty thousand black African troops served with distinction in both colonial armies and as units within regular French units during World War I. Some historians have suggested that the African troops were poorly trained, poorly led, poorly equipped, and were sent to their deaths by a military administration that regarded them as cannon fodder. Charles Balesi estimates that some ten battalions of Senegalese riflemen were wiped out in Belgium between 25 October and 16 November 1914.[2] There is a perception that the French high command wasted these soldiers' lives and did little to prepare them for combat, suggesting, at best, a contemptuous attitude toward the capabilities of black African troops.

A popular image of the French is that of a people who are remarkably free of racial prejudice. Yet, as William S. Cohen has argued, "in regard to blacks, the tradition of racial inequality was dominant in French history." Cohen characterizes the views of explorers, administrators, and soldiers in Africa as repeating "centuries-old complaints about African laziness, lasciviousness, godlessness, and savagery." Tzvetan Todorov argues that, among French intellectuals influenced by Social Darwinism, there was a tendency to disparage blacks as inferior.[3] In the nineteenth century, the French had various ways to obtain information about Africa and its black population. Popular newspapers such as the Petit Journal *and* Petit Parisien *were widely read in both Paris and the provinces. They not only published regular articles on Africa during the early years of the Third Republic but also published weekly illustrated literary supplements. Images of the black Africans as savages, even cannibals, had been commonplace in popular newspapers and illustrated magazines. William H. Schneider tells us that there were regular ethnographic exhibitions after 1877 at the Jardin D'Acclamatation that displayed "Asians, Africans and American Indians in model dwellings." By 1877, when West Africans began to appear in these exhibitions, the emphasis had shifted to the savage and bizarre.*[4] *Some French believed that blacks were horrible cannibals, an image sanctioned by official propaganda during World War I in an effort to undermine the morale of German troops. The French government often portrayed black African troops as "ferocious, bloodthirsty maniacs on the field."*[5] *At best, black Africans might be portrayed as innocent children and loyal servants.*

The story of a black African soldier from Senegal who survived the horrible slaughter of the fall of 1914 during the War of Movement and how he was perceived by a French line officer is particularly interesting in part because of the way it suggests both racial stereotyping and genuine admiration for that soldier. Lécluse's memoir is devoid of the type of racist comments commonplace at the time. He speaks admiringly of the courage of the Senegalese soldier. Both Lécluse's wife and daughter cry when the soldier leaves the hospital, and their interaction suggests genuine friendship rather than fear, suspicion, or dislike. The fact that the author felt no need to comment negatively on Mama Pleya's flirtation with his twelve-year-old daughter can be interpreted variously. Yet, the author's comments about Mama Pleya's lack of civilization, his loyalty, his courage under fire, and his childlike innocence are reflective of another tradition, which depicts Africans as "noble savages."[6] *Once again the translator has retained the author's use of broken French by the Senegalese soldier in the English translation.]*

To my daughter Odette, who became Mama's good friend.

"Good morning, Mama, is everything all right?" the nurse asked.

"Thank you, Missy, Mama happy" was the reply of the infantryman, displaying his ever present smile — such a smile, thirty-two teeth as white as ivory, splitting this pitch-black mask from ear-to-ear.

Mama Pleya, an infantryman from Dakar, Senegal, always wore that smile. He was always happy, whether strolling in the sun, leaning on

Fig. 14. Senegalese soldiers. *Copyright SIRPA/ECPA France.*

his walking stick and smoking his pipe of wild cherry wood, or savoring his favorite drink (an awful concoction of milk turned gray by an abundance of pepper) or giving a hand to the cook by peeling potatoes, which he handed back one by one when done while saying with a strong accent: "other one!"

Seriously wounded in the foot, Mama had been at the hospital in Paramé since the first days of the war. At that time he was wearing beads, all types of amulets, and rolls of parchment inscribed with cabalistic formulas. His large chest was covered with them.

His first encounter with the nurses who were to become his friends was rather stormy. He was carrying a long oak staff, full of knots and covered with moss. It was as big around as your fist and was some two meters long. When he came into the room where his bed was located, leaning on his immense stick like a shepherd out of the past, Miss L.D., the blond Alsacien who was assigned to take care of him, tried to relieve him of his cumbersome weapon. The Senegalese, out of a sudden anger, began to rant and rave in such a way that everyone backed away from him. . . .

Mama, at that time, could neither utter nor understand a single word of French. The stand-off threatened to be lengthy, but, fortunately,

one of his compatriots being treated in the next room was able to inter-
vene and calm him down while explaining to us that he would never
part with his club. He had chopped it himself in a forest in the Savoy
region while on his way to the front from Marseilles.[7] It had never left
his side since, even under enemy fire, at which time he carried it tied to
his pack.

We immediately granted this seemingly harmless request and
Mama, his staff leaning against the head of his bed, quickly became as
docile as a lamb. He turned out to be, without a doubt, the easiest
patient to care for, as well as the friendliest, in the entire hospital.

Later on, when he learned to communicate somewhat, he was able
to give us other reasons for this attachment. As far as he was concerned,
this enormous stick was not just a memento of his trip to the front.

> "You see, Missy," he used to say "is veree good for zee Boches!"
> "Why, Mama, did you fight with this stick?"
> "Ah no, Missy, Mama fight with gun and bayonet . . . Bayonet
> veree good! Dig! Dig! Also good big knife."

You should have seen the enormous knife which Mama would display at that moment. The blade was long enough to kill a cow!

> "But zee stick, for later . . ."
> "What do you mean, for later?"
> "You see, Missy. Zee battle finish, many Boches everee where
> . . . Mama take big stick and go look for Boches. When Boches
> move, me hit Boches on head . . . Ah! Ah! Boches no move no
> more, you see!"

Then the black man would burst out in resounding laughter upon
seeing the earnest bewilderment, if not outright fear of his interlocutress.

In order to excuse some of these rather barbaric behaviors, you
must remember that our courageous African soldiers were not yet accustomed to our way of life. Upon his arrival, Mama was still an uncivilized
man. Taken from his native bush to come and fight in France, he knew
nothing about culture. Plates and glasses were just mysterious objects to
him. He used a fork for the very first time. . . . He even replayed, to the
great amusement of his audience, the classic scene of the monkey in
front of the mirror.

The hospital in Paramé had taken over the casino building, and
large mirrors lined many of the walls. In the first room where Mama

entered, he found himself staring at a large black man who looked as if he could have been his brother. He gave him a gracious smile which was immediately returned. Encouraged by this response, he walked deliberately toward his counterpart until his flat nose was almost touching the mirror. How can one describe the utter stupefaction on his face and the cries of laughter surrounding him! Cautiously, Mama felt the mirror with his fingers, pulled them back quickly because of the coldness of the glass and blew on them. Then he looked back to us with a look of dismay and consternation. We were all overcome with uncontrollable laughter.

It is easy to understand why this big child, whose soul was as simple and naive as his mind, rapidly became the favorite of the nurses. He rightfully deserved this, for he was always well-groomed, meticulously clean, easy to please, accommodating and well-behaved, and above all, he was, like all of his compatriots, a slave to orders no matter what their nature, a blind follower of orders.

He became civilized and adopted our ways with surprising speed considering his unpolished origins. He also had learned a rudimentary though peculiar French, which could be readily understood. In this endeavor as in all others, he fell victim to many pranksters who taught him crude expressions. At times it was fortunate that he mispronounced them because one of the first words he uttered was a vile expression whose only heroic context might have been when it was repeated by the last remaining soldiers in the battle of Waterloo!

Among all of his new found friends to whom he extended both smiles and greetings, Mama also had his favorites. They were Madame de L., an employee in the office which oversaw the hospital kitchen, and especially her daughter, the young Odette, twelve, who always had her way with the big Senegalese.[8] Do not think for a minute that this fondness was motivated in any way by Mama's fondness for good food, a situation which would have easily been forgiven in the case of such a grown-up child. Mama was not that way and, other than his milk with pepper, he did not seek sweets or special delicacies. Actually, this cordial relationship with the head cook could be attributed to the heat generated by the stove. The poor African found our French sun much too pale and not nearly warm enough for his taste. He found the first days of Autumn much too cold. This explains why his silhouette could often be seen in the doorway of the kitchen where he came to offer his self-interested services. He would reach for his pipe and ask in a nice way, "Me can,

Missy?" He thanked her politely for her permission to smoke saying, "There is good from stove." Seated next to the stove, he would peel some vegetables while humming a monotonous song or telling a few stories about his homeland or about the war.

Among these war stories, there was one which I would feel remiss if I did not share it. A compatriot of Mama's who was hospitalized with him is the main hero.[9] It offers a typical example of this extraordinary and almost unassuming self-control and courage which General Baratier so aptly describes in his books dealing with the African epic.

One day, in Lorraine, a cavalry lieutenant was sent to make a reconnaissance in a village which appeared to have been abandoned by the enemy. He approached it cautiously, ventured along its main street and reached the square located in the middle of town. To his great disbelief, he found a handsome infantryman peacefully seated on the church steps, smoking a pipe and holding his gun across his lap. A broad grin exposing his white teeth, the black man stood up to get into a more proper position.

> "What in the devil are you doing here by yourself?" the officer asked. The other answered unpretentiously:
> "Me occupy village."
> "What are you telling me? Where are your comrades?"
> "Me no have camrades. Me alone. Me occupy village."

Faced with such aplomb, the officer, knowing that nothing was impossible with men of such caliber asked him what had happened. . . . There was nothing to say, the infantryman was telling the truth. He had taken over the village and had chased away the enemy single-handedly!

He related that, in the heat of combat a few hours ago, he found himself separated from his unit and ended up all alone. . . . So he walked straight ahead, counting on his luck, toward where the Boches should be and he arrived at the village. He walked in, his bayonet affixed to his gun barrel. In the town square he found himself face to face with a sizable German patrol. . . . Both sides were greatly surprised but the black man was the first to regain his composure. He pretended to yell commands to soldiers following him and then suddenly attacked, firing on the group, knocking one of their horsemen to the ground. He proceeded to charge the Boches with his bayonet while screaming like a demon. The Germans, scared to death and never thinking that he could be acting alone, turned their horses around and took off galloping. . . . The infantryman stopped, shot at the runaways until he had no more bullets, walked back to the fallen horseman and finished him with his bayonet. Having made sure that the enemy was nowhere present, he went and sat in the middle of the town square and, as he repeated with great satisfaction, "He occupied the village. . . ." Such is the story told by Mama to "Missy the cook," although he told it in a much more colorful manner.

His great passion was "Mizelle Odette." Since she had given him a pocket mirror and a small comb for his little goatee, the black man revered her and became her slave. She was the only one who was allowed to play with his amulets and his gris-gris[10]. . . . Then, little by little, Mama, who was not frightened by the young age of his idol, fell in love with her and one day, to the great joy of the young girl, he just asked to marry her! This amusing dialogue followed:

> "But Mama, come on, I am much too young, much too young!"
>
> "That matters, Mizelle? Good for Mama little white woman."
>
> "Well tell me, aren't you already married? You also have children."
>
> "That true, Mama have wife in Dakar, little boy, little girl, and other in Casablanca, little boy, too."
>
> "Well! How do I fit in?"
>
> "You, Mizelle, you be little white wife in France! Other two all black like Mama."
>
> "What will the other ones have to say?"
>
> "Is nothing to say, Mizelle. Black wifes work for little white wife, and you take stick to make them obey."

In spite of these particular conditions and this truly privileged situation, the young Odette had to turn down Mama's offer. He never really understood why and so renewed it on several occasions. It was one of those rare moments when he expressed that he was "not happy."

These decent blacks are blessed with a sensitivity and a faithfulness which is quite admirable. It was evident the day when one of Mama's compatriots, his inseparable friend Damba, left the hospital. His despair was very touching, and he openly displayed it without feigning embarrassment. His little friend Odette had all the difficulty in the world to console him. He was sobbing like a child, his head on her shoulder, repeating endlessly as he caressed her cheeks with his large black hands: "Oh! Mama sad! Mama veree sad!"

Finally, completely healed, it was Mama's turn to leave. His large stick in one hand, Mama said good-bye to the hospital staff, expressing his gratitude as best he could. Then he went down for the last time to the kitchen where he knew he could find his two favorite friends. They were greatly surprised that instead of an outpouring of grief and of tears, Mama was all smiles.

"So, Mama, are you so happy to be leaving? Weren't you well treated here?" asks Missy, the cook, somewhat surprised.

"Yes, Missy, every one veree nice, Mama happy with everee body!"

"Well, then, why are you so happy?"

The face of the infantryman became somber and standing proudly, a glow of valor in his eyes, as matter-of-factly as his comrade had said that he was "occupying the village," and not realizing that he was uttering something beautiful and profound, he answered:

"Here, Missy, Mama veree good, always happy, but over there, is veree good battle!"

Paramé Hospital
(Saône et Vilaine)
Fall 1914

27

Brambles

[Editor's Note: This is a very brief, undated chapter dedicated to Theodore Botrel, a poet whom Lécluse identified as the "bard of Brittany." Here, in a chapter that the author identifies as a "poem in prose," the literary intention is obvious and fundamental.]

To the bard from my Brittany, to my friend Theodore Botrel.

In the hollow of valleys, on slopes of hills, across the countryside, across the forests, crawling for miles and miles, the brambles have grown, treacherous and aggressive! They run along the lines of trenches, slyly hidden in folds of the tall grasses or wrapping themselves like ivy on the trunk of a tree, along the wooden posts and iron stakes. . . . Everywhere, like hideous octopuses lurking after their prey, they throw their nets of barbed vines, spiders' webs with their monstrous folds, where death clutches you, horrible and sterile!

Cowardly, like the Boches hiding behind them, the vile snare choking the deer as he runs with his powerful antlers or the light roe-deer, they break the superb speed of the charging men, the dizzying flight of the light bayonets, a nasty branch of brambles snatches a passing foot, and here are our heroes leaping toward glory, brought down to the ground, useless and bloody! Their eerie branches with sad, rusty tints have no leaves at all, but sometimes bear unusual fruit: heaving bodies, macabre debris, stiff shapes, in crimson clusters, are suspended from the brambles and, with eyes enlarged from horror and from terror, the lookout contemplates them across the crenelations[1]. . . .

O brambles of the War, with your bloody barbs, so much of the soil of our sweet France, like a veil of death thrown on to nature, spreads the network of your sinister branches. . . . May the day finally come at last when, happily, towards the sky, the prairie grasses will grow with their wild flowers, when the heavy spears of golden wheat and blue alfalfa will be able to suffocate you, o murderous Brambles, o breath of beneficial and serene Peace, o Sun of Glory and Freedom!

[No date or location]

28

The Stage-Set

[Editor's Note: The next four chapters were originally grouped together as one single chapter under the label "Landscapes." They dealt with physical objects, inanimate nature, and the corpse of an unknown soldier. Other chapters that had some association with a specific individual were dedicated to that person. These have no dedications.

This particular chapter may have had special poignancy for the author since he was an amateur actor and singer who often performed at impromptu gatherings, masses, musical reviews, and plays. We also know that he wrote a play, found among his papers, set in a military unit. This chapter, dated simply as November 1915, was likely written shortly after the incident at the Hole of Death. Unfortunately, there is no corresponding entry in the author's diary to compare to this chapter or to identify the date and place more precisely.]

Between our shelters of Saint-Pancrace and the ruined village of Bures,[1] where our kitchens and our aid station were located and where our trench line began, if you wanted to avoid a fairly long detour by the large communications trench which went down to the la Fontasse farm, you had to cross a hill whose north slope was exposed to German view and their fire. However, wherever possible, the path had been laid out behind the shelter of hedges, fence rows and orchards. But, over a distance of some forty meters, no natural curtain was available to hide the people coming and going between the two lines, dispatch runners, cooks, relief or work details. It was therefore necessary, as always, in such circumstance, to hide the road, but what was most unusual was the type of camouflage used here and the surprise one felt is rather understandable, when all of a sudden, at the end of a hedge, we emerged from behind the superstructure of a theater!

Yes! it was truly a stage background, and not a natural background, but from a true theater, with a backdrop and backstage. . . . From what café-concert of a little town or what fashionable salon I can not say, but it was there all right, neatly set up and maintained in place by taut ropes.

It represented a classic forest, an undergrowth illuminated here and there by the rays of the sun, from the small trees with brown or gray trunks, with somewhat conventional foliage, a few holly bushes and some reddish rocks emerging from the moss and grass. The scene was brand new, as far as I could determine, and it had been recently painted.

Such unusual destiny for people and things. I could picture Sylvette, wearing a mask and hiding behind the supports, waiting to enter on stage to utter her reply, or a little girl, pale with emotion, listening to the last advice of the Mother Superior and restraining the beating of her heart before going to recite her compliments to Monsieur the Mayor, the day when school awards are handed out. . . . And now the peaceful scene, brought into a real tragedy, had become a "war accessory," and served to deceive the enemy, to fend off his fire, and save human lives!

Alas! poor stage-set, still standing proudly, your days are numbered! Winter is coming, the rude winter of Lorraine! The rain, the snow and the hoar-frost will quickly tarnish your colors and shred into shapeless rags your coquettish painted canvas. . . . But as long as a piece of canvas hangs on this frame, you will fulfill your role, then you will collapse some day, knocked over by a last squall, and you who were meant to echo only poetic speeches, laughter and songs, after having vibrated from the whistling of bullets and the wind caused by shells, turned away from your peaceful destiny, carried away in the great storm, as so many people and so many things, you will perish as they, obscure victim of this disastrous war, without even a second look nor a word of regret on the part of those whose lives you will have so often saved!

Bures
(Lorraine)
November 1915

29

Moonlight

*[Editor's Note: Dated August 1915, this chapter may well have been writ-
ten following the night of 25-26 August 1915. The diary entry says simply:
"It was so clear that for the first time — and that ought to be unique —
I was able to go to the edge of the woods to my hut* without a pocket
lamp" (author's emphasis). *This was only ten days after the author's
troops raided enemy trenches at Ammerzwiller, for which action the author would later receive the croix de guerre. This is an excellent example
of a tranquil sector at its best. Particularly interesting (and not unusual)
is the resentment expressed by a French soldier toward an artilleryman on
his own side, who disturbed "the beauty of that incomparable moment."]*

Oh! the beautiful night, serene and clear! The moonlight was enchanting.
. . . I never had seen another night shine with such brilliancy. . . . The
moon was like a polished silver disc whose glow made our eyes look
away. . . .

To use the standard cliché, "it was as clear as mid-day," but we were far
enough from the enemy that they did not disturb our nocturnal work, and
we came out of the trench, my officers and I, to supervise the construction
of new gabions which served at the same time as crenelations for firing.[1]

The Boches were also at work on their side. So profound was the
silence, we could clearly hear their mallet blows sinking stakes, the roll-
ing of their carts unloading concrete, and . . . even the noise of their
scythes cutting the grass in front of their iron wire.

On both sides, the gunners had the good taste to respect the peace
of this wonderful night, and we were all able to leisurely savor some of
its bliss. We stretched out in front of the iron wire network, in the thick,
soft and scented grass. Our hands crossed under the napes of our necks,
cigarettes in our mouths, while following with our eyes the columns of
blue smoke climbing toward the starry sky, keeping silent to avoid ruin-

ing the divine silence where each collected his thoughts. We slid slowly down the slopes of this reverie, away from the present and far from the landscape which surrounded us. . . . Wasn't this beautiful summer night similar to many others whose charm and poetry we once savored without after thought? To make the illusion even more complete, from time to time the sound of the scythes cutting in the tall grass reached us. . . . Countryside, sweetness of the evening, contemplation of beings and things, all united to deceive us, and minutes passed, soothing and sweet, as we numbed little by little in a delicious torpor. . . .

Alas! Time to wake up! A silhouette loomed in front of me, the cursed telephone operator, more often a carrier of bad than good news! "Captain, we were told that the heavy artillery is going to fire for effect on Burnhaupt and we must bring in the workers return for fear of reprisals. . . ."

Huh! what! to the devil with the intruder and the gunner, and his firing! Undoubtedly, the gunner's heartburn that evening had ruined for him the poetry of the moonlight and the beauty of this incomparable moment. . . . "Go! Let's move, men!" We picked up our tools and returned to our tomb-like burrows to finish there this divine evening, sitting on our benches or on our straw mattresses, in the heavy and smoky air, and the depressing flicker of our Argand lamps. . . . What the hell! It was the war, after all. We had almost forgotten it, some even completely, but the gunner was on top of things, he was going to bring us back to reality!

Forgive us, o sweet night! Men are evil beasts! They take pleasure in ruining the most beautiful things! Scorn their ridiculous tumults and their impotent rage, for they do not know what they do!

For a few minutes, they will vent their anger, filling the tranquil sky with howling whistling and tremendous explosions. . . . And then this din will suddenly cease, as if out of breath, and your majestic silence and your pure light, o night, will regain possession of the space, symbol of the consoling and Divine Peace that will come in time, to rock in victory the hearts of men. . . .

Psannestiehl
(Haute-Alsace)
August 1915

30

The Bus

[Editor's Note: This is the third of four chapters grouped together under the heading "Landscapes." Dated December 1914, this chapter was subtitled "The Bus." As the author reflected on the role played by buses during the Battle of the Marne (known as the Taxicab War), he mentioned the various military purposes to which buses had been adapted. It reminded him of Paris and the possibility that he, too, will never see that city again. He compares himself to the bus, both of whom would end their careers discarded. He also drew from this encounter the hope that he would fulfill his military duty and go off proud and resigned in the "serenity of duty accomplished."]

If I had expected to find in the course of the campaign, some old acquaintances, it would not have been you, my old "Madeleine-Bastille," coming down the main street of an Artois village with a great clanking noise! But, I remember they had told me that you, the good Parisian buses, had also deserted the streets and boulevards of the capital to go to the front. In order to satisfy the ever-growing needs of this gigantic war, it was necessary to call on all the devotion to duty, all the good will, all the services, and, even old territorials[1] had to run to the front line to support their young comrades and plug holes. We also saw taxis supplement railroads and trucks to transport the army of Maunaury, and here you were now, their big brothers, ingeniously transformed by the Supply Service into "meat wagons!" In a blink of an eye, you had been adapted to your new role: benches removed, metallic shades replacing the windows, a few strong hooks fixed to the ceiling, and you were on your way, still wearing your respective names and your "Full" sign at the rear, but transporting now, instead of frail models or nice, chubby ladies, some sheep, hams and quarters of beef!

What a fall from grace, some will say! Quite to the contrary, your passage brought out the touched and grateful smile of a poilu, especially when you were "Full" . . . of good "meat" for his stew pot. . . . It was said that the French soldier was the only one who fought and fought well on an empty stomach. It was still appropriate to avoid putting him in that situation as much as possible and you were there to help in that endeavor.

At times also, even though it was against the rules, you even picked up an officer along the road, going to do his shopping in the neighboring town. When that happened, he needed to be contented with a place on the rear platform. That was all that the poilu, butcher by trade, who played the classic role of the driver, could offer him. It was true that it was "on the hush," and nothing was more amusing than to recall, while leaning against the rear balustrade, the errands which we used to run across Paris, in this same vehicle, which now played its humble role in the Great Epic. . . .

Poor, brave bus on which I made such an unforeseen trip, God willing, I would see at least, this Paris which we used to see together, barely a few months ago, but as for you, you have bid farewell to Paris forever! What a hard life you led, on roads full of potholes, abandoned at night under the rain and the snow, no longer able to enjoy the protective shelter of the comfortable garage, patched up as well as one could in the case of accident or breakdown. Your days were numbered! Already your motor was not running right. Your body was falling apart. . . . One day you would remain on the road forever, and once discharged, you would be going to the junk yard, unless you ended up in a roadside ditch!

And it was that ending which I wished for you! If things have souls, you would be saddened undoubtedly by recollections of the past, by your long rides in clear, sunlit mornings, along the tumultuous boulevards of your old Paris, but you would console yourself also by thinking of what surprises destiny had reserved for you, instead of the vulgar and pitiful ending of the servant forcibly-retired, the warrior who, proud and resigned, left in the serenity of having accomplished his duty. . . .

Bouchers-sur-Cauche
December 1914
(Artois)

31

The Comrade

[Editor's Note: Dated 18 October 1915, this incident supposedly occurred a week after the incident at the Hole of Death on 6 October 1915. Such suggests the date should be the thirteenth, not the eighteenth. In this chapter, one of Lécluse's men spotted the body of a French soldier shot earlier. He asked permission to retrieve the body, and Lécluse told him to take two armed men and a stretcher. Despite the fact that the Germans were nearby and the mission was dangerous, his men were eager to retrieve the corpse. The author and his lieutenant accompanied the men to the lookout posts. Once again, this scene reminded the author of his own mortality.]

"Captain" D——n said to me, "Can we get another one?"
"Ah? and where's that?"

The man led me to an opening in the parapet.

"Here, to the right of the broken tree, next to the large white stone, do you see a grayish, white spot? It is there, along the hedge."
"Hum! It is quite a ways!"
"Oh! Captain, there is no danger! . . . This evening, just before the moon appears, we will take him in one fell swoop. I'll take the responsibility. Is that all right with you, Captain?"

I looked at the man. He was brave, agile, resourceful. He had enough faults that the least we could do was give him credit for at least these qualities! A week ago, at the Hole of Death, he picked up a wounded man, carried him on his back to the aid station across a frightening barrage of fire, and all he could say with his slow, Parisian drawl: "There's no reason that these brutes should keep quiet, but still we have to tend to my buddy!" The next day, he got drunk and raised havoc in the bivouac, and I had to give him a good scolding. It was obvious he wanted to be forgiven. So, after glancing outside again, I granted his request. . . .

"I'll go along. You will take three comrades with you, two with weapons, and one with a stretcher."

"Thank you, Captain."

"But I will be the one who will give you the signal and who will decide at the last moment if you can leave. I do not intend to risk a hair of one of my men to pick up a corpse whom I do not even know!"

For, you might have guessed, this was not some kind of game, a hare or rabbit surprised at his burrow, which we had to go and get in front of our lines, but the corpse of one of ours, sad remains of the last offensive. When we arrived to occupy the sector, the infantrymen we replaced, benefiting from darkness, had already picked up all the bodies which could be reached safely. Viot's cuirassiers,[1] who preceded me at the trench, had brought back a few who were farther from the parapet, and it seemed possible to reach this one even though it was a bit more perilous, because the Boches across from us were not very far away. Right away my men, with this splendid solidarity, let's say with this marvelous "generosity" which was in the heart of each of them, had decided to take a chance. They would not have hesitated, had I not kept them under control, to risk their lives to bring back to our lines and give a suitable burial to the body of this unknown who meant nothing to them. But he was a Frenchman, a "buddy," as D——n said.

The night was slowly falling. The moon had yet to appear, and the moment had come. But there was already a faint light which did not please me. Finally, we went away. We would be able to find our way better and act more quickly.

The men were there, with their stretcher. I went along with them, as well as my lieutenant Rouxel. One by one, silently, we crossed the parapet, at a place where the bushes masked us somewhat. Bent over, the stretcher-bearers went toward the front, flanked by their armed comrades. Lieutenant Rouxel and I stood watch, our ears alert. Our eyes had grown accustomed to the semi-darkness and we could see distinctly our men advancing rapidly, but carefully, towards the bush which we had carefully marked, reach it, bend over towards the earth, and already they were on their way back with their morbid burden. "It's an officer" one of the bearers whispered upon arriving at the trench, where ten arms reached out for the stretcher to pass it over the parapet. With a pain in my heart, I saluted it as an atrocious odor slapped me in the face from the corpse. . . . The moment was truly eerie! But, everything had gone without a hitch and I re-entered the trench feeling very satisfied.

Now, Rouxel and I proceeded with the identification of the corpse before sending it on to the second line. I presided over the task from a distance, I must confess, because the corpse was already in a horrible state. . . . It was a colonial infantry lieutenant, quite young, with blond hair. . . . That's all we could notice in the case of this hideous form where the flesh, the leather equipment, the cloth of the uniform already formed only a darkish and pestilent mass. . . . Courageously, Rouxel, a handkerchief tied over his nostrils, searched the pockets of the dead and gathered his papers and his personal objects. . . . Then, the men took up the stretcher again, and left by the communications trench of the command post. The moon was now high and bright, and the chalky plain seemed snow-covered as far as the eye could see. The night was truly beautiful, but now all its charm was gone for me. I could see too well the poor comrade we had just brought back. I thought that hardly a month ago, he had come as we did in this awful corner of Champagne, full of life, enthusiasm, hope. . . and now!

But at least, in his case, he fell in full charge, in the intoxication of battle, under the illusion of success, of the breakthrough, of the Victory. Now, he was going to sleep near his companions of arms. Later on, he would be able to rest next to his kin. . . . Will we have the same opportunity? And is it not better to say rather, as the sailor of Yann Nibor:

"He rests gently under his six feet of earth. . . . Will we rest there? That is something we do not know!

Opposite the Butte de Souain
(Champagne)
18 October 1915

32

The Last Column

[Editor's Note: This chapter describes in agonizing detail the death of a Senegalese soldier named Badji-Djendo. In contrast to the sense of paternalism and cultural superiority implicit in the author's description of Mama Pleya in chapter 26, the description of this soldier is sad and respectful. In fact, the deliberate association of Guy de Lécluse with Badji-Djendo and the suggestion that the black African troops are "magnificent and impeccable soldiers" joined together in the "assault on Paradise" indicate that the author's admiration for these men and his compassion for human beings diverges sharply from the emphasis on racial differences and supposed black inferiority commonplace in the late nineteenth century.

    In these respects, Lécluse may well have been reflective of the attitudes of other French army officers who encountered black African troops on the western front. Melvin E. Page indicates that the qualities of black soldiers were "recognized by their French comrades-in-arms." Joe Harris Lunn puts it more bluntly: "Slaves were treated as equals with their former masters."[1] The sources indicate that black African troops were admired by other troops for their courage under fire while white French citizens regarded the service of these colonial troops with considerable pride.

    There is evidence that, during World War I, the image of black Africans evolved from one racial stereotype and toward another. Marc Michel argues, "Literature intended for the public at large tended to substitute for the image of the Negro as 'savage' that of the Negro as a 'big child,' obedient but proud, honest, brave and carefree at the same time."[2] That same stereotype of the "big child" existed in Lécluse's chapter on Mama Pleya which was based on an encounter in 1914. However, his encounter with Badji-Djendo in 1917 is relayed much differently. Badji-Djendo is not regarded as a "big child" but as an individual filled with personal suffering and a deep love for his family. Alternatively, it is possible that these two chapters simply reflect two different, simultaneous attitudes toward black Africans. We believe, however, that the author's habit of reproducing in his memoir the text and spirit of his diary entries

*and personal letters argues in favor of a possible change in attitude to-
ward black African troops, influenced strongly by the death of his own
son from tuberculosis.]*

> *To the memory of my son Guy de Lécluse who died
> in the service of his country and who rests in the
> cemetery of Arcachon, at the head of "the last column."*[3]

Lying in his little hospital bed, the rifleman Badji-Djendo agonized
slowly. . . . The major, during his morning visit, had declared that he
would not survive the day. . . . The sinister tuberculosis had done its
work. Slowly, but surely, it had gotten the best of the ebony giant whom
grapeshot had not been able to destroy, and it had reduced him to a
pitiful skeleton as he went to his tomb!

From time to time, a nurse approached, wiped the sweat which
drenched the face of the moribund with a light hand, moistened his dry
lips with a bit of water, then went to other invalids, for whom her cares
were so much more needed. . . . Here there was nothing left to do than
to await Death. . . .

Poor Badji-Djendo! A year ago, in Dakar, he embarked, free and
happy, with so many good friends on the big steamship which took
them to this magical country, France, and this intoxicating life, the War!
Since then, what recollections have filled his memory which he never
will retell! The landing in Bordeaux[4] on platforms swarming like ant-
hills, the crossing of France and its wonderful surprises at every turn in
the road, then the first contact with the enemy, the bayonet charge
across a hurricane of iron and fire, followed by the horrible war of holes,
to which it was so hard to get used, the dismal guard duty in the night
and in the mud, the rough winter of the Argonne where so many Africans contracted the germs of this sickness which was to mow them down
by the hundreds, and all at once, the waning strength, the hoarse cough
tearing lungs, the fever which ate at you slowly, and Death which comes
to reclaim its prey, all despite the science of the doctors and the care of
the good women of the Red-Cross. . . . In vain the black man came, as
so many of his compatriots, to ask for the pure air of Arcachon to chase
from his chest the awful pain which gnawed at it. . . . Neither the sun,
nor the ocean breeze, nor emanations of the firs had been able to save
him, and now Badji-Djendo had only a few minutes to live. . . . Follow-

ing a monotonous rhythm, his large, black head rolled back and forth from one side to the other of the pillow, and his emaciated hands seemed to claw at the white sheet, with the mechanical motion of one who was about to die. . . .

But, beyond the walls of this still room where night was steadily falling, far from France, from beyond the seas, his thoughts took flight one last time. . . . He saw again his native country, the wild brush at the edge of the great river, the path which caravans followed, his thatched hut, where "Mrs. Rifleman" awaited him, where he planned on returning covered with glory, where little black children played on the sand, while their father agonized hundreds of miles away. . . . He kept his eyes closed, as if he wanted to hang on to this precious vision, but two large tears rolled from his eyelids and flowed down slowly on his hollow cheeks. . . . Then, little by little, his features relaxed, a great serenity spread over his ebony face. . . . Stoically, without a twitch, without a complaint, the Senegalese was dead. . . .

Poor innocent victim of the Great War, you came to offer us your life, loyally, almost happily, perhaps without really understanding why! We had taught you that it was necessary to live and die for a flag with three colors which was the flag of the country of your leaders. You did not question further. The least you deserved, as a brave soldier, was to fall facing the enemy on the battlefield. . . . But your sacrifice was even greater, the most painful of all for a warrior like you: disease, suffering, slow death without glory. With the same resignation of your countrymen, you have accepted it without a complaint.

Badji-Djendo, humble black rifleman, France thanks you and blesses you! Its great soul hovers above your death bed and will watch over you at the edge of your tomb. . . . Sleep in peace in the bosom of this new homeland which you barely got to know and for which you gave your life!

And now, through the pines of the City of Winter, Badji-Djendo went to his last resting place. . . . Behind the coffin, covered with a large tricolor flag, the Senegalese, preceded by their priest, walked slowly in two long lines. . . . They sang a sorrowful chant, based on six notes which were repeated indefinitely. . . . At the cemetery, they crouched down in a circle around the pit next to which the priest alone stood and they formed a ring by holding each other's hands and uttered prayers interrupted from time to time by a guttural invocation which the priest cried out loudly. . . . During that time, one of them jumped them into the pit and lined up the coffin according to the ritual, which was to say almost vertical and facing the rising sun. Then he piled up the sand and the earth with his hands until the wood of the coffin disappeared. Then he rejoined his comrades, and, after a last invocation to Allah, the Senegalese withdrew in silence, impassable as statues of bronze.

I have visited several times and always with the same emotion, this corner of the cemetery of Arcachon reserved for the riflemen. I have seen it quite frequently, alas! in my dreams, since we brought there in his turn, on a radiant June morning, the small dear French soldier to whom I piously dedicate these lines! Cut down like so many of his black comrades, by the same implacable evil, our poor little fellow rests with them, at the head of "their last column." That is the poignant impression which you felt at first sight, never to be erased. . . . A black post rose above each rifleman's tomb, supporting a sign with only a name and a date. The dates followed closely, because the ranks of the blacks grew rapidly, in the cemetery of Arcachon, harvested by the grim reaper. . . . We read for example:

Moussa Bamba — Tir. Sen.[5] 10 October 1916
Mamadon Taraore — Tir. Sen. 21 October 1916
Ousman Dumba — Tir. Sen. 25 October 1916
Goundo Gana — Tir. Sen. 2 November 1916

and so on. . . . Heartbreaking litany, lamentable slaughter, without honor, without glory! But this forest of poles, aligned in long lines of four abreast, looked exactly like a column of black soldiers on the march. . . . And that's what they are, to tell the truth, the "last column" of the riflemen! As if still under arms, they preserve in death the same martial attitude which they had on maneuvers or on the battlefield. They remain forever what they were so proudly, magnificent and impeccable soldiers, and formed in columns for eternity. They march, aligned like at a parade, in the assault on Paradise!

Cemetery of Arcachon
1917

33

The Living Dead

[Editor's Note: Not listed as an independent chapter in the memoir, this undated poem follows the previous chapter in the manuscript. We know that this poem was written by Lécluse in France, presumably by 11 August 1916.[1] It was inspired by a phrase borrowed from the conservative politician and patriot, Maurice Barrés, who wrote about the "living dead." Originally, this was a reference to a traditional call to soldiers upon reveille: "On your feet, you dead!" Mystical, religious, patriotic, and sorrowful, this poem proclaims the author's belief that the sacrifices of these men will not have been in vain and that their souls will live on.]

To my comrades, to my soldiers who died for France.

They died, a smile on their lips and without a complaint,
Holding back with their bodies the invading tide,
And so to see triumph the holy and just Cause
As some give their gold, they gave their blood.

They died far from those they loved, far from "home,"[2]
Where cherished ones will await them in vain,
And their bodies scattered about the woods and stubble fields
Do not have even a cross to honor their final hour!

They died, blessed artisans of Victory,
Wall of flesh rising up before the accursed Huns,
And the God of Battle, calling them to his glory
Has, with all these martyrs, swelled his Paradise. . . .

They died! They will live on in the history books
Our children will read, and, in turn, their children recite.

They brought such glory to these sublime pages
That our eyes are startled as we read.

They died, proud of their ultimate sacrifice,
And, so that their hope not be ignored,
The scale which Eternal Justice holds
Tipped toward us under the weight of their virtue.

They died! But is this word not blasphemy?
Death has not taken everything, the souls and the bodies!
To bring them back to life, one doesn't need
A hero's voice calling: "On your feet! You Dead!"[3]

They are here, next to us, finishing up their task,
Still dedicating themselves beyond the tomb,
Exalting our hopes, doubling our courage,
Superhuman apostles of the noblest of Duty!

Toward the ideal goal they show us the path,
The path which the victors have marked out for us. . . .
If our ardor wavers and our faith is doubting,
To the call of our dead let us open up our hearts!

When we feel passing over our mournful soul
Something akin to a breath from Above floating in the wind,
Let us tell ourselves: It is their soul, invisible and present!
Let us no longer speak of the Dead, for the dead Are Alive!

Conclusion

To put this memoir into its proper context, we need to compare the Lécluse manuscript to the diaries and memoirs of other line officers. Restricting our sample to captains and commandants born between 1864 and 1870 (three years before and after Lécluse's birth year) we can find the diaries and memoirs of five men close in age and rank to our author: Commandant Paul Lefebvre-Dibon, Commandant Sylvain-Eugène Raynal, Commandant Pierre-Louis-Georges Bréant, Captain Charles Laurent Delvert and Captain Joseph-Charles Ouÿ-Vernazobres. All of these officers served in front-line units during WWI. All were patriots. All regarded their men as heroes. All demonstrated great pride in their unit. All tended to express hated for the Germans. All hoped for revenge when one of their men was killed or seriously wounded. And the similarities do not end there.

The dedications of these officers' books are remarkably similar. Lécluse dedicated his book "To my comrades of the 9th Light Group and the 2d Light Group." The same impulse to memorialize the men who served under him is reflected by Commandant Lefebvre-Dibon, who dedicated his book: "To the dead and to my comrades from the Battalion."[1] Ouÿ-Vernazobres dedicated his book to "My comrades from the First Cavalry Corps." Thus, Lécluse's dedication is consistent with this practice. Furthermore, these authors' texts show remarkable similarities in terms of the stories told and the attitudes expressed.

Commandant Raynal was a national hero for the defense of Verdun.[2] For seven days he commanded the Fort de Vaux during which the Germans attacked in force, penetrated the fort, and finally captured it after heavy fighting. Greatly outnumbered, Raynal and his men were completely cut off from help. Holding out against impossible odds, the French soldiers fought hand-to-hand against rifle fire, machine guns, hand grenades, artillery fire and flame throwers. Their cistern damaged and their water spoiled by decaying bodies, the men were forced to drink their own urine. Later, Crown Prince Rupert of Bavaria asked to see Commandant Raynal, commended him for his bravery, and presented him with a sword (which Rupert mistakenly thought belonged to Raynal) as a symbol of Rupert's respect.

In *Journal d'un officier de cavalerie,* Ouÿ-Vernazobres told the story of the War of Movement. A cavalry officer, he commanded a squadron during the Race to the Sea and described being greeted by the patriotic inhabitants of French cities, who threw flowers in their path. He commented: "Each knows well that peaceful France, hammered for fifteen years by kicks from the boot, would not be able to submit for long to the German spur." An ardent Catholic, he reflected on church bells ringing in the distance and said: "And the thought comes to us . . . the Church, immutable, calls its faithful to its ritual hours to its offices to its prayers. . . . It seems to us clearly, then, that she alone, in the world, is truly a power." Like Lécluse, he was deeply troubled by the deaths of his men. Seeing only three men exit the woods where one of his squads had been attacked, he said, "my heart saddens at the thought that they were the only ones who survived that beautiful squad."[3]

We see examples of unbridled patriotism as Ouÿ-Vernazobres quoted the words of Henri Lavedan "which pass from hand to hand in our bivouacs:"

> I believe in the courage of our soldiers, in the skill and devotion
>   of our leaders.
> I believe in the force of law, in the crusade of the civilized, in
>   France eternal, imperishable and necessary. . . .
> I believe in the prayers of wives, in the heroic insomnia of
>   spouses, in the purity of our cause, in the immaculate glory of
>   our flags. . . .
> I believe in us. I believe in God. I believe. I believe. And, right up
>   to the end, whenever it arrives, I will not cease to recite this act
>   of faith which is my chant, my litany, my alleluia![4]

Like Lécluse, Ouÿ-Vernazobres encountered houses and even towns that had been "broken, torn, cut into a thousand pieces." He complained, "Senlis has been pillaged and burned.[5] It is lamentable. Only the hospital and the Grand-Cerf remain standing." He spoke at length of dogs shot; works of art and antique furniture stolen from houses; women's hose, perfume, and lace stolen. He recounted tales of atrocities in Péronne and was indignant over the bombardment of the cathedral at Reims. He talked about the Germans supposedly cutting off the noses and ears of little children and the breasts of women.[6] He also recounted what appears to be the same tale told by Lécluse in "Mama Pleya, Rifleman":

> Lieutenant Rupied's squad . . . recounted that it encountered at Liban a superb black rifleman. What was this Negro doing so far from his unit, all alone? He was armed with a rifle and said to the officer who interrogated him: "Lieutenant, I am occupying the village.". . . The squad charges a dozen uhlans, killing one of them, wounding two of them and taking several horses. . . . During the alert, the black rifleman had not budged and he repeated . . . I am occupying the village."[7]

One officer whose path may have crossed that of Lécluse is Commandant Bréant, author of *De l'Alsace à la Somme*. He served both at Verdun and the Somme and was at the Trou Bricot and the Butte de Tahure on 27 September 1915, the precise location where Lécluse's men suffered heavy casualties on 6 October 1915. Whether they ever met is impossible to determine.

A patriot, Bréant and was fiercely proud of his men. He exulted in the killing of one enemy soldier and the capture of two others on 4 August 1914 and said, "The joy of our soldiers is exuberant." On his entry into Alsace on 7 August 1914, Bréant was deeply moved and stated, "We will never forget this day." He described the burial of one of his men and commented about the "three colors of our flag . . . transforming the poor ditch into a bed of glory." Bréant's colonel offered a eulogy, describing the soldier as "one of the first victims of our war, the war of civilization, liberty and law against barbarism, slavery and criminality." The night of 16 August 1914, Bréant received a letter addressed to "Mulhouse. Alsace. France." and said "I cried."[8]

As with Lécluse, Bréant believed rumors of German atrocities. He repeated the story that "some hussards . . . found a farm boy put on a cross by these savages." He indicated that the mayor of Senlis, M Odent, had been shot by the Germans "in order to terrorize the population." In an incident similar to that described in "The Hole of Death," Bréant wrote about the killing of sixty men and a dozen officers by heavy artillery fire on "one of the most frightful days of the campaign."

When Bréant's men took heavy casualties at Verdun, he went to mass and received communion "for my men and for me." Bréant seemed to believe that he was favored by Divine Providence as he wrote, "Yes, certainly, I have been protected, yesterday and today." He, too, visited a cemetery, read an inscription to a "dear and regretted captain," and commented, "It is that which he wanted to be. To be that only: loved by his men."[9] As with Lécluse, there was nothing vainglorious about Bréant, whose memoir says more about his men than about himself. In fact, these commandants and captains told the story of their units without attempting to enhance their own individual reputations.

Perhaps the one officer who came closest in spirit to Captain de Lécluse was Captain Delvert. Delvert fought at Fort de Vaux during May and June 1916. He and his men fought off five enemy assaults in a four-day period. At one point, the enemy reached within three meters of the trenches manned by Delvert and his men, and destroyed most of the company. His depiction of combat is horrifying and his descriptions of dead bodies putrefying in the open air is disgusting. Nowhere is there a sense that war is glorious or combat bloodless.

Delvert hated the enemy with a passion reminiscent of Lécluse. In *Quelques héros,* he described the Germans as "the savage horde," "assassins of women," and "torturers of the elderly and of children." Commenting on a young machine-gunner from Lille named Fleurquin, he said, "He knows the horrors that the Boche have committed, the pillage, the arson, the theft, the deportations. . . ."[10]

As he comments on the suffering of his men, Delvert evokes the heroic myth so often found in officers' diaries, "It is pitiful to see what our poor troopers have to eat. . . . They do not complain and they accept everything with stoicism. I said to them today at the report, that their good humor in face of these hardships was part of their duty as soldiers. They have nearly applauded me. I heard the beating of hands."

There is even an encounter with a statue of Christ whose arms appeared to be extended toward the front lines. To Delvert they seemed to say, "Come! Come accomplish the secular dream! Chase away that horde which presses upon me. . . ." In a scene reminiscent of Lécluse's chapter "The Sentinels," Delvert told of leaving the dead along the top of the trenches as "lugubrious sentinels" who guard "this corner of French soil which they seem, in death, to want still to interdict to the enemy."[11]

Delvert's sense of humor was strikingly similar to that of Lécluse. He recounted the story of Rouzeaud who fired an illumination flare toward the enemy. Unfortunately, that flare drifted back over French lines, illuminating Rouzeaud's position. The enemy fired a few rifle shots. The French dove for cover and the Germans burst out with laughter. Rouzeaud repeated his folly again with the same results. The sense of humor implicit in this story reminds one of Lécluse's chapter, "The Mad Escapade." Like Lécluse, Delvert commented at length on beautiful and ruined churches. He described the upper valley of the Marne in great detail. He wept at the death of his men; he described in detail the beauty of the surrounding countryside; and he referred to his soldiers as "pauvres petits." He also told a story of his worst day, 29 May 1916, when he sent out fifty-four men to work on a communications trench. The unit was assembled outside of the command post when it was hit by an artillery shell that caused a terrible explosion. He heard his men cry out, and he heard their death rattles. Ten men were killed, twelve were seriously wounded, and another dozen suffered minor wounds.[12] The next morning, he went to the scene of the massacre and commented,

> A long pool of violet and glue-like blood is congealed near the trunk of a tree. Some helmets full of blood, some bags torn open, some shovels, some rifles splattered with blood. A shirt all red emerged, spotted with blood, from a mass of shapeless debris. Near a tree, a head . . . which is doubtlessly that of our poor little D. . . .
> Over this carnage, buzzed a swarm of fat blue flies who were filling

themselves with blood.[13]
But the most lasting impression one gets from reading Delvert's two books is that his men were genuine heroes. In *Histoire d'une compagnie,* he wrote about a stretcher-bearer named Levêque who had gone three days without eating or drinking but still continued to perform his hazardous duty without complaint:

> One speaks continually of heroes. Here is one and one of the most authentic. He has no croix de guerre. He is a good man, very modest, who does his duty without concern for the bullets and the shells, who does his duty to the point of exhaustion. He is a true hero.

Elsewhere, he said "they defend to their last breath the corner of French soil assigned to them." They fight and "die at their post because their duty is to be there . . . because they are men and they would feel . . .

worthy of being called 'sissies' if they flinched; because . . . they are
aware of being citizens of a great, free country which defends liberty."[14]
When compared to these other line officers, Henri de Lécluse appears to
have been highly representative of his class and caste.

If the books written by line officers provide evidence of the courage
of the men, their patriotism, and their religious devotion, the works
published by common soldiers and staff officers offer very different perceptions of the war. At one extreme, Corporal Louis Barthas *(Les carnets
de guerre de Louis Barthas, tonnelier, 1914-1918)* expressed open hostility
to the high command. He refers to the "criminal obstinacy of our general staff." He described soldiers fleeing the enemy in panic. He noted
the executions of men for cowardice under fire. He spoke of his own
insubordination when ordered to do meaningless and dangerous hard
work. Barthas detested certain officers who demanded strict application
of the military code, or who punished soldiers who missed mass on
Easter.[15] He ridiculed the false communiqués released by government
and military propaganda organizations. He criticized doctors for lack of
concern for the men and stretcher bearers for failing to carry out their
duty. He complained bitterly of the better food and quarters enjoyed by
the officers and of the hardships endured by enlisted men. Yet Barthas
had a strong sense of responsibility. He explained that "when one accepts
a rank, as minuscule as that of corporal, one must accept all the responsibility and rise to accomplish one's duty up to the sacrifice of one's life,
if it is necessary." He insisted that appeals to the soldiers' patriotism fell
on deaf ears. Barthas maintained that the squad had an intimacy and
closeness that excluded all officers and noncommissioned officers.

Perhaps the most telling difference between Barthas's account and
that of the four captains and commandants described above is that Barthas
provides strong evidence of a deep mistrust between the enlisted men and
the officers. Frequently, men were ordered to move forward toward enemy
lines and were told that they were to attack only at the last minute. While
officers had their orders to carry out, the men were preoccupied with
saving their own skins and minimizing the risk of injury or death.[16]
Barthas clearly suggests that there was a deep rift between the officers and
enlisted men. There were, however, some exceptions. Barthas deeply admired his own captain (although he detested his colonel). We are told that
officers who shared the risks of the men and who exhibited genuine concern for their welfare were loved by their men in return.

David Englander points out that the French army in World War I lost 19 percent of its officers and 16 percent of its enlisted men. The courage under fire of the officer corps was not in question. It was, instead, a matter of their "humanity." Englander tells us that enlisted men had difficulty adjusting to a "loss of comfort, privacy and freedom" in the military. He argues that they resented "endless parades and pointless training exercises." The poilu's lack of food, drink, shelter, and comfort contrasted with the better food and more comfortable quarters of the officer corps, a fact that led to considerable grumbling among the men. Poor pay and insufficient leave were also major sources of conflict between officers and men. Englander writes:

> The contrast between their own miserable condition and the relative comfort of their superiors made a deep impression on the men. Inequalities born of military necessity were generally accepted. Privilege based on non-military considerations, however, was bitterly contested. Many soldiers felt abandoned by their officers who seemed pre-occupied with their own well-being.[17]

Under these circumstances, an officer like Captain de Lécluse, who exhibited genuine concern and affection for his men, might be expected to be loved by them in return.

At another extreme, Lieutenant-Colonel Simon Bourguet, in *L'Aube Sanglante,* makes little mention of the physical discomforts of the trenches that dominate the works of common soldiers.[18] The first half of *L'Aube Sanglante* is dedicated to Bourguet's service as an artillery officer from September 1914 through March 1915. Bourguet complains bitterly that his family has not written him in his first five weeks at the front. He comments that the Breton cooks are incompetent. He notes that he is sleeping in an "excellent sleeping bag" on a bed of straw. He was preoccupied with his prospects for promotion. While he does comment on the ubiquitous mud, there is no mention of rats, cold, rain, or lice. There is hardly any mention of casualties and no sense of the unrelenting horror of heavy bombardment. In the second half of his book, Bourguet is transferred to an infantry unit upon his request where he commands a regiment. His days are filled with preparing bombardments, maintaining communications with other units, arranging for transportation of men and equipment. In short, he appears to have been focused on his administrative duties rather than on the harsh realities of combat and life at the front.

Lécluse's memoir was based on the combat diary written from 6

December 1914 through 22 August 1916. We can compare the memoir to both his diary and to a series of eighty letters that he wrote to his wife and daughter during that same period. With the single exception of the conclusion to "The Mad Escapade," there is little difference between these three different sources in terms of the way Lécluse characterized specific events. Specific phrases and sentences found in the author's diary and in his letters to his family are reproduced faithfully in the memoir.

Properly speaking, this is not the history of the Fourth Squadron, Ninth Light Group, or the Tenth Squadron, Second Light Group, nor is it one man's account of his own exploits. Instead, it is a captain's attempt to memorialize the men who fought and died for France as well as an effort to describe the central experience of his military career.

Some readers may find Lécluse's patriotism and hatred of the enemy quite disturbing. They are, however, quite typical of his age and rank. Moreover, the chapters that tend to reflect these feelings come late in the memoir and were written, for the most part, during 1918. In that year, two events tended to generate outraged nationalism and hatred of the enemy: the retreat of civilians in the face of the German advance in May, and the Armistice on 11 November. Thus, the retrospective chapters that conclude the memoir may be reflective of the heightened sense of patriotism and hatred of the enemy, which existed in northern France during the last six months of the war.

How do we assess the combat memoir of Henri de Lécluse? This passionate, often patriotic account of war is far from objective. *Comrades-in-Arms* is the work of a French cavalry officer trained at Saint-Cyr and Saumur, steeped in the traditions of his caste and class. His well-told tales reflect themes dominant in the literature of World War I: camaraderie between common soldiers, fear of death, contempt for high command, dislike for politicians and journalists, and devotion to duty. For Lécluse, as for so many war veterans, the experience of combat was the central psychological experience of their public careers and continued to dominate their consciousness for the rest of their lives. Perhaps to cope with his own anguish toward the end of the war, Captain de Lécluse decided to transform his diary into a memoir. Thanks to that effort, we have not only an eloquent and moving account of combat on the Western Front in 1915–16, but also a very important insight into the way in which one line officer coped with the responsibility of command as well as his own personal sense of grief and anger.

APPENDIXES

Genealogy

The following information has been provided by M Stéphane de Lestrade de Conty, Captain de Lécluse's grandnephew.

The Lécluse family originated in a town called Crusley, near Laigle, in Normandy. Before 1868, the name was written as Delescluse. Thanks to a fortune derived from commerce, the family enjoyed upward social mobility. One of its branches, based at Saint Lo in the seventeenth century, had a large number of decendants, two of whom settled in Quimper, in Brittany. One of those, François-Léon Delescluse, gave rise to the Trévoëdal branch. Born in 1710 in Quimper, he had a son named Christophe-Léon. The latter, a merchant in Audierne, married Louise Vrignaux and produced several children, among them, Jean-Pierre.

Jean-Pierre (1799–1884) benefitted from an imperial decree of 17 June 1868 authorizing him and his two sons, Amédée and Emile, to separate the letters "de" from his name. Five months later, 13 November 1868, Jean-Pierre Delescluse, the mayor of Audierne, added the name Trévoëdal. From this time forward, the family name became known as Lécluse-Trévoëdal. Properly speaking, the family was part of the Imperial nobility and had a silver coat of arms with two crowned dolphins at the top and a pine cone at the bottom.

Jean-Pierre's son, Amédée, was born in 1836 and died in 1898. He also was mayor of Audierne and later became Counsellor General of Finistère. He married Henriette Le Meneuste and they had a son, Henri-Pierre-Marie. The mother was born in 1846 and died on 25 November 1900 at the age of fifty-four at the family chateau in Loqueran in Finistère. Henri was commissioned as an officer on 1 January 1893 and married Jeanne Bertrande Labrousse de Beauregard later that year. They had a son, Guy, born in 1895 who died at the age of twenty-two on 14 June 1917 in Arachon. Their daughter, Odette, was born in 1902 and died in 1989 in Grinnell, Iowa.

Henri's wife, Jeanne Bertrande, was the daughter of Pierre-Adolphe

Labrousse de Beauregard and Jenny Boersch, and the great-great-grand-daughter of Louis IX, Langrave of Hesse-Darmstadt. The family trees of both families have been reproduced below.

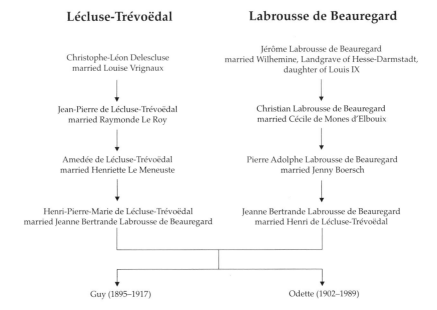

Lécluse-Trévoëdal   **Labrousse de Beauregard**

Christophe-Léon Delescluse   Jérôme Labrousse de Beauregard
married Louise Vrignaux   married Wilhemine, Landgrave of Hesse-Darmstadt,
                                      daughter of Louis IX

Jean-Pierre de Lécluse-Trévoëdal   Christian Labrousse de Beauregard
married Raymonde Le Roy   married Cécile de Mones d'Elbouix

Amedée de Lécluse-Trévoëdal   Pierre Adolphe Labrousse de Beauregard
married Henriette Le Meneuste   married Jenny Boersch

Henri-Pierre-Marie de Lécluse-Trévoëdal   Jeanne Bertrande Labrousse de Beauregard
married Jeanne Bertrande Labrousse de Beauregard   married Henri de Lécluse-Trévoëdal

Guy (1895–1917)   Odette (1902–1989)

French Text of "Brambles"

LES RONCES (poème en prose)

Au barde de ma Bretagne, à mon ami Théodore Botrel.

Dans le creux des vallons, aux pentes des collines, — à travers la campagne, à travers les forêts, — rampant pendant des lieues et encore des lieues, — les ronces ont poussé, traitresses et hargneuses! . . .

Elles courent le long des lignes de tranchées, — sournoisement cachées aux plis des hautes herbes, — ou s'enroulant comme un lierre au tronc des arbres, — le long des pieux de bois et des piquets de fer. . . .

Partout, pieuvre hideuses à l'affut de sa proie, — et jete le filet des lianes barbelées, — la toile d'araignée aux replis monstrueux, — où la mort vous agrippe, odieuse et stérile! . . .

Lâches comme le Boche accroupi derrière elles, — le vil collet étranglant dans sa course — le cerf aux bois puissants ou le chevreuil léger, — elles brisent l'élan superbe de la charge, — le vol vertigineux des claires baïonnettes, — un méchant brin de ronce happe un pied au passage, — et voilà le héros bondissant vers la gloire, — abattu sur le vol, inutile et sanglant! . . .

Leurs lugubres rameaux aux tristes tons de rouille — n'ont point de feuilles, mais parfois des fruits étranges: — corps pantelants, débris macabres, formes raides, — en grappes empourprés sont suspendus aux ronces, — et, les yeux agrandis d'horreur et d'épouvante, — le guetteur les contemplent à travers le créneau. . . .

O ronces de la Guerre, aux bardes ensanglantes, — tant et tant de sol de notre douce France, — comme un voile de mort jeté sur la nature, — se déploie le réseau de vos sinistres branches. . . . — Qu'il vienne enfin le jour où, gaiement, vers le ciel — poussera l'herbe folle avec la fleur sauvage, — où les lourds épis d'or et les luzernes bleues — pourraient vous étouffer, ô Ronces meurtrières, — au souffle de la Paix sereine et bienfaisante, — au Soleil de la Gloire et de la Liberté! . . .

French Text of "The Living Dead"

Les Morts vivants

A mes camarades, à mes soldats morts pour la France

Ils sont morts, le sourire aux lèvres et sans plainte,
Endiguant de leurs corps le flot envahissant,
Et pour voir triompher la Cause juste et sainte
Comme on donne son or, ils ont donné leur sang.

Ils sont morts loin de ceux qu'ils aimaient, loin du "home,"
Où des êtres chéris les attendront en vain,
Et leurs corps dispersés par les bois et les chaumes
N'ont pas même une croix pour honorer leur fin!

Ils sont morts, artisans sacrés de la Victoire
Mur de chair se dressant devant les Huns maudits,
Et le Dieu des combats, les prenant dans sa gloire
A, de tous les martyrs, peuplé son Paradis. . . .

Ils sont morts, dans l'orgueil du dernier sacrifice,
Et, pour que leur espoir ne fût pas méconnu,
La balance que tient l'Eternelle Justice
S'est inclinée vers nous du poids de leur vertu.

Ils sont morts! . . . Ils vivront dans la sublime histoire
Qu'apprendront nos enfants, que rediront leurs fils..
Aux pages de ce livre ils ont mis tant de gloire
Qu'en les lisant nos yeux demeurent éblouis! . . .

Ils sont morts! . . . Mais ce mot n'est-il pas une blasphème?
La mort n'a pas tout pris, les âmes et les corps! . . .
Pour les ressusciter, il n'est pas besoin même
De la voix d'un héros criant: "Debout! Les Morts!"

Ils sont là, près de nous, achevant leur ouvrage,
Se dévouant encore au delà du tombeau,
Exaltant notre espoir, doublant notre courage,
Apôtres surhumains du Devoir le plus beau! . . .

Vers le but idéal ils nous montrent la route,
La route que nous ont jalonnée ces vainqueurs. . . .

Si notre ardeur charnelle et notre foi doute,
A l'appel de nos morts ouvrons tout grand nos coeurs!

Quand nous sentons passer sur notre âme dolente
Comme un souffle d'En Haut qui flotte dans le vent,
Disons-nous: C'est leur Ame, invisible et présente! . . .
Ne parlons plus des Morts, car ces morts Sont Vivants!

NOTES

Introduction

1. R. Ernest Dupuy and Trevor N. Dupuy, *The Encyclopedia of Military History from 3500 B.C. to the Present*, 949.

2. Col. Leonard P. Ayers, *The War with Germany: a Statistical Study*, 149.

3. Typically, soldiers whose ranks varied from private to captain have been included in definitions of "common soldiers" in World War I literature.

4. The British literature of World War I has been described in detail by Paul Fussell, *The Great War in Modern Memory;* Tony Ashworth, *Trench Warfare, 1914-1918: The Live and Let Live System;* and Denis Winter, *Death's Men;* while the French literature has been studied by Jean Norton Cru, *Témoins: Essai d'analyse et de critique des souvenirs de combattants édités en Français de 1915 à 1928,* and Stéphane Audoin-Rouzeau, *Men at War, 1914-1918: National Sentiment and Trench Journalism in France during the First World War.*

5. Ashworth, *Trench Warfare,* 2.

6. Depending on circumstances, the French often used a trench located five to ten meters behind the firing trench to provide covering fire. In the literature this is usually identified as a covering trench.

7. Winter, *Death's Men,* 81.

8. Ashworth, *Trench Warfare,* 15, 21-22.

9. Leonard V. Smith, "The Disciplinary Dilemma of French Military Justice, September 1914-April 1917: The Case of the 5e Division d'Infanterie," 51.

10. Ashworth, *Trench Warfare,* 82.

11. Ibid., 102.

12. Paul Gerbod, "L'Ethique héroic en France (1870-1914)," 409-10.

13. R. D. Anderson, *France, 1870-1914: Politics and Society,* 26.

14. Maurice Agulhon, *The French Republic, 1879-1992,* 137-38.

15. Raoul Girardet, *Le Nationalisme français,* 224; Eugen Joseph Weber, *The Nationalist Revival in France, 1905-1914,* 11.

16. See, for example, J.-J. Becker, "A Lille au début de la guerre de 1914," *Historique,* 256, no. 1 (1976): 89-116.

17. James Friguglietti, "Albert Mathiez, an Historian at War," 574.

18. Becker, *La France en Guerre,* 1914-1918, 22-24.

19. Ibid., 25-36. See also Gérard Cholvy and Yves-Marie Hilaire, *Histoire religieuse de la France contemporaine, 1880-1930,* 240.

20. Cholvy and Hilaire, *Histoire religieuse,* 236-44.

21. Henri Desagneaux, *A French Soldier's War Diary, 1914-1918,* 4-5.

22. Jean-Jacques Becker, *La France en Guerre, 1914-1918,* 112.

23. Vincent Suard, "La Justice militaire française et la peine de mort au début de la première guerre mondiale," 141.

24. Jean Galtier-Bossière, *En rase campagne,* 40-46, as quoted in Jean Norton Cru, *War Books: A Study in Historical Criticism,* 111-12.

25. Audoin-Rouzeau, *Men at War,* 73.

26. Winter, *Death's Men,* 117.

27. Ibid., 118, 181, 227.

28. Audoin-Rouzeau, *Men at War,* 9, 130.

29. Ibid., 95.

30. Ibid., 61-63, 95, 57.

31. On the surface, this is strange and unlikely. During the ten years before the outbreak of World War I, there had been a Catholic revival, especially among intellectuals. The fierce battles between clericals and anticlericals had polarized France after 1900 over such issues as the expulsion of religious teaching orders and the separation of church and state. Describing this period, Adrien Dansette writes: "We are in the presence of a great spiritualist revival, at time Christian, which extends little by little to all branches of knowledge. It also animates literature." Adrien Dansette, *Histoire religieuse de la France contemporaine,* 698. See also Pierre Paraf, "Les Français devant dieu, les religions, la libre pensée," 91-99, in *La France de 1914: Le passé et l'avenir nous parlent,* 91, 97.

32. David Englander, "The French Soldier, 1914-1918," No. 1, 64.

33. Winter, *Death's Men,* 209-10.

34. Ruth Harris, "The Child of the Barbarian: Rape, Race, and Nationalism in France during World War I," 170-205. Although Harris was not specific, presumably this was the Comité d'Études et Documents sur la Guerre headed by Ernest Lavisse with Émile Durkheim as secretary.

35. Joseph Bédier, *Crimes allemandes d'après des témoinages allemandes,* as cited in Harris. See Harris, "Child of the Barbarian," 182-83. Arnold Toynbee also described German atrocities in his book, *The German Terror in France,* which drew much of its information from the Bryce Report.

36. John Horne and Alan Kramer, "German 'Atrocities' and Franco-German Opinion, 1914: The Evidence of the German Soldiers' Diaries," 7, 23-24. Horne and Kramer state, "Half the incidents described by Bédier concern summary executions of civilians, frequently accompanied by the deliberate firing of buildings, from isolated farm houses to whole villages and towns. . . ." The authors also indicate that "a third of the total incidents involved pillage and incendiarism." They state that "the rest in general concerned the killing of wounded Allied soldiers and prisoners of war" (7).

37. Pierre Miquel, *La Grande Guerre,* 115-28.

38. Winter, 23-35.

39. According to the copy of the marriage contract in the "Dossier d'un officier" at the Military Archives at Vincennes (France, Service Historique de l'Armée de la Terre, dossier No 150.378), Lécluse's personal property was worth five thousand francs while his wife's was worth twenty thousand. His parents gave the couple property worth four hundred thousand francs and a guaranteed lifetime income of fifteen thousand francs. Jeanne Bertrand's widowed mother gave them four hundred thousand francs, mostly in the form of railway shares and debt obligations.

40. From 1894 to 1897, his commanding officer gave the young lieutenant a series of negative performance reviews, calling attention to his great wealth, his lack of interest in riding horses while off duty, and his general lack of enthusiasm for a military career. Later commanders would call Lécluse a very good horseman. Apparently, a personal conflict between Lécluse and his commander played a major role in his eventual resignation.

41. Ralph Gibson, *A Social History of French Catholicism, 1789-1914*, 271, 194.

42. Ralph Gibson, "The French nobility in the nineteenth century — particularly in the Dordogne," in J. Howorth and P. Cerny, eds., *Elites in France*, 11.

43. Ibid., 29, 36, 8.

44. Andrew Sinclair, *The Last of the Best: The Aristocracy of Europe in the Nineteenth Century*, 27-29.

45. Eric Mension-Rigau, *Aristocrates et grandes bourgeois. Education, traditions, valeurs*, 22-27.

46. Ibid., 50-52, 61.

47. Dominic Lieven, *The Aristocracy in Europe, 1815-1914*, 39.

48. Christophe Charle, *A Social History of France in the Nineteenth Century*, 165; Theodore Zeldin, "France," in David Spring, ed., *European Landed Elites in the Nineteenth Century*, 190-93.

49. French cavalry squadrons usually consisted of 160 men organized into four platoons of forty each. However, these mixed squadrons were fixed at five officers and 147 men. They were often formed into light groups within each division. In this case, the Ninth Cavalry Division gave rise to the Ninth Light Group. For a discussion of the experiences of cavalry squadrons in the Second Cavalry Division see Francis Latour, "La deuxième division de cavalerie pendant la Grande Guerre," 137. Also see "French Cavalry in August 1914" and "The French Cavalry After August 1914," as well as Colonel Pierre Guinard, et al., *Inventaire Sommaire des Archives de la Guerre*, Série N: 1872-1919, 138.

50. Dunkerque (59183) is the capital of the arrondissement by the same name and is in the department of the Nord.

51. A light cavalry unit was trained for scouting, screening, and pursuit. Typically, they might be lightly armed and equipped. According to "The French Cavalry After August 1914," cavalry squadrons facing a shortage of horses were given bicycles and from October to December 1914 were organized into Light

Groups. Squadrons were permanently assigned to their regiments but temporarily assigned to these Light Groups.

52. Letters sent to his wife during August 1916 speak directly to this point.
Lécluse was quite content to get the assignment but missed his unit. In the new
assignment, he would be close to his wife and her mother. The author viewed
this assignment as a favor, not as a demotion or criticism of him as a soldier.
However, he complained bitterly of being discarded when he felt he had more
to contribute.

53. *Dossier d'un officier,* SHAT, 150.378.

54. Ammerzwiller (68006), located in the Haut-Rhin in the arrondissement
of Altkirch in the canton of Dannemarie, was near the German border in 1914.

55. France's highest military decoration, the croix de guerre is comparable to
the Congressional Medal of Honor in the United States, the Victoria Cross in
England, and the Iron Cross in Germany.

56. These include the continuation of the First Battle of Champagne from
1 January through 30 March 1915, which saw offensives in both Artois and
Champagne, and the Second Battle of Champagne from 25 September through
26 November 1915.

57. As a result of naturalization, Captain de Lécluse was forced to change his
legal name from Henri-Pierre-Marie de Lécluse-Trévoëdal to Henry de Lécluse.
Apparently, he had already anglicized his first name and had dropped the names
Pierre and Marie. However, the presiding judge refused to allow the hyphena-
tion of his last name.

58. Anonymous, *Historique du 3ᵉ Dragons pendant la campagne 1914–1918,* 24.

59. Longeville-devant-Bar appears to be called Longeville-en-Barrois today
(55302) and is located in the Meuse in the arrondissement and canton of Bar-
le-duc. Nançois-Tronville (55372) is located in the Meuse and is part of the
commune of Nançois-sur-Ornan. Naives-devant-Bar (55369), located in the
Meuse in the arrondissement of Bar-le-duc in the Canton of Vavincourt, is
called Naives-Rosières today. Merles-sur-Loison (55336) is in the arrondissement
of Verdun, the canton of Damvillers, and the department of the Meuse.
Neufchâteau (88321) is located in the Vosges.

60. Paliseul is located seventy kilometers northwest of Luxembourg and
twenty kilometers west-northwest of Neufchâteau. It is not listed in the current
Dictionnaire des Communes but can still be located on recent maps.

61. Presumably this is Châlons-sur-Marne (51108), the capital city of the
department of the Marne. Soudé-Saint-Croix (51555) is located in the Marne
in the arrondissement of Vitry-le-François. Sommesous (51545) is also located
in the Marne in the arrondissement of Vitry-le-François, some thirty-two kilometers west of that town. Suippes (51559) is located in the Marne in the
arrondissement of Châlons-sur-Marne, some thirty kilometers west of Sainte-
Memehould. *Historique du 3ᵉ Dragons,* 9. Ecueil (51225) is located in the Marne

in the arrondissement of Reims in the canton of Ville-en-Tardenois. Compiègne (60159) is the capital of the arrondissement by the same name in the department of the Oise.

62. Hollebeke is located just southeast of Ypres.

63. *Historique du 3ᵉ Dragons,* 14.

64. Latour, 134.

65. Ibid., 137–41.

66. Saint-Pol (62767) is located in the Pas-de-Calais. Humières (62468) is also located in the Pas-de-Calais, in the arrondissement of Arras in the canton of Saint-Pol-sur-Ternoise. *Historique du 3ᵉ Dragons,* 16.

67. Both Royallieu and Jaux are located in the Oise and are now part of the commune of Compiègne (60159). The Bois des Loges is located directly south of Les Loges, which is south of Roye. Les Loges (52290) is in the arrondissement of Langres, in the canton of Fayl-la-Forêt, in the department of the Haute-Marne.

68. Burnhaupt-le-Haut lies some twenty kilometers west of Mulhouse. It is one kilometer north-northwest of Burnhaupt-le-Bas and 4.5 kilometers north-northwest of Ammerzwiller in the arrondissement of Altkirch, canton of Dannemarie, in the department of the Haut-Rhin. Saint-Dizier (52448) is the capital of the arrondissement by the same name in the department of the Haute-Marne, some twenty-two kilometers southwest of Bar-le-duc.

69. Saint-Julien-de-Courtisols (51193) is located in the Marne and is part of the commune of Courtisols. *Historique du 3ᵉ Dragons,* 18.

70. Lunéville (54329) is the capital of the arrondissement of the same name in the department of the Meurthe-et-Moselle. The Parroy forest is located south of the Marne river, some fifteen kilometers northeast of Lunéville and near the border of Lorraine. Parroy (54418) is in the Meurthe-et-Moselle in the arrondissement of Lunéville in the canton of Arracourt.

71. This includes the first cousin of Captain de Lécluse, 2d Lt. Alexandre de Lestrade de Conty, who was killed in action on 30 September 1914 at Auberive-sur-Suippes (Marne) and posthumously received the Order of the Brigade.

72. This diary consists of hastily written personal notes of pages of varying size and thickness, suggesting that he used whatever paper was available. Unfortunately, much of that paper was transparent and Lécluse wrote on both sides. The ink frequently bled through, making it difficult to produce an accurate transcription of the entire diary. However, M Stéphane de Lestrade de Conty did a masterful job of transcribing the text, which has been used extensively in preparing the memoir for publication.

73. The memoir was written on the blank, lined pages of a separate book. The dates of individual chapters are those based on diary entries and not on the date on which they were written in the memoir. The handwriting is neater, suggesting a more self-conscious effort.

74. Onésime Reclus, *Lâchons l'Asie, Prenons l'Afrique,* as cited in Christopher

M. Andrew and A. S. Kanya-Forstner, *The Climax of French Imperial Expansion, 1914–1924,* 35.

75. Ibid., 134, 140.

76. The term *Senegalese* was applied to all black African troops serving in the French army in World War I regardless of their actual origins.

1. The Mud

1. The Berthonval farm is located northwest of Arras and west of Vimy. The woods are located one kilometer north of the farm.

2. Captain de Lécluse served initially with the Ninth Light Group of the Third Regiment (Bourbon), which originated from Nantes. This was part of the Ninth Cavalry Division, Thirtieth Army Corps. While on duty with the reserves, he received notice dated 6 October 1914 that orders were being prepared for him to join his regiment at the front. Those orders were dated 31 October 1914. He appears to have reached his unit by either 6 or 12 December 1914, although this is unclear. Later, after the formal dissolution of the Ninth Light Group on 22 May 1914, Lécluse remained with the Third Regiment, assigned to the Second Light Group until he was transferred to the Twentieth Regiment of Dragoons on 22 August 1916.

3. A sap is a crude, shallow trench that usually stretches from the forward trench toward enemy lines. Here, Lécluse is apparently referring to a shallow communications trench.

4. A pejorative label for the Germans. Apparently, it was derived from "Allemoche," a slang term for "Allemand" (German), which became corrupted into "Alboche" (before 1870). The "b" came from "caboche" (cabbage) and from "tête de bois" (wood head). In short, the equivalent terms in contemporary American slang would seem to be "cabbage head" or "block head," suggesting someone thick-headed or hard-headed, and certainly not very bright. Alfred Dauzat, Jean Dubois, and Henri Mitterand, *Dictionnaire étymologique et historique du Français,* 87. Jean Norton Cru maintains that the term *boche* did not exist in August–September 1914, and that it began to replace *Alboche* between September and December of 1914. Cru, *Témoins,* 569.

5. According to the author, Second Lieutenant Couespel du Menil accompanied Lécluse from Nantes. He transferred to the infantry on 28 May 1915 and was killed on 21 June.

6. Mont Saint-Eloi is located some five kilometers west-southwest of the Bois de Berthonval.

7. This was a wooded hillside, and Lécluse's men were located at the edge of the plain just east of the woods.

2. The False Alert

1. This suggests that Chapter 2 was written before February 1917, well before the end of the war.

2. A popular French card game resembling canasta.

3. Lécluse identifies this officer as "Lieutenant Grandjean, who commanded the light squadron of the first dragoons . . . [and] has since been killed."

4. In his notes, Lécluse identifies this officer as Second Lieutenant de Peyronnet who later transferred to aviation and had been promoted to captain.

5. A reference to the Roman Catholic practice of making the sign of the cross on one's forehead, chest, and both shoulders.

6. Some sources claim barbed wire did not make its appearance until 1916. However, Paddy Griffith's *Battle Tactics of the Western Front,* 29, refers to barbed wire in use in 1914. There are times, however, when the author uses the term *iron wire* and we have retained that expression.

7. According to the author, this was Captain Delaire, who later would be named squadron leader.

8. The word *poilu* literally means "hairy," but the word is associated with the idea of an "homme robuste" in French military slang (ca. 1875) and with a "combattant" in 1910, according to Alfred Dauzat, et al., *Dictionnaire étymologique,* 594. Cornélis De Witt Willcox *A French-English Military Technical Dictionary,* 562, indicates that the term had "connotations of virile qualities." Apparently, most common soldiers preferred the term *soldat.*

3. The Lair

1. In his notes, Lécluse writes that until it was dissolved, Captain Delacour was commander of the light squadron of the Twenty-fifth Dragoons, the Sixth Squadron of the Ninth Light Group, and the Twelfth Squadron of the Second Light Regiment.

2. A flat area behind the parapet that can be used for mounting guns.

3. Lécluse identifies him as "Lieutenant de Gasté, machine gunner with the Fifth Cavalry."

4. According to the author, Lieutenant Pavy was a machine gunner with the Twenty-fourth Dragoons, assigned to his command.

4. The Mass of the Catacombs

1. See *Histoire de la France religieuse sous la direction de Jacques Le Goff et René Rémond,* especially vol. 4, *Societé secularisée et renouveau religieux,* 119.

2. Dansette, 711-12; Cholvy and Hilaire, 240; *Histoire de la France religieuse,* 122.

3. Gibson, *Social History of French Catholicism,* 181, 174-75.

4. In his notes, Lécluse writes that Peyronnet was promoted to captain after transferring to aviation.

5. The author used the English word *home* in the text instead of the French word *maison.*

6. The term *God of Armies* is not unique to the author. Second Lieutenant

Jacques Jartel refers to a priest saying mass in a note in the 28 February 1915 entry of his *Journal* and says, "he brings to us the God of Armies." The Blessed Virgin, for example, was often invoked as "Our Lady of the Trenches." *Histoire de la France religieuse*, 120.

7. According to the author, Lieutenant-Colonel de la Tour of the Eighth Cuirassiers commanded the sectors occupied by the Ninth Cavalry Division at Canny-sur-Matz and the Bois des Loges from March through May 1915 and was later promoted to general.

5. The Good Thieves

1. In his notes, Lécluse indicates that Second Lieutenant Durat had been transferred to his squadron from the Eighth Cuirassiers in December 1914. He later returned to his regiment and subsequently transferred to aviation.

2. Lécluse explains that "Lieutenant Grandjean, temporary commandant of the light squadron of the First Dragoons, transferred into the infantry and was killed shortly afterwards in the Forest of Apremont," located just southeast of Saint-Mihiel.

6. The Sentinels

1. Conchy-les-Pots (60160) is located in the Oise in the arrondissement of Compiègne in the arrondissement of Ressons-sur-Matz.

2. See, for example, Henri Desagneaux, *A French Soldier's War Diary,* where the author describes "two burnt corpses, black, unrecognizable. Further on, bunches of men, legs twisted and mangled, or with gaping holes in their bodies, their eyeballs dangling out of their sockets, half their jaws missing, with terror written all over them" (86).

3. According to the author, Lieutenant de la Villéon of the Twenty-fifth Dragoons, joined the Ninth Light Group as a machine-gunner in September 1915 and then was assigned to the Second Light Group until its dissolution. He later transferred into the infantry with the rank of captain.

7. In Boche Country

1. Mulhouse (68224) is the capital of the arrondissement of the same name in the department of the Haut-Rhin.

2. Roye-au-Bois, currently known as Roye-sur-Matz, is located south of the Bois des Loges and southeast of Canny-sur-Matz at the intersections of the modern departmental routes 27 and 938 (shown on map 3).

3. Only Hecken (68125) could be found on current maps. It is located in the department of the Haut-Rhin, in the arrondissement of Altkirch, and in the canton of Dannemarie.

4. In his notes, Lécluse writes that Destressou was a second lieutenant with the Fifth Cuirassiers, attached to the Fourth Squadron of the Ninth Light Group, who later transferred upon his own request to the chassiers à pied.

5. Lille (59350) is the capital city of the department of the Nord. Cambrai (59122) is the chief city of the arrondissement in the department of the Nord. Saint-Quentin (02691) is the chief city of the arrondissement in the department of the Aisne. Laon (02408) is the capital of the department of the Aisne.

6. Although it is not clear when this particular chapter was written, it seems evident that it must have been composed before November 1918.

7. Presumably 1870,when that territory was reconquered by the Prussians.

8. Longpré-le-Corps-Saints (80488) is in the arrondissement of Abbeville and the canton of Hellencourt in the department of the Somme. Amiens (80021) is the capital city of the department of the Somme. Belfort (90010) is in the Territory of Belfort. Nantes (44109) is the capital city of the Loire-et-Atlantique.

9. Bretten (68052) is in the Haut-Rhin in the arrondissement of Altkirch in the canton of Dannemarie.

8. Moment of Anguish

1. Lécluse explains, "Corporal d'Ollendon, mortally wounded at Ammerzwiller on the 15th of August 1915, died three days later at the hospital at Belfort."

2. August 15 is the Feast of the Assumption and is celebrated by Roman Catholics.

3. This river flows from east to west just south of Burnhaupt-le Bas. (See map 4.)

4. According to the author, Lieutenant Boisfleury from the Third Dragoons' horse regiment was assigned to Lécluse's squadron to serve with the machine-gun section.

5. Gabions were a form of protective screen made up of wood and brush, two feet high and two feet, six inches wide. Apparently, seventy-five pounds of wood and brush were used in their construction. A gabionnade is a series of screens made up of brush and wood and filled with dirt. It is designed to shelter a gun emplacement or to provide protection in the trenches from small arms fire.

6. In his notes, Lécluse writes that Second Lieutenant Cossou of the Fifth Cuirassiers was transferred to the Ninth Light Group, then to the Second Light, and was killed in 1918.

7. Lécluse explains that Second-Lieutenant Billet had transferred to his squadron a few days before. He remained under Lécluse's command until the dissolution of the Second Light Group and then was assigned to the Twenty-seventh Dragoons.

8. According to the author, this was a passage wide enough for only one man. It zigzagged through the coils of iron wire.

9. The author writes that Second Lieutenant Ehrmann had been recently transferred to the Ninth Light Group and never returned to duty as a result of his wound.

9. Forgetting About Time

1. Chamouilley (52099) is in the arrondissement of Saint-Dizier, in the canton of Saint-Dizier Sud-Est, in the department of the Haute-Marne.

2. Lécluse indicates that Lieutenant de Lorgereil of the Twenty-fourth Dragoons' foot squadron was transferred to the Ninth Light Group and then to the Second Light Group until its dissolution.

3. Located in the Marne.

4. Saint-Dizier (52448) is capital of the arrondissement in the department of the Haute-Marne, southeast of Châlons-sur-Marne.

10. In Chalkland

1. Maison Forestière (55266) is located in the Meuse and is part of the commune of Lachalade.

2. Sermaize-les-Bains (51531) is located south of the Ornain River, fifteen miles east-northeast of Vitry-le-François. Sermaize is thirteen kilometers east-southeast of Les Loges, where the author spent considerable time during World War I, and is 5.5 kilometers northwest of Noyon. Vassincourt (55531) is located in the Meuse in the arrondissement of Bar-le-duc in the canton of Revigny-sur-Ornan.

11. The Hole of Death

1. Supposedly a term coined by Napoleon himself, the term *grogneurs* or *grognards* refers to Napoleonic war veterans. Literally meaning a "grumbler," more figuratively an "old soldier," it implied a soldier of the Imperial Old Guard who served with Napoleon during the Russian Campaign of 1812. Wilcox, 210; Dauzat, et al., *Dictionnaire étymologique,* 355; and Terry W. Strieter, "The 'Old Grumblers' of Napoleon's Army: Rates of Promotion Before and After 1815," 63.

2. In fact, twelve died in that explosion and thirty-three others were wounded.

12. Brothers-in-Arms

1. In his notes, Lécluse writes that Lieutenant Levylier had been a member of Lécluse's foot squadron since its formation, and that "Moissec was a private in the foot squadron of the Ninth Dragoons."

2. These were light troops trained for rapid movement, either infantry or cavalry.

3. According to the author, Second-Lieutenant Rouxel, paymaster of the Third Dragoons, joined Lécluse's squadron in Alsace in August 1915 and was assigned to the First Light Group at the time of the dissolution of the Second Light Group.

4. Leggings of leather or cloth worn over the shins.

5. In his notes, Lécluse indicates that Major Roqueplane, a physician,

joined the Ninth Light Group as a replacement for Doctor Barandon in October 1915 and left for the Army of the East in 1916 at the time of the dissolution of the Second Light Group.

6. Lécluse explains, "Mabrilet was decorated with the croix de guerre for his work on 6 October 1915 at the 'Trou de la mort' and returned there on his own several days later with volunteers and, despite a violent bombardment, retrieved the bodies of soldiers left there."

13. In the Field of Crosses

1. According to the author, Captain Delaire was assigned to the command of the Ninth Light Group at the time of its creation in December 1914 and was later promoted to squadron leader during their April 1915 stay at the Bois des Loges (Oise). He was decorated with the croix de guerre in Alsace in August 1915 and was killed in action in the trenches at the Camp d'Aiguille in Champagne on 6 October 1915.

2. In his notes, Lécluse writes that Lieutenant Laroche was in the first squadron of the Ninth Light Group.

3. Here, Lécluse is referring to Commandant Chevassu, commander of an infantry battalion.

4. Lécluse is referring to the death of the commandant's daughter about which he had been informed at Canny-sur-Matz in February 1915.

14. Accompaniment in Music

1. In his notes, Lécluse indicates that Lieutenant Bellot of the Third Regiment joined the Ninth Light Group in August 1915 and was assigned to the Second Light Group until its dissolution.

2. Cuirassiers are heavy cavalry and previously wore body armor.

15. The Croix de Guerre

1. Lécluse explains: "Lefevre reported on 7 October 1915 to take command of the Ninth Light Group as a replacement for Commandant Delaire, killed the previous day. At the formation of the Second Light Group, Lefevre took command of the Third Battalion, including the foot squadrons of the First, Ninth, Twenty-fourth and Twenty-fifth Dragoons."

2. Torpedoes were metal cases, often self-propelled, containing explosives that could be exploded on contact or by electricity.

3. Revetments are retaining walls made up of various materials and intended to support the dirt walls of the trenches.

4. According to the author, General du Frétay commanded the brigade of Dragoons of the First and Third Regiments under the Ninth Army Corps. Subsequently, Frétay commanded the sector at the Parroy Forest. Parisot is identified as another captain in Lécluse's regiment.

5. In the notes, Lécluse identifies Captain Maud'huit as Commandant Lefevre's assistant "who joined the Light Group at the same time as Lefevre to replace Captain Montergon, wounded 6 October 1915. Mauduit remained with the unit until the dissolution of the Second Light Group."

16. The Heartbroken Christ

1. Arracourt (54023), a cantonal capital, is located in the Meurthe-et-Moselle in the arrondissement of Lunéville, some twenty-eight kilometers east of Nancy and twenty kilometers north of Lunéville, very close to the German border. It is also directly north of Crion and Sionviller.

2. According to Lécluse, Captain Viot de Roquefeuil was commandant of the foot squadron of the 8th Regiment of cuirassiers and the 8th Squadron of the Second Light Group until its dissolution.

3. The text suggests that this chapter was written prior to the end of the war.

17. The Mad Escapade

1. Suard, "La Justice militaire français," 141–42.

2. Bures (54106) is located in the Meurthe-et-Moselle in the arrondissement of Lunéville in the canton of Arracourt.

3. According to the author, this pond was located in the Parroy forest, north of Lunéville.

18. A Winter in Lorraine

1. Both Crion (54147) and Sionviller (54507) are located in the Meurthe-et-Moselle in the arrondissement of Lunéville and are at the western edge of the Parroy Forest, where Lécluse spent several months.

2. This pond is located on the northern edge of the Parroy Forest, southeast of Arracourt and northeast of Lunéville.

3. The Mondon Forest is located directly south of the Parroy Forest, between routes 4 and 59, and lies east-southeast of Lunéville.

4. Baville is located approximately four kilometers northwest of Crion.

5. This suggests that the Germans avoided firing on French positions in order to create or to maintain an "unofficial truce" as part of a "live and let live" attitude. However, Lécluse seems not to have understood their intentions.

6. Literally "Burned House."

19. The Farewell

1. This diary entry is dated 1 July 1916.

2. Blainville (54076) is located in the Meurthe-et-Moselle. Vigneuilles (54565) is located in the Meurthe-et-Moselle in the arrondissement of Lunéville in the canton of Bayon. Gray (70280) is located in the Haute-Saône in the arrondissement of Vesoul, some forty kilometers northwest of Besançon.

3. In his notes, Lécluse indicates that General Baratier, "the heroic companion of Marchand," had been a colonel at the beginning of the war and was subsequently promoted to brigadier general. He died at the front in 1917. Marchand was a colonel who commanded an infantry brigade in the Saint-Mihiel sector in September 1914. Their heroic defense earned for them the admiration of their enemies.

4. Lécluse's notes indicate that this was Colonel Forqueray, commandant of the Second Light Group.

5. According to the author, this was General de Ruyer of the Third Cavalry Corps.

6. Lécluse identifies this officer as General Baralio.

7. The kepi is a soft form of uniform hat worn by French soldiers.

20. The Woodsmen

1. According to the author, Lieutenant de Mont replaced Lieutenant Grandjean in February 1915 as the commander of the foot squadron of the First Regiment of Dragoons (the Third Platoon of the Ninth Light Group) and remained in that capacity until the dissolution of the Ninth Cavalry Division and the Ninth Light Group in May 1916.

21. The Tombs

1. Lécluse indicates that Narroy is close to Vitry-le-François in the Marne.

2. The phrase "when the hour of Justice has arrived" suggests that Chapter 21 was written before the end of the war.

22. Pataud

1. According to the author, Rochefordière joined the Light Squadron of the Third Dragoons in August 1915 and remained with the unit until the dissolution of the Second Light Group.

23. Ruins

1. Gerbéviller (54222) is located in the Meurthe-et-Moselle in the arrondissement of Lunéville, approximately fourteen kilometers south of Lunéville.

2. Pierre Miquel, *La Grande Guerre*, 117. Englander insists that soldiers "encountering the destruction of the occupied districts, were angry and vengeful" (65).

3. Montergon was commandant of the Ninth Light Group until he was transferred. Lécluse's personal papers include a poem published by Captain de Montergon, and evidence exists that these two men were close friends.

4. There are three towns with the name Pargny, each of which might be the "Pargny" mentioned by Lécluse. This is probably Pargny-sur-Saulx (51423) in the arrondissement of Vitry-le-François, in the canton of Thiéblemont-

Farémont, in the department of the Marne, near Sermaize-les-Bains. Pargny-les-Reims (51422) is found in the arrondissement of Reims, in the canton of Ville-en-Tardenois, in the department of the Marne. Another Pargny (80616) is located in the arrondissement of Péronne, in the canton of Nesle, in the department of the Somme.

5. This language suggests that Lécluse had intended to write and publish his memoirs in France for the benefit of his countrymen.

24. Missing-in-Action
1. In his notes, Lécluse indicates that Captain Rollin joined the Ninth Light Group in the beginning of 1916. Described as a poet of "great talent," Rollin apparently received the acclamation of the Academie Française.

2. Paimpol (22162) is located in the Côtes d'Armor in the arrondissement of Saint-Brieux.

3. Cancale (35049) is located in the arrondissement of Saint-Malo in the department of the Ille-et-Vilaine.

4. Henri Bataille, "La divine Tragédie."

25. Settling a Score
1. Paramé (35288) is part of St Malo.

2. Harris, "Child of the Barbarian," 172-73, 186.

3. A reference to the narrator's wife, Jeanne Bertrande Labrousse de Beauregard.

4. Among the regular French army stationed in France, white colonial troops and the French foreign legion were often regarded as disorderly and ill-disciplined elements who fought well but lacked the skill in fighting European-style wars.

5. The original word was *gold* which communicated well when the manuscript was written but is less expressive today.

6. This indicates that the sergeant's original intention had been to capture prisoners, not to kill them.

7. Lécluse added the following note at the end: "This story, rigorously authenticated, was told to me while I was on leave, by Sergeant S.m.t of the Colonial Infantry."

26. Mama Pleya, Rifleman
1. Charles Balesi, "West African Influence in the French Army of World War I," in G. Wesley Johnson, ed., *Double Impact: France and Africa in the Age of Imperialism,* 104n. 32. Balesi cites the work of Marc Michel, "Le Recrutement de tirailleurs en A.O.F. pendant la première Guerre mondiale: essai de bilan statistique," in *Revue Français d'histoire d'outre-mer* 60 (1973): 644-60; Tyler Edward Stovall, *Paris Noir: African Americans in the City of Light,* 4-7.

2. Balesi, 99.

3. William S. Cohen, *The French Encounter with Africans: White Response to Blacks, 1530–1880*, x, 283; Tzvetan Todorov, *Nous et les autres: la réflexion française sur la diversité humaine*, 110, 131.

4. William H. Schneider, *An Empire for the Masses: The French Popular Image of Africa, 1870–1900*, 5–9, 203.

5. Stovall, 19.

6. Balesi tells us that black troops were seen by the French in 1918 as "newly adopted children," an attitude consistent with the Lécluse text. Balesi, "West African Influence," 101.

7. Marseille (13055) is the capital of the department of the Bouches-du-Rhône.

8. Reference to the author's wife and daughter.

9. It is possible that the apparent hero of the story may have actually been in the hospital at Paramé. There is no information to confirm that claim.

10. A leather pouch often worn around the neck or on a shirt that contains writing intended to provide the wearer with protection against harm.

27. Brambles

1. *Crenelations* refers to the openings in the parapets which resemble the tops of old castle walls. These allowed a view of the battlefield and an opportunity to aim a rifle at the enemy.

28. The Stage-Set

1. Saint-Pancrace is a tiny hamlet located one kilometer west of Bures. Although found on current maps, it is not listed in the current *Dictionnaire national des communes*.

29. Moonlight

1. These gabions, set close to one another, would have provided narrow firing slits and, collectively, would have formed the familiar pattern termed *crenelations*.

30. The Bus

1. An obvious reference to himself.

31. The Comrade

1. According to the author, Captain Viot commanded the second squadron of the Light Group.

32. The Last Column

1. Melvin E. Page, "Introduction: Black Men in a White Man's War," in

Africa and the First World War, 9. Joe Harris Lunn, "Kande Kamara Speaks: An Oral History of the West African Experience in France 1914–1918," p. 37 in Page, ed., *Africa and the First World War.*

2. Marc Michel, *L'Appel à l'Afrique (1914–1919),* 395.

3. Arcachon (33009) is located in the arrondissement of Bordeaux and is the chief city of the canton in the department of the Gironde.

4. Bordeaux (33063) is the capital city of the department of the Gironde.

5. "Tir. Sen" means "Senegalese rifleman."

33. The Living Dead

1. The poem was translated by Charlotte Kelsey and edited by Jacques Dubois.

2. Here Lécluse used the English word *home* not the French word *maison.*

3. This phrase was often used by sergeants waking up troops at reveille. It also became mythologized in an apocryphal tale told by soldiers at the front.

Conclusion

1. Captain Charles Laurent Delvert, *Quelques héros.* Delvert dedicated his book: "To my father, a combatant of 1870." Commandant Paul Lefebvre-Dibon, *Quatre Pages du 3ᵉ bataillon du 74ᵉ R.I. Extrait d'un carnet de campagne, 1914–1916.*

2. Commandant Sylvain-Eugène Raynal, *Journal du Commandant Raynal. Le Fort de Vaux.*

3. Captain Joseph-Charles Ouÿ-Vernazobres, *Journal d'un officier de cavalerie,* 16, 17, 33.

4. Henri Lavedan, as quoted in Ouÿ-Vernazobres, *Journal d'un officier,* 47–48.

5. Senlis (60612) is located in the Oise, thirty-five kilometers northeast of Paris.

6. Ouÿ-Vernazobres, *Journal d'un officier,* 54–56, 76.

7. Ibid., 8, 11. This incident supposedly took place on 11 August 1914 at Sart.

8. Commandant Pierre-Louis-Georges Bréant, *De L'Alsace à la Somme. Souvenirs du front (août 1914–janvier 1917),* 5–7, 33–34, 40.

9. Ibid., 65, 73, 84–87, 216, 223, 231.

10. Delvert, *Quelques héros,* 10, 93.

11. Ibid., 145, 149–50, 268–69.

12. Ibid., 153, 161–62, 189, 191, 286, 219, 238–39.

13. Ibid., 240.

14. Capt. Charles Laurent Delvert, *Histoire d'un compagnie,* 265.

15. Corporal Louis Barthas, *Les Carnets de guerre de Louis Barthas, tonnelier, 1914–1918,* xii, 115, 117–18, 123–25.

16. Ibid., 59, 175, 179.

17. Englander, *The French Soldier,* 59.

18. Lieutenant-Colonel Simon Bourguet, *L'Aube Sanglante. De La Boiselle (octobre 1914) à Tahure (septembre 1915).*

BIBLIOGRAPHY

Agulhon, Maurice. *The French Republic, 1879-1992*. Oxford: Blackwell, 1993.

Anderson, R. D. *France, 1870-1914: Politics and Society*. London: Routledge and Kegan Paul, 1977.

Andrew, Christopher M. and A. S. Kanya-Forstner. *The Climax of French Imperial Expansion, 1914-1924*. Stanford: Stanford University Press, 1981.

Ashworth, Tony. *Trench Warfare, 1914-1918: The Live and Let Live System*. New York: Holmes and Meier, 1980.

Audoin-Rouzeau, Stéphane. *Men At War, 1914-1918: National Sentiment and Trench Journalism in France during the First World War*. Providence, R.I.: Berg, 1992.

Ayers, Leonard P. (Colonel). *The War with Germany: A Statistical Study*. Washington, D.C.: GPO, 1919.

Barthas, Louis (Corporal). *Les Carnets de guerre de Louis Barthas, tonnelier, 1914-1918*. Paris: Éditions la Découverte, 1992.

Balesi, Charles. "West African Influence in the French Army of World War I," in *Double Impact*, by G. Wesley Johnson, 93-104.

Becker, Jean-Jacques. *La France en Guerre, 1914-1918*. Paris: Presses Universitaires Françaises, 1988.

———. "A Lille au début de la guerre de 1914." *Revue Historique* 256, no. 1 (1976): 89-116.

Bédier, Joseph. *Crimes allemandes d'après des témoinages allemandes*. Paris: Comité d'Ètudes et Documents sur la Guerre, 1915.

Bloch, Marc. *Memoires of War*. Translated with an introduction by Carole Fink. New York: Cambridge University Press, 1988.

Blunden, Edmund. *Undertones of War*. Garden City, N.Y.: Doubleday, Doran, 1929.

Bourguet, Simon (Lieutenant Colonel). *L'Aube Sanglante. De La Boiselle (octobre 1914) à Tahure (septembre 1915)*. Paris: Berger-Levrault, 1917.

Bréant, Pierre-Louis-Georges (Commandant). *De l'Alsace à la Somme. Souvenirs du front (août 1914-janvier 1917)*. Paris: Hachette, 1917.

Charle, Christophe. *A Social History of France in the Nineteenth Century*. Oxford: Berg, 1994.

Cholvy, Gérard, and Yves-Marie Hilaire. *Histoire religieuse de la France contemporaine, 1880-1930*. Paris: Bibliothèque historique Privat, 1989.

Cohen, William S. *The French Encounter with Africans: White Response to Blacks, 1530-1880.* Bloomington: Indiana University Press, 1980.

Cru, Jean Norton. *Témoins: Essai d'analyse et de critique des souvenirs de combattants édités en Français de 1915 à 1928.* Paris: Les étincelles, 1929.

————. *War Books: A Study in Historical Criticism.* San Diego: San Diego State University Press, 1988.

Dansette, Adrien. *Histoire religieuse de la France contemporaine.* Paris: Flammarion, 1965.

Dauzat, Alfred, Jean Dubois, and Henri Mitterand. *Dictionnaire étymologique et historique du Français.* Paris: Larousse, 1993.

Delvert, Charles Laurent (Captain). *Histoire d'un compagnie.* Paris: Berger-Levrault, 1918.

————. *Quelques Héros.* Paris: Berger-Levrault, 1917.

Desagneaux, Henri, *A French Soldier's War Diary, 1914-1918.* Morley, Yorkshire: Elmfield Press, 1975.

Dictionnarie national des communes de France: donnent la nomenclaturecomplète des communes et des principaux villages, hameaux, écarts, et lieux dits habités avec le canton, et le renseignements sur la population, les perceptions, la poste, les chemins de fer voyageux, les télécommunications, les messageries, les zones industrielles, la distance à la bretelle d'autoroute la plus proche et le code postal. Paris: A. Michel, Berger-Levrault, 1992.

Dupuy, R. Ernest, and Trevor N. Dupuy. *The Encyclopedia of Military History from 3500 B.C. to the Present.* New York: Harper and Row, 1986.

Englander, David. "The French Soldier, 1914-1918." *French History* 1, no. 1 (March 1987): 49-67.

Ettinger, Albert M. and A. Churchill Ettinger. *A Doughboy with the Fighting 69th.* New York: Pocket Books, 1992.

France, Armée, "État-Major, Service Historique." Archives de la guerre, *L'Inventaire des archives conservées au Service historique de l'État-major de l'armée. Château de Vincennes (Archives Modernes).* 2e éd. rev. complété par Marc-André Fabre, Ateliers d'impressions de l'armée, 1954.

France, Armée, État-Major, Service Historique de L'Armée de la Terre. *Dossier d'un officier* (manuscript series), No 150.378, n.d.

————. "Service historique." *Bibliographie des historiques des régiments de l'armée français: de 1914 à l'époque contemporaine.* Ministère des armées, État-major de l'armée de la terre, Service historique. Vincennes, 1973-.

France, Ministère de la guerre, État-Major de l'Armée, Service historique. *Les Armées français dans la grande guerre.* Paris: Imprimèrie Nationale, 1922-37.

"The French Cavalry in August 1914." *Tactical Notebook,* April 1992.

"The French Cavalry After August 1914." *Tactical Notebook,* October 1992.

Friguglietti, James. "Albert Mathiez, an Historian at War," *French Historical Studies* 7, no. 4 (Fall 1972): 570-86.

Fussell, Paul. *The Great War in Modern Memory.* New York: Oxford University Press, 1975.

Gerbod, Paul. "L'Ethique héroic en France (1870-1914)." *Revue Historique.* 268, no. 2 (1982): 409-29.

Gibson, Ralph. *A Social History of French Catholicism, 1789-1914.* New York: Routledge, 1989.

Gilbert, Martin. *Atlas of World War I: The Complete History.* Oxford: Oxford University Press, 1994.

Girardet, Raoul. *Le Nationalisme français.* Paris: Armand Colin, 1966.

Graves, Robert. *Good-bye to All That.* Garden City, N.Y.: Anchor Books, 1985.

Griffith, Paddy. *Battle Tactics of the Western Front: The British Army's Art of Attack, 1916-1918.* New Haven: Yale University Press, 1994.

Gunard, Pierre (Colonel), et al. *Inventaire Sommaire des Archives de la Guerre.* Serié N, 1872-1919. Vincennes: Ministère de la Defense, Service Historique de l'Armee de Terre, 1875.

Harris, Ruth. "The Child of the Barbarian: Rape, Race and Nationalism in France during World War I." *Past and Present* 141 (1993): 170-206.

Haythornthwaite, Philip J., *The World War One Source Book.* London: Arms and Armour, 1993.

Historique de 3^e Dragons pendant la campagne 1914-1918. Paris: Charles-Lavauzelle, 1920.

Horne, John, and Alan Kramer. "German 'Atrocities' and Franco-German Opinion, 1914: The Evidence of German Soldiers' Diaries." *Journal of Modern History* 66, no. 1 (March 1994): 1-33.

Howorth, J. and P. Cerney, eds. *Elites in France.* New York: St. Martin's Press, 1981.

Johnson, G. Wesley, ed. *Double Impact: France and Africa in the Age of Imperialism.* Westport, Conn.: Greenwood Press, 1985.

La Gorce, Paul-Marie de. *La Première guerre mondiale.* Paris: Flammarion, 1991.

Latour, Francis. "La deuxième division de cavalerie pendant la Grande Guerre." *Guerres mondiales et conflits contemporaines* 167 (1992): 133-47.

Lefevre-Dibon, Paul (Commandant). *Quatre Pages du 3e bataillon du 74e R.I. Extrait d'un carnet de campagne, 1914-1916.* Paris: Berger-Levrault, 1921.

Le Goff, Jacques, and René Remond. *Histoire de la France religieuse sous la direction de Jacques Le Goff et René Remond.* Vol. 4, *Société secularisée et renouveau religieux.* Paris: Editions du Seuil, 1992.

Lieven, Dominic. *The Aristocracy in Europe, 1815-1914.* New York: Columbia University Press, 1993.

Livesey, Anthony. *Great Battles of World War I.* New York: Marshall Editions Limited, 1989.

Lyons, Michael J. *World War I: A Short History.* Englewood Cliffs, N.J.: Prentice-Hall, 1994.

Mension-Rigau, Eric. *Aristocrates et grandes bourgeois. Education, traditions, valeurs*. Paris: Plon, 1994.

Michel, Marc. *L'Appel à l'Afrique (1914-1919)*. vol. 6. Afrique Series. Paris: Publications de la Sorbonne, 1982.

Miquel, Pierre. *La Grande Guerre*. Paris: Fayard, 1983.

Nicot, Jean, Philippe Schillinger, and Josette Ficat. *Inventaire sommaire des archives de la guerre, 1914-1919. Grand quartier général des armées alliées*. Troyes: Imprimèrie La Renaissance, 1972.

————. "Le Recrutement de tirailleurs en A.O.F. pendant le première Guerre mondiale: essai de bilan statistique," in *Revue Français d'histoire d'outre-mer* 60 (1973): 644-60.

Ouÿ-Vernazobres, Joseph-Charles (Captain). *Journal d'un officier de cavalerie*. Paris: Berger-Levrault, 1917.

Page, Melvin E., ed. *Africa and the First World War*. New York: St. Martin's Press, 1987.

Paraf, Pierre. *La France de 1914: Le passé et l'avenir nous parlent*. Paris: Editions du Sorbier, 1981.

Raynal, Sylvain-Eugène (Commandant). *Journal du Commandant Raynal: Le Fort de Vaux*. Paris: Albin-Michel, 1919.

Sassoon, Siegfried. *Sherston's Progress*. Garden City, N.Y.: Doubleday, Doran, 1936.

Schneider, William H. *An Empire for the Masses: The French Popular Image of Africa, 1870-1900*. Wesport, Conn.: Greenwood Press, 1982.

Sinclair, Andrew. *The Last of the Best: The Aristocracy of Europe in the Nineteenth Century*. London: Weidenfeld and Nicolson, 1969.

Smith, Leonard V. "The Disciplinary Dilemma of French Military Justice, September 1914-April 1917: The Case of the 5ᵉ Division d'Infanterie." *The Journal of Military History* 55 (January 1991): 47-68.

Smith, Michael Douglas. *Poets and Poems of the First World War: The English*. Washington: University Press of America, 1978.

Spring, David. *European Landed Elites in the Nineteenth Century*. Baltimore: The Johns Hopkins University Press, 1977.

Stovall, Tyler Edward. *Paris Noir: African Americans in the City of Light*. Boston: Houghton Mifflin, 1996.

Strieter, Terry W. "The 'Old Grumblers' of Napoleon's Army: Rates of Promotion Before and After 1815." *The Historian* 53, no. 1 (Autumn, 1990): 63-75.

Suard, Vincent. "La Justice militaire française et la peine de mort au début de la première guerre mondiale." *Revue Historique Moderne et Contemporaine* 41, no. 1 (Jan.-Mar. 1994): 136-153.

Todorov, Tzvetan. *Nous et les autres: la réflexion française sur la diversité humaine*. Translated by Catherine Porter, Cambridge, Ma.: Harvard University Press, 1993.

Toynbee, Arnold Joseph. *The German Terror in France*. London: Hodder and
    Stoughton, 1917.
Weber, Eugen Joseph. *The Nationalist Revival in France, 1905-1914*. Berkeley:
    University of California Press, 1968.
Willcox, Cornélis De Witt. *A French-English Military Technical Dictionary*.
    Washington, D.C.: Government Printing Office, 1917.
Winter, Denis. *Death's Men*. London: Penguin Books, 1979.
Winter, J. M. *The Experience of World War I*. New York: Oxford University
    Press, 1995.

INDEX